BROKEN

BROKEN

A Memoir

EMMA WHITE

M

MELBOURNE BOOKS

Published by Melbourne Books
Level 9, 100 Collins Street,
Melbourne, VIC 3000
Australia
www.melbournebooks.com.au
info@melbournebooks.com.au

National Library of Australia
Cataloguing-in-Publication entry
Author: Emma White
Title: Broken: A Memoir
ISBN: 9781925556124 (paperback)
Subjects: White, Emma,
Accident victims--Australia--Biography.
Accident victims--Psychological aspects.
Paraplegics--Biography.
Paraplegics--Travel--Australia.

Printed in Singapore

FOR KEV

CONTENTS

PART I

COLLAPSE

I

I am painting a henna butterfly across the brown leathery breasts of a wild silver-haired nudist at the time Kev's back is breaking. Not that I know that yet, of course. I have no blinding flashes or intuitions that my life is about to be radically altered — no freaky visions of my boyfriend lying broken and smashed at the base of a rugged cliff: small, vulnerable and alone, lost beneath a thick coniferous carpet unfolding endlessly to the horizon. Eyes level with nipples the size of poached eggs, I concentrate, squinting to gauge if the elaborate wings spanning her torso are symmetrical, despite a clearly non-symmetrical canvas. It's not an occupational challenge I'd ever anticipated encountering but then again, I hadn't expected to be a henna body artist either. It's the second day of the Nelson Street Festival in British Columbia, Canada, and my summer stretches ahead as a series of festivals and markets, bursting with warm skin ripe for staining. And then, everything changes with a call.

It comes once the fierce sun has dropped from the sky and colourful tents are closed for the day; when artists, musicians and performers have melted from the streets and the wilted, sunburnt crowds have vanished into campervans and squats in the thick, damp forest. Erratic campfire shadows dance upon laughing faces and reflected fire burns in amber bottles held by cramping, russet-stained fingers when the call shatters a tremendous sky full of foreign stars.

'There has been an accident,' says Diane.

Her voice is thick with worry and immediately I assume she is overreacting. She sees zebras when there are only horses. I can see her small, huddled figure, stocky like a toddler, blue dressing gown draped and loosely tied over her long nightie, her hair a grey, frizzy cloud above her head, eyes huge and scared as her fingers twirl the phone cord anxiously.

'Don and I are driving out to Kamloops,' she says. 'Will you meet us there?'

Oh man, now I have to hitchhike to Kamloops, over 450 kilometres north-west, and miss the rest of the festival. Likely Kev just broke his arm or his leg — which sucks, but he'll be back out in the bush in no time.

'Okay, I'll figure out some way to get there. I'll call the hospital now.'

Around the fire, the other body-art girls hush and my boss continues to slowly sift greenish-brown henna powder into a large bowl on the steps of her caravan.

'That was my boyfriend's mum. He's doing bush work up near Clearwater and apparently he's just driven a motorbike off a cliff,' I say, to commiserations and reassurances, while flipping the phone closed.

My boss stretches out her hand. 'I'm so sorry, I don't have much credit left … you'll have to find a phone booth.'

I pass her the phone and unease pierces my beer-buzz as I

prowl the darkened streets of Nelson for a payphone. I call Alex, owner of the geophysical company that employs Kev to run mineral exploration surveys in the Northern British Columbian wilderness.

'Alex, it's Emma. What's going on? How is he doing?'

'Oh, hi Em. The doctors think he's broken his leg but he also suffered some chest trauma and is having difficulty breathing. The doctors are with him at the moment. Hang on, he wants to talk to you.'

Alex briefly passes the phone to Kev who repeats, 'I love you, I love you,' his voice slow and drugged. Standing in the narrow phone booth, the night contracts around me and despite the warmth of the evening my arms erupt in goose pimples. Kev isn't the type of man to endlessly tell me he loves me and instead offers up *I love you*'s with ceremony, like little presents. It took six months before he said he loved me in a smoky Northern Albertan bar, his shirt wet from where he'd leant across the beer-soaked table to touch my hand as though proposing. Now, his frantic medicated declarations chill me. It feels as though he doesn't think he'll see me again.

I stand for a moment, unsure of what to do. In my pocket, my fingers find a pair of delicately designed silver rings purchased hours earlier from an old man in the adjoining tent: one small and one so much larger that the smaller ring fits perfectly inside. I'd bought the rings on impulse without assigning any meaning to them — they were just funky and cool — but on some level, they were also something else: a commitment. I had immigrated to Canada, far from my home and family in Australia, which made things more serious between Kev and me. To me, the rings meant forever.

Half a world away in Melbourne, my parents are making lunch and Dad answers when I call. In the background, I hear Mum's muffled voice asking, 'Do you want a cup of tea, Gordon?' Visualising them making tea and sandwiches in their sunny kitchen, I feel small and alone.

'Dad, it's me. Kev's had an accident. He was doing fieldwork and the motorbike he was riding went off a cliff. It took them ages to find him and he was just lying there alone. Diane is freaking out and Kev sounds really bad. What if it is really bad?'

'Well it can't be too serious, otherwise he would be dead already.' I can hear him chewing as he gives me the type of reassurance that can only come from a pathologist. 'It will be okay, Floss.'

News trickles in during the night: the CAT scan machine broken in Kamloops; no sacral response to stimuli; breathing weak. I stick to the phone, ringing anyone and everyone just to hear voices and mute the feelings of loneliness and fear. Kev is being transported to Vancouver by jet. That is not good. Jets are not used for broken legs. Jets are heavy. Jets are serious.

Alex drives through the night from Kamloops and arrives early to pick me up. It takes us most of the day to reach Vancouver and conversation is kept light and peppered with forced joviality, both avoiding speaking our fears lest they eventuate. As we approach the town of Hope, Alex's phone shrieks in the console and I snatch it before he piles distraction onto exhaustion to further deteriorate his driving.

'Em?' Diane's voice is soft and on the verge of tears.

'Oh, hi Diane. Alex and I are just passing Hope and should be there within a couple of hours or so,' I say, my voice laced with laughter that fills the car. From my tone, I could've been on my way to a Sunday afternoon barbecue asking whether I should pick anything up. Alex darts me a smile.

'Em, I've just seen Kev in emergency.' She takes a huge shuddering breath, audibly exhaling as though slowly breathing into a balloon, and I deflate. Words follow but they need not have. 'They did a CAT scan.' And now she cries, 'Kev's spinal cord has been damaged … they … they don't know how badly. More tests are scheduled and then they'll know better but it doesn't look good.'

'Okay, thanks,' my voice is a faint shadow.

Outside, the misty coniferous forest smudges into a green blur and, blinking angrily, I glare past my reflection and see nothing. Alex watches nervously as I stab my palm with a thumbnail and clench my cheek viciously between molars till I feel deep imprints with my tongue.

2

18 JULY 2004

Vancouver General Hospital looms huge and grey and rimmed with pyjama-wearing smokers wheeling IVs around like balls and chains. On the spinal ward, only the incessant beep of heart-rate monitors, the gentle rustle of paperwork from the nursing station and the slap of my dusty sandals on vinyl cuts the silence of the fluorescent-lit hallways. A nurse directs me to a room in the intensive care section where the soft glow of seemingly infinite monitoring devices provides the only light. Breathing apparatuses and important-looking machines crowd the bed where Kev lies motionless, as around him, machines pump, suck, drip and keep him alive. Dirt, blood and pine needles mat his long hair and his face, partially obscured by an oxygen mask, is scratched and coated in mud.

For the first time, I realise he could die. He could actually die. How can this be happening to him? To us? To our life together? This is not how it's supposed to be. I stand spellbound for a long moment in the doorway. On some level, I hadn't realised how serious Kev's accident was; part of me hoped he'd be sitting up in bed reading a magazine with a leg cast tethered to pulleys and ropes above his head, greeting me with a hearty, 'It's so good to see you, Baby.' But it's not like that at all. Intravenous tubes coil from needles burrowed into his tanned neck and hands — thick, clever hands, well-formed for holding hammers and wrenches, now so swollen his fingers resemble overcooked sausages on the verge of splitting. They are incongruous beside my own hands, intricately patterned with rich mahogany henna. I stroke his hair, pushing the stray curls behind his ears and feel my tears falling into his red beard, now grown longer than I remember. He opens hollow, bloodshot eyes.

'Don't cry, pretty girl,' he whispers hoarsely through cracked and bleeding lips. And a great, heavy pressure settles around my chest and steals my breath. One corner of his mouth twitches almost imperceptibly in an attempted smile, and ever so slowly he brushes the back of his dirty, scraped and swollen hand against my cheek; I squeeze my eyes closed.

'They say I've broken my back.' I stop him before he can go any further.

'I know, I know. Everything will be okay.' Pulling the larger of the two silver rings — the one with the wave pattern — from my pocket, I try to jam it onto his grotesquely misshapen finger. 'I love you, Kev; nothing will change that.'

'But what if my back really is broken and I am paralysed? You said you could never be with a disabled man.'

Shit!

'I said that almost four years ago. Anyway, I say things I don't mean all the time — stupid things, you know that.'

It had been on a warm summer evening, about six months after we got together, that in response to a friend's multiple sclerosis diagnosis Kev had asked, 'What would you do if I ended up in a wheelchair?' We were crossing a high bridge spanning a ravine in Edmonton, swinging our linked hands on our way home from the pub, admiring the faint ghostly glow of the Aurora Borealis flowing through the sky above.

'Would you stay with me?' He'd asked.

'Nah, I would definitely leave you,' I replied emphatically with the absolute conviction of a twenty-three-year-old. 'I haven't signed up for that.'

'Cast me aside to be refunded like a defective product? "My boyfriend broke, I need a new one".'

'Something like that,' I murmured.

And then we had laughed because the whole hypothetical situation seemed so preposterously remote.

I had not thought of the blithe conversation in years, but since his fall, Kev has thought of little else. He paws the oxygen mask from his face and it hisses faintly into the tangled hair of his throat.

'I didn't want you to see me looking all messed up, didn't want to freak you out … I just kept thinking how you'd never stay with me if I was paralysed, so I had them take out this tube in my throat that made me look really bad. I kept gagging, I couldn't breathe … but most of all, I didn't want to scare you.'

'Oh Kev. No, Babe, you don't look too bad. You're going to be fine.' I grip his hand harder than intended, using my thumb to rub the back of his hand. I laugh, more maniacally than calming.

'I knew at the base of the cliff I had a spinal injury. I was scared of not being able to walk, but also scared of losing you.'

'You're not going to lose me Kev, I'm right here.' I glance at his legs, hidden under the thin hospital sheets, noticing for the first time that they have not moved since I entered the room; not a single twitch.

'And anyway, you won't be in a wheelchair,' I try again to put the ring on his finger, my own fingers working clumsily in my haste, but it's no use.

'You keep it safe for me, Babe,' he says closing my fingers over the ring and I slip it back into my pocket as his eyes close. Dragging a chair to his bedside, I hold his hand and stroke his face as he drifts in and out of consciousness.

Time passes. Blasting air conditioning chills the air and I wrap my naked arms around my shoulders. I see dimly as though looking through mist and feel a rising panic. I have always been good at the false bravado, seen as strong and composed although I am just better at hiding my craziness than most. Stepping outside into the hall, my composure breaks. Suddenly I feel hot, my throat raspy as if recovering from a cold, and I'm breathing irregularly as though hyperventilating. I've never felt panic as acute as this. I feel like I'm going to throw up. *What the fuck? What the fuck? What the fuck?* I want to find a little box somewhere to crawl into: a warm Goldilocks bed where I can pull the covers over my head and pretend this is not happening.

Kev's parents, Don and Diane, appear, looking horribly old with worry, and enfold me in their arms.

'He's alive. At least he's alive. Thank God for that!' Says Diane, gripping my shoulders as though for stability, her face worn and puffy with the disoriented look of someone woken unexpectedly before slipping on their glasses: a searching, shrunken look. Again, she buries her face in my shoulder and her hair is a soft boll of cotton against my chin.

'Em … he's strong; the doctors say he's strong,' says Don, clasping Diane and me tighter than is comfortable.

* * *

A tall, fair-haired man dressed in blue surgical scrubs with a clipboard tucked into his armpit slips into Kev's room.

'Kevin, hello. I'm Dr Meyer. I'm an orthopaedic surgeon,' he says.

'Hi,' says Kev, rolling his head towards the voice.

'Kevin, I've taken a look at your scans: you've severely fractured your T6 and T7 vertebrae. My main concern is stabilising the area so I'd like to operate as soon as possible.' He briefly fiddles with an identical clipboard hanging on the end of Kev's bed.

'I can't move my legs; will the surgery fix that?'

'From the images, it appears that your spinal cord has been damaged, which is consistent with the lack of response to stimuli,' he pauses for a heartbeat. 'Frankly, it looks like it's been smashed with the blunt side of an axe, but I can't see a break so it appears incomplete. I'm going to put your body in a position where it has the best chance to heal by inserting titanium rods along your spine, fusing your vertebrae from T4 to T9.' With his thumb, he points to a spot on his chest approximately level with his shoulders, spreads his hand wide and with his little finger, indicates a place mid-stomach. 'I've got the permission forms here for you to sign,' he says, laying his clipboard on the wheeled table stretching over Kev's bed. Barely looking, Kev signs the forms scheduling surgery for the morning.

I sleep on a Therm-a-Rest mattress on the floor of Kev's room, waking every hour for his blood-pressure test and whenever nurses bustle in to check equipment, only lulled back to a sleep-like state by the white noise of all the beeping, humming machines.

During the night, Kev frequently wakes panicked. He has nightmares from the drugs and the pain, calling for me in the night and leaving my nerves jangling and sharp. I'm unable to sleep, feeling like I'm the one facing surgery in the morning. Kev continually hacks phlegm into a suction hose, similar to the type used at a dentist's office, because his lungs collapsed due to chest trauma and, he now lacks muscular control to cough up the mucus. It's a long, disgusting process accompanied by dire sounding noises that bring to mind the final stages of a terminal lung disease. Without a solid cough, only a fraction of the phlegm comes up at a time, leaving Kev with the constant unfulfilled desire to cough deeply and he feels as if he's drowning and suffocating. The night drags on forever as I watch the clock and wait for them to come for him.

Kev's anxious as they wheel him from the prep room to the operating theatre. He doesn't want to release my hand and I'm dragged beside his bed for several steps before his grip finally loosens. We are both apprehensive about what this surgery means: about the outcome and what may be discovered and lost. Once he has disappeared into the operating theatre I'm unsure what to do. Should I wait here? Am I even allowed to wait here? The nurse decides for me, ushering me gently from the prep room.

'The surgeon will be in touch within a few hours,' she says.

3

As I find myself walking through the early morning rush to the hotel where Don and Diane are staying, passing the ranks of well-dressed energetic people making their way busily to work, my mind journeys back four years. Fresh out of a BA in Classics I'd travelled to Canada to spend a year working out what to do with my life. So, with my snowboard under my arm, I drifted up to Big White Ski Resort in British Columbia searching for snow.

The first time I saw Kev it was January — always a cold, slow month for the ski industry. Standing at the top of the chairlift, I was trying my best to look like an attentive ski-lift operator, while mentally calculating the angle to sit so I could smoke a cigarette without being seen by my boss in the administration building behind me. Up the chairlift came a young ski instructor in a red uniform beside three breathtakingly tiny kids on skis. Long blond curls escaped from under his black beanie and upon his flat, previously broken, nose rested a pair of decidedly unfashionable silver sunglasses. He was solid, with ski-racing legs that his pants struggled to contain and I almost expected to hear a tremendous rip as he stood up, leaving me with a view of his underpants as he skied away.

He in turn saw a girl slouching against the lift shack, quietly appraising him. I wore the blue-and-yellow uniform of a lift operator and the hair around my freckled face was dirty blond and matted with dreadlocks that hung to my shoulders. A pair of brown sunglasses hid my blue eyes and I cultivated a slight lip curl, which I hoped conveyed both indifference and sexiness. Leather Sorel boots warmed my feet and, leaning my shoulder against the doorjamb of the shack, I kicked a hole in the snow with my toe. I should have been digging, smoothing or de-icing the offload ramp, but I wasn't. My job was only important enough for me to not actively try to get fired, but not important enough to worry about if I was. With the sun shining in the huge azure sky, I worked on my tan instead of the ramp — like any reasonable ski bum.

The young ski instructor avoided eye contact as his chair glided past me and I mistook his shyness for arrogance; *jerk–off can't even say hi! He must be one of those snobby you-lifties-are-so-far-beneath-me instructors.* As the chair reached the top, he stood and skied down the ramp with a child under each arm and the remaining one landed in a twisted pile on the down slope slightly below me. I slowed the chair, allowing him to swoop back and carry the kid away, receiving a brief shy smile in return. Lighting a cigarette, I promptly forgot about him and pondered more important matters, such as where tonight's beer money would come from when I earned $7 an hour yet paid $400 a month for the privilege of living with thirteen other Australians in a four bedroom house.

Snowshoe Sam's mountain bar was packed when I met Kev again a few weeks later and we chatted around the foosball table over a couple of drinks as my roommate hit on his friend. Stripped of his beanie and sunglasses, deeply set eyes peered from beneath a prominent brow, giving him a serious look and when he smiled I could see his pointy eye teeth poking out from under plump lips. His round cheeks — that I longed to pinch — looked too young to be covered in red stubble and his hair fell in ringlets more befitting a tutu-wearing little girl than a young man. But it was his unusually light, clear blue eyes that were remarkable and caused me to notice him in the crowded bar.

He was taking a year off university while debating whether to return to study or pursue a career in the ski industry. Passionate about the outdoors, he spent his summers hiking and biking and his winters were consumed with skiing. On the walk home, he offered his hand up the steep section of the track where the ice was smooth and blue, and we dawdled behind our drunken friends who were yelling and throwing each other in snow banks. He escorted me to my door, where he kissed me next to the overflowing garbage bins and huge piles of beer cans lining our driveway — much to the glee of my housemates spying out the window.

* * *

Don, Diane and I are waiting at the hotel reception when the surgeon's call comes through and Diane passes the phone to me — an official recognition of my relationship with their son.

'Things have gone well,' the surgeon says. Kev is in recovery and although he's still pretty out of it, we can go and see him. I feel that 'things have gone well' means that Kev will get better, that they have somehow fixed him, and the heady feeling of hope envelopes me. But I don't realise that in a surgeon's vocabulary 'going well' means not bleeding excessively, vomiting copiously or dying. Don, Diane and I have been waiting in Kev's room for an hour-and-a-half when the orderlies finally wheel him back in, still groggy from the surgery. He, too, hopes that they have fixed him, and we bask in a positive 'post-surgery' glow.

As the anaesthetic wears off, I watch Kev willing his feet to move, begging his brain to remember his lower body exists. My fingers stroke his freckled calf, tugging gently on the long, fair hairs of his leg.

'Can you feel that?' I ask softly.

'Feel what?' He says.

Later, the surgeon arrives to assess Kev's recovery, lifting the blanket draped across his legs and poking him with the lid of a pen.

'Can you feel this?' The surgeon asks, running a pen lid along each of Kev's legs in a manner that should tickle, making a 'humph' sound at each answer, signalling neither pleasure nor displeasure. 'How is your pain level?' He asks, inspecting Kev's surgical incision and arranging the blanket gently over Kev's legs.

'Manageable,' Kev says, indicating his morphine drip.

'Ok, everything looks good,' the surgeon says, preparing to leave.

Kev and I exchange glances. What do the noises mean? Has Kev done well? At Dad's recommendation, I'd written down all my questions so I could get answers before the surgeon left. There's so much I want to know.

'Will he get better? How often do people get better with this particular injury? Is it a good thing that his legs spasm? What will he be able to do? When will we see recovery if we are going to? When should we accept that he's not going to get better? Will he ever be able to have children?'

The surgeon has heard all of my questions and many more from numerous anxious families and he fields them all deftly with answers such as, 'It is too early to say, recovery is different for everyone'; 'the nervous system is very complicated'; 'I can't say'; and the honest, 'I don't know'. All I want is some hope. A little kernel of 'perhaps', or of 'maybe'; a mere possibility. I want the surgeon to say that the spasms mean his neurological system is trying to reconnect itself, working like busy little nano-bots on rebuilding the information superhighway: a council construction crew on speed. I want him to say the injury is not final, not irreversible, and that Kev can recover. But he doesn't. To him it is simple: Kev's spine has snapped as clearly as a stick snaps under force and for it to spontaneously heal, for the break to vanish, is almost impossible. He assumes we are on the same page but I am still chapters behind. I haven't even accepted the break.

* * *

Two days ago, Kev was supervising a month-long geophysical survey, living in cork boots and quick-dry clothing, the skin at his sleeves and waistband red and swollen from bug bites and legs solid and muscled from long days hauling equipment through the thick northern British Columbian forest. On the morning of his accident, Kev drove the work truck with a three-man crew as a fourth guy followed behind on a trail-bike to the field site where the equipment had been left the previous day. The day was unremarkable: he hiked the survey line, pounding electrodes into the ground, rolled Drum cigarettes while the measurements registered and periodically fixed wire snapped by moose, bear or vandals. Later, coiling cables and packing the truck in the soft afternoon light, Kev decided to ride the motorbike back to camp and skidded away as the rest of the crew piled into the truck.

The road was a cut line falling away steeply on one side and he dodged potholes and jarred across washboard as he wound through dense, dark green pines. Rounding a bend, Kev was blinded by sun blasting through clear-cut regrowth.

His foot fell to the brake but the exceptionally severe corrugations rippling the road wrenched the bike sideways onto the grass where it bounced off a boulder and over the cliff.

'The next thing I knew, the bike was falling — I was falling. Huge boulders were rushing towards me and all I could think was, "fuck this is going to be really bad". It's hard to describe … time seemed to slow momentarily and I was suspended in the air. But then I hit the ground and the impact was … electric: all-consuming.'

And spine shattering, I think, transfixed by his description of a pain I can't comprehend.

The impact knocked him unconscious for a time and he woke, mind reeling in disbelief, lying at the base of a cliff enclosed by cold, grey boulders. Shadows were long and threatening, the dirt around him was reddened with blood and the only sounds were the distant burbling of a creek and the lonely far-away cry of a solitary crow. Even the insects, which had been unbearable all day, had mostly retreated.

'I could see my stomach and see myself touching it but I couldn't feel it … it felt like a slab of beef, detached from the rest of my body. Trying to move my feet I kept thinking, "this is not good, oh man this is really, really not good". There was not too much pain — shock or adrenaline I guess.'

Hearing the work truck trundle past on the forestry road far above, he yelled for help, trying for assertive instead of weak and wounded, his thoughts shifting to the many bears and wolves he'd seen nearby. But the sound soon faded and he was alone. With an hour's drive back to camp ahead of them, it would take several hours for the guys to backtrack and find him and he knew he had to stay conscious — though while the shock was subsiding, pain was taking over.

'Never have I felt so vulnerable. I wanted to yell but I couldn't move and was terrified a bear or cougar would stumble upon me. I was prey.'

Hours passed.

'I thought I was going to die … I was reflecting on my life, travels … you … It's funny, it was almost calming in a way; not nearly as scary as I thought it would be, you know?'

I don't know. I have no idea. Yet I nod wisely, stroking the valley of flesh between his index finger and his thumb.

It had long been dark by the time Kev heard the low murmur of a truck driving slowly along the track above and he yelled for help with a thin voice he didn't recognize, words shattering the extended silence. Hearing yelling in return, he allowed himself to hope.

One of the guys from the crew climbed and skidded down the cliff as another shouted frantically into a satellite phone. Too dark for a helicopter landing, by the time the ambulance arrived, Kev had been lying motionless for six hours, struggling to breathe and unable to feel his lower body. As around him, working by torchlight, the crew felled trees and cleared scrub to make a path to the road. And the pain was monstrous.

'The ambos couldn't give me anything for pain because my breathing wasn't strong enough, and we had to drive rough forestry roads for hours. I kept saying, "how much longer, how much longer?" It was ten hours after my accident when I finally reached hospital.' He sighs and smiles wanly, 'I should have just got in the fucking truck.'

* * *

Within a day or so of Kev's surgery, a team of nurses, physiotherapists, occupational therapists, on-call neurology residents and social workers are assembled to aid him on his recovery journey; the physical and emotional rollercoaster he'll face over the coming months. The person we interact with most is his principal physiotherapist, Kristi, a tall, thin, red-head in her early thirties. She is enthusiastic, vivacious and passionate about her work.

On day two, I corner Kristi in the hall.

'Is there any hope that Kev will regain movement? Have you seen people with his injury recover?'

Her eyes are full of compassion as she says slowly, 'There is always hope.' She smiles, 'I know it's difficult but we just have to wait and see. Often, after a spinal injury, people experience some form of recovery as everything settles down. Usually it occurs fairly rapidly after surgery but sometimes incremental recovery can take as long as a year, but after that it's unusual for any spontaneous motor or sensory changes. There is still time.'

A surge of optimism fills me as I follow Kristi into Kev's room and watch her roll down his compression stockings and prick his legs with pins as she has for the past two days. I hate the exercise because Kev's inability to feel the pins is tangible evidence of his injury, proof that something is terribly, terribly wrong. I shoot expectant looks at his face as another pin punctures the thick muscles of his legs. He doesn't register feeling, let alone pain, but simply frowns, trying to decide between sharp, dull, hot, or cold, or whether he feels anything at all. I realise with a shock he's simply guessing.

'The surgeon said Kev has an incomplete spinal injury; that's good news, right? It's not really a break so he'll get better, right?' I had asked Dad the day after Kev's surgery.

'Well, not necessarily, Floss. Hopefully he will, but even when a spinal cord is not completely severed and it remains relatively intact, it can be so badly damaged that it might as well have been severed.'

With an incomplete injury, signals can still reach the injured part of the body, leaving the patient with some function or feeling below the injury level; whereas with a complete injury, no signals are received below the injury level.

'Think of a thick rope,' Dad had said. 'Now you can use a knife to completely cut the rope and you'll have two pieces which is like a complete spinal injury. But you can also take a hammer and smash the hell out of the rope until it's flattened and fraying and not much good for anything anymore, and that's an incomplete spinal injury.'

An incomplete injury is a double-edged sword; it allows Kev to feel sensation and increases his spatial awareness, but results in alarmingly severe spasms shuddering through his body like earthquakes. As painful and horrible as the spasms may be, they could serve a useful purpose increasing the circulation, retaining muscle mass and if he suffers injury the spasms go berserk alerting him to the fact that something is wrong, even if he cannot tell precisely what it is.

Kev feels sensation in his lower body but it's similar to the numbness of pins-and-needles caused by the immobility of a limb for a time: a maddening buzzing, not so much pain as an unpleasantly alien feeling. When I touch his legs, he can't tell precisely what's going on with his lower body, only that someone or something is interfering with it. I could sear his feet with a blowtorch and he would only be alerted by his spasticity, a feeling of 'something happening', and the stench of burning flesh. It is both incredible and horrifying at the same time.

Squeezing his eyes closed, Kev concentrates; his brain attempts to interpret new signals arriving from below the injury into something plausible, transforming the weird feeling back to normal. I move his toes back and forth and obsessively ask, 'Can you feel this? This? This?' And whenever he guesses the correct toe, I feel a bolt of triumph. The doctors are wrong: he is getting better.

The first few days after Kev's accident smear together. Kev's older brother, Sandy, arrives from North Carolina and his heavily pregnant sister, Jocelyn, from Calgary. Friends are calling, cards arriving, and Kev's room has blossomed into a verdant oasis of flowers. I'm at the hospital constantly; time is meaningless. I don't care where I sleep, what — or even if — I eat and I'm certainly not in a frame of mind to think about practicalities. But in the background, Kev's parents are organising the logistics and settling in for a long stay in Vancouver.

A man of few words and accustomed to being in control, Don is lost. In Kev's room, Don stands, then sits, then stands, then sits, pacing impatiently and looking out the window while leaving his coat on, debating whether the parking meter will have expired and bumping, flustered, into wall-mounted medical equipment. He feels most useful when given a specific task: finding an apartment is something Don can do, whereas healing his son, as he aches to, he cannot. After a day or so of searching, Don finds a vacant apartment across the street from the emergency department of Vancouver General Hospital, negotiating a flexible lease due to the uncertainty of Kev's situation. I sleep in the hospital but the apartment provides somewhere to shower and eat. Each evening I make the fifty-meter commute from Vancouver General across the street and up three flights of narrow stairs to the small, bland apartment.

By the third evening, I'm exhausted. I can't think, my life seems unreal — a dream, or a terrible hallucinogenic effect of copious amounts of magic mushrooms. Slumping on the pink toilet seat in the cramped, mouldy bathroom, I fall apart. My body heaves and shakes uncontrollably as I cry in pain and frustration, in fear and anguish, for dreams lost and shattered, unfulfilled and unimagined. I don't cry prettily or daintily, but convulsively, uncontrollably and painfully, breathing in great, heaving gasps with my eyes and nose running, breaking and ripping inside; an artesian well of misery.

Falling forward onto the tiled floor, I pull my knees into my chest and gently rock back and forth, curling my hands into fists and shaking with simple, ineffectual rage. Numbly, I climb into the bath and let the warm water rain down upon me, sitting with my arms wrapped tightly around my knees, tears streaming down my cheeks. My pants and shirt, now soaked, cling to my body like a wetsuit, my eyes are squeezed shut and a silent scream suffocates me. I sink into the grimy porcelain and the water washes away my cares and momentarily I feel like a Zen Master. And like the crazy person that I am, I lie fully clothed in the shower, lost within a cloud of steam with my hair plastered to my face and my clothing stuck to my skin, and somewhat strengthened, I finally smile.

4

LATE JULY 2004

In the days following Kev's surgery my conviction he'll recover begins to waver and doubts seep in. I hope, despite knowing it's likely futile: the way a condemned inmate hopes of reprieve — fervently, but realistically. Time passing without recovery terrifies me. Kristi had said recovery usually happens fast, so every passing day makes it less likely.

'Isn't there something you can do to try and reverse the damage, considering the injury only happened two days ago?' I had asked one of the neurology residents as he examined Kev's lower body sensation.

'Two days is a long time in terms of a spinal injury,' he had replied, meeting my eyes across Kev's motionless legs. 'If a patient reaches hospital within a couple of hours of their injury then we're able to administer high-dose steroids in an attempt to reduce inflammation that may cause additional damage. But after that window of eight hours or so … there's not a lot that can be done.' He had shrugged his shoulders and delicately tucked Kev's feet back underneath the thin white blankets. The injury only just happened, how can it be too late for recovery already?

Kev is awake for longer stretches of time and has periods of lucidity where I feel I can talk to him and he understands what I'm saying. It's hard for me to push all of my doubts and fears to the back of my mind so I can tell him everything is going to be okay, when I am pretty sure that everything is *not going to be okay*. I have to pretend that I'm whole, that I'm fine, that I'm coping and strong, when I'm just as scared, broken and confused as he is. In my screwed-up state, I can't stop visualising the image of a large brown snake with a broken back I'd seen when I was a little girl. It was summer and I'd been lurking on the fence beside our henhouse, trying to put salt on a sparrow's tail because Gramps had told me sparrows can't fly with salt on their tail. Maybe it interfered with their aerodynamics or threw off their balance. Or maybe it was bullshit and Gramps thought it was hilarious watching me sit for hours on the burning roof vainly trying to sprinkle salt on birds.

As I was crawling along the fence line, a flash of movement seized my gaze and a large brown snake emerged from the long grass directly below me. I froze mid-crawl like a convict in a searchlight, watching with sick dread as it slid effortlessly underneath me, well within striking distance of my pale, terrified face. As a farm kid, I knew enough about snakes to recognise a brown snake; one of the deadliest snakes in Australia.

'Dad,' I whispered hoarsely, 'Daaaaaaaaaddd.' Dad was building stuff in the shed and making a hell of a racket. 'Snake,' I croaked louder and Dad burst from the shed, shovel held high above his head, and gave the snake an almighty whack on the back. The impact clearly broke the snake's back and as the front half of the snake thrashed furiously, lunging violently at the shovel and the man wielding it, whipping around in angry hurt circles, the back section of the snake lay ominously quiet, completely, utterly still. I could see the exact spot where the snake's spine had been severed.

Thinking about the snake and its furiously thrashing top half while sitting in Kev's hospital room, I feel sick. I simply can't get the image of the whipping snake out of my head — like the Buddhist meditation technique of trying not to think about a white bear for a full minute, then all you can think about is a white bear. *Don't mention this to Kev*, I chant silently as a mantra, but when he asks what I'm thinking about I blurt out the story of the broken-backed snake in a rush.

'So now I'm that snake, is that what you mean?' Kev asks in bewilderment.

'I don't know; I don't know what I mean. I think it is just a thought.' I wish with all my heart I had never started this conversation. But once committed, I plough on inexplicably madly about the snake. 'Maybe you are just like the snake,' I say. 'Your back is broken, too.' He is looking at me in incredulous horror as if to say, 'Yeah, so what the hell is your point?' I become desperate. I'm trying to make sense of what has happened, searching for some explanation or something to identify with Kev's situation because no one I know has ever broken their back or neck, or anything much more serious than an arm or a collar-bone. The snake is the only living being I can definitively identify as having suffered a spinal injury.

Of course, I have seen people in wheelchairs but I assumed they were born into them, arriving screaming into the world and immediately issued with a wheelchair — not someone like me or Kev who had just suffered a particularly serious accident. But with the snake analogy, I have failed miserably, completely and emphatically. Kev is not ready to discuss the philosophical implications of his injury. He doesn't even want to see or associate himself with other people in wheelchairs yet, and he certainly does not want to identify himself with a bloody, broken-backed brown snake living its last mortal moments in terror and pain. What the hell is the matter with me? Why can't I act like a normal person and not mention every single wildly inappropriate thought that pops into my head? Kev ponders what I have said for a while and we descend into an uncomfortable silence, both contemplating the story of the snake and my tactlessness.

'Did the snake die?' Kev asks eventually.

'Yes,' I answer reluctantly, 'Dad chopped off its head with the shovel.'

* * *

Kristi and her team of assistants visit several times a day, checking the changes in Kev's sensation, probing for any new movement and stretching and massaging his legs. He's been elevated somewhat with pillows stuffed behind his back in order to alleviate breathing difficulties and fluid build-up due to his collapsed lung, but he hasn't actually moved from his bed since being deposited in it post-surgery.

Most of Kev's tubes have been removed, he's healing well and Kristi is keen for him to try to sit up in a chair. When two physiotherapists and two nurses each take a corner of the sheet on which Kev lies and heave him into the reclined total lift chair (TLC), he can't help but cry out as pain radiates from the shattered vertebrae and arcs through his mangled nervous system. I squeeze my eyes closed. Initially, the chair lies flat like a bed and Kristi slowly adjusts the tilt with a hand-held control button, bringing Kev closer and closer to a sitting position, his face growing redder and sweatier with every increased angle.

'Do you have a headache? Are you feeling faint? Can you handle a little longer?' Krisi asks.

'No ... a bit ... yes.' Kev's replies are forced puffs of words. He only tolerates the TLC for several minutes before he has an episode of autonomic dysreflexia: a reaction of the autonomic nervous system to overstimulation. Autonomic dysreflexia is thought to be triggered by nerve signals that have originated below injury level sending messages to the spinal cord. Kristi quickly lowers him back to a supine position.

After Kev's first experience in the TLC, Kristi attempts to sit him up several times each day and his tolerance increases. After a couple of days, Kristi is keen to try Kev in one of the many huge hospital wheelchairs clogging the hallways and at first, he lasts only minutes, but forces himself to remain sitting for longer and longer periods. Each day, the period Kev sits up increases a little and once he can stay in the wheelchair for half an hour or so, he can have his first real shower since his injury a week ago.

Still coated in dirt, pine needles and blood, with the areas cleaned for surgery smeared in orange antiseptic wipe, his hair looks like a grotesque parody of the French swirl: flat on one side and bouffant on the other. A team of nurses load Kev onto the shower wheelchair — a large plastic chair with a hole cut out in the base so that his bottom sticks through like an old-fashioned commode chair. A nurse carefully peels the sheets used to lift him out from underneath and wheels him through the halls. When ill and hospitalised, a shower seems such a simple pure pleasure and a self-confidence-lifting joy.

* * *

Dr Symons is a neurosurgery resident and he tells Kev, somewhat apologetically, that he will never walk again: for this, I hate him.

'It's been a week since my surgery and I haven't had any recovery yet, does that mean I'm not going to?' I hear Kev ask Dr Symons from within his room and I pause at the door. Dr Symons jabs the back of his neck with two fingers, like he has an ache, and stands within touching distance of Kev. Snug in a high-backed wheelchair with a blue cotton blanket spread across his knees, Kev looks up at Dr Symons with eyes slightly narrowed as though pierced by sunlight.

Outside, clouds the colour of gravel gather and rain begins to spit on the wide window panes: fat drops, racing each other to the bottom.

'In my experience, if recovery occurs, it generally occurs quite rapidly after surgery, once swelling has receded.'

Kev closes his eyes and swallows several times, his mouth a flat, lipless slit.

'How rapidly?' He asks, cheeks contracting and eyes tightening further.

'Usually within a day or so … It's quite unlikely you'll have substantial motor recovery at this stage if you haven't already noticed improvements.'

'So I'm not going to walk again?'

'It's very unlikely, I'm sorry.'

I don't want to listen. I want to prove him wrong, to shove Kev's miraculous recovery into his statistically-minded face. All I care about is Kev getting better and going on with our lives.

Then, slowly, it starts to hit me that Kev isn't going to make a miraculous recovery and walk out of the front doors of the hospital on his own two legs, with just the lingering scent of antiseptic and a new appreciation for the fragility of life to remind him of the entire experience before it fades to an unpleasant memory. This is real. This is actually happening and there is absolutely nothing I can do to change it. It's a horribly empty and desolate feeling, not unlike a sucker-punch in the abdomen. Through my tunnel vision, Dr Symons appears in front of me as I lean against the doorway of Kev's room, and, unaware I had been listening, advises me to, 'Give him some time alone because he has just received some bad news.'

Ignoring him, I push into the room where Kev sits, tears rolling down his blotchy red cheeks, hands clenching and unclenching in his lap and mouth opening and closing, seemingly unconsciously. He looks up at me desperately, despairingly, chest convulsing and breathing laboured, his Adam's apple bouncing up and down spasmodically and lips forming soundless words. He looks at me like a man who has abandoned all hope; a man lost in darkness. He is unable to speak and I am glad because I have no answers to offer him. I stand behind him, wrapping my arms around his heaving shoulders, feeling his hiccups and the bubbling, terrified hysteria underneath, and try to squeeze the pain from him. I hate seeing him so vulnerable because he's always been the strong one, he's always calm when I am a tempest. It's as though an icy wind has wrapped around us, sweeping away all the joy in the room — all the joy in the entire world.

And then it is over. Kev wipes his face with the back of his hand in the rough, angry manner of men wiping away tears, repeatedly blows his nose loudly, takes several long, shuddering breaths and asks me to fetch him some juice from the patient's kitchen. As I close the refrigerator door I pause for a moment, juice in hand, to peer out of the kitchen window. The clouds are clearing and far below a small park is full of people going about their daily business, playing games, lounging and laughing. It seems inconceivable to me that life can simply go on normally for people when my own life feels so ruined and shattered. I want to smash my fists through the plate glass to allow pain to slice through this novocaine fog. I want my environment to be as decimated as my life.

Exhausted and heavily medicated, Kev sleeps. But it's a restless, fitful sleep, and I wake often, rising from the chair I have claimed as my bed, to stand beside him in the soft darkness as he moans and stirs, his face spasming in response to some unseen stimulus. Then his face softens, the muscles framing his eyes relax and his bandaged hand curls softly around the sucky-hose the way a child cradles a favoured toy. Mouth slightly open, he makes gentle snoring noises — more an indication of the amount of medication coursing through his veins than of a serene slumberous state. His blue gown is slightly askew on one shoulder, exposing the curly mat of black hair on his chest. He looks so peaceful that I want to touch him. I haven't seen his face totally relaxed for so long; the muscles are usually tense and tight with pain, pinching and creasing at the corners of his eyes like he's squinting against wood smoke. Standing beside him in the shadows, I run my hands over his hair and forehead, slightly above him so that I'm not touching him and won't wake him, but still feel as if he's absorbing my touch. He's always tried to look in control, so I've always loved watching him sleep, watching his defences drop and seeing him vulnerable. It makes me see in him the little boy he once was.

At the end of the ski season at Big White, we had said goodbye in a Kelowna carpark as our friends pretended not to watch. I was going to Jasper to find work and he was returning to Edmonton to finish his geophysics degree; we both felt like it was the end. With our foreheads touching, Kev stroked my cheek, 'Everything will be okay, Baby,' he said sadly.

Now, as I watch him sleeping in his hospital bed, I remember his words and they give me hope that everything will eventually, somehow, be okay.

5

In the days that follow, we try to accept what Dr Symons has said and attempt to make it more palatable.

'Perhaps you'll only need to use a wheelchair for a couple of years before you get better,' I say hopefully.

'Yeah,' Kev agrees quickly, 'even if I have to walk with crutches or a cane that would be okay.' Thinking of the wheelchair as a temporary solution is much easier to accept than the fact that Kev will never walk again. Nonetheless, deep down Kev knows that the wheelchair is not a temporary solution.

'I don't want to be described as the guy in a wheelchair,' he says to me.

'You won't,' I say, knowing that he will.

He feels that his life will now become urban: unable to travel far from smooth concrete footpaths, wheelchair ramps and curb cutaways — the mountains, wilderness and outdoor sports forever lost to him. Are we going to be able to travel? I've no idea. I've no idea how Kev will even do the simplest things such as getting dressed, showering or going to the bathroom, let alone backpacking, mountain biking and skiing.

I also find it hard to accept the concept of forever. My young, strong boyfriend has suddenly become weak, frail and injured. How will my perception of him change? He'd been capable of skiing with me on his back, of lifting heavy stuff, of hiking and biking all day — capable of so much. What is he capable of now? Am I going to find him attractive now that he's disabled? And what about sex? Is that even possible? I'd said in the invulnerability of youth that I'd not signed up to be with a disabled man, but the declaration I'd made so emphatically four years previously was not quite that simple now that I knew I loved him. So many relationships barely survive day-to-day life, let alone the paralysis of one partner; how are we going to deal with this? The accident may have happened to Kev, but it also happened to me.

It all still seems so fantastical. Even though the wound is a thick twenty-centimetre slice up his back, it doesn't seem big and gruesome enough to have affected him so dramatically, so permanently. He doesn't feel fragile and hurt and paralysed when I lay my head on his broad chest, crammed together in the narrow hospital bed. He feels like Kev, the way he always has with his large, rough hands tickling my wrist. I feel residual strength in those hands I hold, while telling him lies I need to believe and willing that strength to radiate into the rest of his body like healing ripples. My fingers stroke his sturdy legs in which the memory of motion still lingers, the muscles slowly relaxing and winding down like the cooling engine of a car on a hot day, ticking and clicking as the engine stills. It's a slow release, similar to the gentle exhale of a long-held yogic breath. His body is adjusting to the new circumstances and his legs no longer move on command but instead flex and jerk spasmodically trying desperately to reconnect with his brain, searching frantically for instructions as they march unbidden and leaderless.

* * *

The doctors predict Kev will remain at Vancouver General for six to eight weeks before transferring to a rehabilitation hospital and it's surprising how quickly I adapt to the strange new situation. After a week or so, life on the spinal ward becomes normality. At first, the activity swirling around me was so sharp and focused that I turned whenever a gurney trundled by the open door, startled each time a nurse breezed into the room. Every yell or curse drew my attention and every unpleasant smell assailed my nostrils. But it didn't take long for the chaos and drama to become blurred and mundane. On the ward, someone always yells angrily or cries in pain, and gradually, I began to tune out the sounds of other people's misery. I stopped noticing the people who didn't get visitors peering at me with pathetically hopeful eyes, and was no longer bothered by those with a constant stream of loud, annoying visitors. There have been so many doctor visits that my initial impulse to rush about madly expecting earth-shattering news was muted as the mystique faded. Most of the time, the visits are routine examinations and follow-ups; a doctor trailing medical students asks about pain and sensation changes, then sticks his finger up Kev's bum to check again whether he can still feel it — quite boring really.

As the days pass, I begin to recognise familiar faces in the visitor's room and around the ward, and we spark up a type of friendship born of shared experience. We are not quite friends because we have absolutely nothing in common except for the paralysis of a loved one — similar to the type of friendships acquired on a long-distance train voyage, or with other dog owners at a dog park. Most conversations revolve around patient's injury level and functionality. If your family member has a higher injury level than theirs, they commiserate with you and vice versa. Hushed conversations are held in the halls whenever a new patient is admitted to the ward, 'He is a C2 quad, it was an ATV accident,' or 'She is a partial-para from a car accident,' is whispered furtively just out of earshot of the new patient's family. Serious injuries such as the high-level quadriplegics are discussed in reverent tones and their arrival sends a collective shudder of relief through the lower level quadriplegics and paraplegics. A high-level quadriplegic is perceived as a benchmark of sorts: as a, 'Oh thank goodness that didn't happen to me,' example of what may have happened had the injury been higher.

Before Kev's accident I knew nothing about spinal injuries. I'd never even met anyone in a wheelchair — except for the old people cloistered together in my Nana's nursing home. So whenever I saw someone on the street in a chair I would think to myself, 'Oh God a disabled person, don't stare at them,' as if they were a temperamental time bomb liable to start screaming obscenities at me if I happened to gaze upon them for a fraction of a second longer than is polite. I didn't want to offend anyone by staring so I did the complete opposite, looking at cracks in the sidewalk and interesting clouds in the sky and pretty much anything else except the person in the wheelchair, and breathed a sigh of relief when they passed me by with barely a glance. I knew some people in wheelchairs had different abilities than others but not the mechanics of spinal injuries or what those abilities were. I assumed quadriplegic meant you couldn't use your arms at all and were essentially a head teetering on top of an immobile body, and that paraplegics all had huge Popeye arms and could wheel themselves around the world like Rick Hansen. Unlike a basic fracture of an arm or leg there is no 'standard textbook' spinal injury; like fingerprints, each one is unique.

The surgeon had explained how the soft spinal cord is covered and protected by the vertebral column — thirty-three bony vertebrae divided into five segments: cervical, thoracic, lumbar, sacral and coccygeal — and consists of nerve fibres that send and receive electrical messages between the body and brain. Nerves branching from high on the spinal cord (cervical segment) control breathing, upper trunk stability and both movement and sensation of the arms. Nerves branching from the thoracic section primarily control trunk stability, and the lumbar and sacral nerves service the legs, bladder, bowel and sexual organs.

'Generally, we define a spinal injury by the vertebrae where damage to the spinal cord occurs, which in your case was six and seven of the thoracic,' the surgeon had stated. 'Depending on height, spinal injuries fall into two categories: quadriplegia and paraplegia. Paraplegia, your situation, results from injury in the thoracic, lumbar, or sacral region and impairs lower limbs and potentially the trunk. Injury to the cord in the cervical section is termed quadriplegia, and impacts, to some degree, the trunk and all four limbs.'

Because everyone suffering serious spinal injuries in British Columbia and the Yukon are sent to Vancouver General Hospital for care, the ward is hopelessly overcrowded. Often, Kev is only separated from one, three or (at one stage) five other patients by a flimsy, gaping curtain. Whenever we have a modicum of privacy with the curtain closed, Kev and I have emotionally charged conversations in stilted whispers. But it's an uneasy form of privacy — akin to a masturbating teenager in an unlocked bathroom. We anxiously watch as feet approach, fully expecting the curtain to be thrown open, displaying us to the entire ward.

Living in such close quarters, we get to know the other patients well. Kev's current roommate is a young father of two from Vancouver Island who broke his neck cruising jumps at the Whistler Mountain Bike Park and became a C5 quadriplegic. After a spinal injury, the doctors often say you may get some form of recovery that could increase your functionality, so he keeps repeating, 'When I get my hands back, I can do that ...' assuming he'll regain use of his hands. It's easier to imagine losing the ability to walk than the ability to feed yourself, write, touch your family, or breathe independently.

A large ability variation exists between low- and high-level quadriplegics. For example, a C7–C8 quad has some hand impairment but essentially the same level of ability as a T1 para, whereas a complete C1 quad can't move his arms or legs at all and requires a ventilator to breathe (like Christopher Reeve). Breaking your neck does not necessarily mean that you cannot walk: some incomplete quadriplegics retain the ability to walk, albeit a little irregularly.

Across the hall is a friendly young man from Northern Canada whose car veered off a stretch of road into a tree late one night. His back broke at a similar level to Kev's. The twelve thoracic vertebrae running from the base of the neck to the lower back (T1–T12) cover the region of the spinal cord that controls the intercostal muscles of the ribs, trunk support and abdominal muscles. Kev's injury occurred at the T6–T7 level, just below the nipples, and as a result, he lacks abdominal control and can no longer suck in his stomach whenever a pretty girl walks by. Although, he has retained his intercostal muscles to assist with breathing — which is almost as important.

A few doors down is a biker, whose gaping hospital gown exposes his scrawny back that is covered in childish, poorly drawn (and possibly prison) tattoos, all of which have been offset by the surgical scar created when his spine was fused back together. I learn through the spinal ward rumour mill that, incredibly, he was injured when mowed down by the irate, truck-driving owner of a motorcycle he'd just ineptly stolen from a garage.

It is among this motley crew of other patients and associated friends and family that Kev and I currently reside. People I may have moved away from had I been sitting beside them on a bus have become fixtures in my life and, even though I may not like some of them, it helps to know that I am not going through this alone. These people understand what Kev and I are experiencing like no one else can. They know the fear, the uncertainty, and the despair we feel because they also face it. They live it. And unlike friends who can commiserate and then put Kev's injury out of their minds while they do their shopping or work their jobs, these people eat, sleep and exist at the hospital, understanding that it can never be put out of mind. No one talks about dreary topics such as the weather or the performance of sporting teams; discussions centre on bodily functions, insurance type, injury, ability and recovery. In no other circumstances is it appropriate to discuss how you have not taken a shit for two weeks, or that you had catastrophically shat your pants the previous day.

Among all the spinal patients on the ward, Kev is the only person who was injured at work and consequently is covered by the Workers' Compensation Board of British Columbian (BC WCB). We both feel extremely fortunate in this respect because Kev is provided with a small stipend to pay for rent and expenses, which allows me to spend my time with him and removes the necessity of working.

As the days pass and become weeks, Kev grows stronger despite muscle spasticity and constipation that distends his stomach till it's hard and round. The physios have mounted a rod to the wall behind Kev's bed so that a triangular grab-bar hangs down over his chest and he can pull himself more upright and assist when the nurses need to move him. The bar also enables him to use his body weight to work-out and strengthen his arms. Over time, using the bar and the sides of the bed, Kev is able to heave himself into a sitting position. But due to lack of core muscles, he can't let go without toppling over, and often experiences severe abdominal spasms that smack him back down onto the bed.

With practice, Kev becomes more mobile in a wheelchair, weakly wheeling around the ward and even occasionally leaving the spinal ward. At first it is just down to the cafe on the second floor, yet he dresses meticulously in a collared shirt and pants that don't display his bottom. He forces his Foley catheter bag down the front of his pants, and I jam his immobile feet into shoes, like chunks of wood. Feeling like a person instead of a hospital inmate, the simple act of wearing normal clothes and sitting at a cafe table with his girlfriend gives him a huge psychological lift. Kev is not supposed to leave hospital grounds, so to get some sunlight and fresh air, he has a choice between sitting in a haze of cigarette smoke outside the main entrance doors of the hospital, or in the little park across the street where his quadriplegic roommate spends hours smoking pot.

'I want to see your new apartment,' Kev says to me one morning. 'I just want to get the hell out of here for a while.'

'Umm, okay.' I'd recently moved into a small, one-bedroom apartment a ten-minute walk from the hospital. It is slightly cheaper than the emergency room apartment and, being ground floor, has the possibility of becoming a longer-term home.

'Let's just go now,' he says, watching a skinny, greyish-looking guy wheeling an oxygen tank behind him light his fourth cigarette.

I can't see where I'm going as I push the wide, high-backed hospital chair like a mule, uphill to sixteenth street. Kev yells instructions as we plough along clearing the footpath of all other traffic: 'right, right, *right*. No, straight, stop — *stop!*'

We've barely been at the apartment long enough for Kev to have a look around before disaster strikes; the immoveable obstruction plaguing Kev since his injury becomes an unstoppable flood. The exertion of the wheel must have finally shaken things loose and Kev's faecal drought breaks in an unspeakably mortifying manner. I keep thinking of *Heart of Darkness* and 'the horror, the horror' as it keeps coming and coming, similar to a tube of toothpaste squeezed gently from the bottom. I run, panicked, to-and-from the bathroom, grabbing towels like an actress in a slapstick comedy trying to stop a leak. Kev's plastic hospital pants are hopelessly overwhelmed.

'Oh fuck, I'm so sorry Em,' says Kev, attempting futile damage control by slouching low in his chair.

'Quick, we have to get back to the hospital. Shove this down your pants,' I gasp, passing him a roll of toilet paper and spinning him towards the door. Potential pants-shitting was not an eventuality we had considered may occur on our first outing from the hospital, and I push him back as fast as my shaking limbs allow. *We will never, ever leave again*, I swear silently, shoving Kev into the foyer and panting while weaving towards the elevators.

An elevator has just arrived and people spill out, surging into the tide of others attempting to push their way in, and I fight desperately. The crowd funnels into the elevator without leaving enough room for Kev, and I am beyond livid. Fuming, I glare at averted faces and wait for someone to offer their space to the guy in a wheelchair.

'Isn't anyone going to offer to get out so the *only* person in a wheelchair can use the elevator?' I demand. 'After all, you all have legs, which presumably work, and walking up a couple of floors wouldn't be too much of a struggle.' The people crammed into the elevator huddle together, look at the ground and refuse to meet my eyes. I feel like Medusa: if they meet my gaze I will turn them to stone. To the immense relief of the elevator occupants, the doors whisper shut and Kev and I are left to await the next one.

'Kevin. Hey!'

I twist from the closed doors. A teenage girl with long, dark hair approaches through the crowd, smiling broadly and shadowed by her mother.

'Oh ... Sarah ... hi,' says Kev, looking as if he's been caught shoplifting condoms in front of his grandmother. *Go away! Go away! Go away!* My mind screams at them.

'We were just coming up to see you. You've met my mum, right?'

Kev carefully readjusts himself in his chair, nonchalantly folding his hands across his lap. 'Yes, I think so. Em, this is Sarah and her mum ...'

'Vicky,' says Mum.

'Vicky, yes, that's right,' says Kev. Alarmed, his eyes dance from me, to Sarah, to Vicky and everywhere in between. 'Sarah was one of the ski racers I coached last season at Big White,' he says, turning to me. I glance at the numbers above the four elevators: seven, four, nine and eleven — all rising as though synchronized. 'And this is my girlfriend, Emma,' he tells Sarah and Vicky. Standing behind Kev, I attempt a smile,

'Nice to meet you.'

'Likewise,' says Vicky, and awkwardness hangs in the air. Vicky knows something's wrong but is unsure of what. Catching our weighted looks, obvious discomfort, and tripping into the type of dense silence that comes after unresolved anger, she obviously assumes Kev and I are in the midst of an epic argument.

Where's the fucking elevator? Drained, I rest my forearms on the handles of Kev's wheelchair and drop my head slightly, allowing my gaze to fall to the gap between the backrest and seat of Kev's chair. With dull horror, I notice considerable leakage caught within a bouquet of toilet paper and blue plastic pant liners, dangerously close to escape. Oh man, it must have squirted out as Kev readjusted himself to appear nonchalant and debonair. The last thing he wants is one of his racer-punks to know he shat his pants. Sarah and the other kids had looked up to Kev as a great skier, fun, capable, always kidding around and, in the eyes of some of the older girls, he was 'kinda cute'. Now, far from the slopes, devoid of jokes, he's sitting crippled in a wheelchair oozing shit and repulsed by the idea of their pity. I see it in his affected smiles and assurances that, 'No really, I'm doing okay.' And it makes me want to cry. Shielding him from hypothetical judgement and looks of pity or disgust consumes me — looks, I fear, I may once have shot him in different circumstances. Any acknowledgement of his accident threatens to release my anger because deep down, smothered by decorum and sensitivity, I too am mortified. Desperately shuffling sideways to block the gap from view, I straighten carefully, my gaze surreptitiously sweeping the waiting throng for anyone who's noticed anything untoward. All eyes avoid mine, but no more than the usual discomfort felt by strangers sharing personal space. Two red splotches have bloomed across Kev's cheeks.

'All the kids know about your accident, we couldn't believe it when we heard,' says Sarah. 'Here, everyone signed a card for you.' She thrusts a card towards Kev.

I lean with him as he delicately reaches for the oversized novelty card, my body forming a barrier around him. An elevator starts its descent: six, five, four.

Kev's hands falter as he opens the card and Sarah leans against the armrest of his chair pointing out various messages and I search her face for evidence of artifice but find only concern. Yet, still, I see her speaking with impish thrill to an enthralled gang of teenagers, 'Yeah, I saw him at the hospital, it was like, so awkward … he shat his pants — I know! Gross, huh.'

Three, two, one: the crowd swells in anticipation. Kev forms a barricade in front of the metal doors and as they slide open, the crowd flows together, shoving and pushing. I am Moses parting the red sea with a wheelchair and people hop and trip out of the way as ankles and shins lose skin. Inside, with personal space non-existent, the smell is unmentionable.

Up glides the elevator. A heavy, wet and unmistakable odour devours the air and we all pretend not to notice.

'Sooo, are you doing any dryland training this summer?' Asks Kev. A brief, involuntary spasm flicks across Vicky's face and a doctor in the corner coughs.

'A bit. We're going to visit my grandparents for six weeks so I can't get too involved.' Sarah speaks with the lack of perception peculiar to young teenagers — only she is oblivious. The elevator shudders, jerking upwards and then grinding onto the third floor. *Oh, please God, please-please-please don't let the bloody elevator break down,* I pray, fingers clenched white on the back of Kev's chair. Two middle-aged ladies all but launch themselves from the elevator — *that'll teach you to walk up three flights of stairs next time,* I think spitefully.

'Well that'll be fun.' Kev sighs, trails off and gives up. Everyone counts with the numbers.

Vicky and Sarah follow us out of the elevator.

'Can you just give me a minute?' Kev gropes around for the unfamiliar lie, 'I just have to …'

'Check in with your physio,' drops soft as butter from my tongue. I catch Vicky's gaze and see understanding.

'Sure,' she says.

We've never been so pleased to see the nurses but they don't experience the same pleasure upon seeing us. Kev's nurse explains that constipation is a very typical response to a spinal injury, and cleaning people's clothes, sheets and wheelchairs really isn't a big deal.

'It's only when I need to clean your curtains it gets nasty,' he says drolly. Clean-up takes over an hour and by the time Kev emerges from his room wearing clean trousers and smelling of baby powder, Sarah and Vicky are gone.

6

I spent a week in Jasper before catching a bus to Edmonton. As soon as I saw him, I knew I'd made the right decision. That summer, Kev and I drove through the Rocky, Kootenay and Selkirk Mountains in search of wild country, and through the midnight sun to Alaska in his 1977 Volkswagen Kombi. It was witches-hat orange, had 'Fuhkengruven' emblazoned across the rear window and rust crept like lichen over its body, but Kev loved it like a woman. We slept along forestry roads and in campsites without gates so we could sneak out early without paying, ate salmon and Arctic grayling caught on Kev's fly rod, and hiked often into the high alpine. The rain fell soft on snow that crunched under our feet, as the eerie sound of shifting glaciers reached our ears. I worried about bears and, after once seeing paw prints in the snow, cougars, but Kev quietly explained the necessary precautions, carried bear spray on his belt, and loudly sang when we approached berry patches. He did the driving while I rolled Drum cigarettes and occasionally climbed into the back to make salami and cheese sandwiches or search out more CDs. Hours were spent buried in the engine and sorting through Volkswagen graveyards for parts when the van inevitably failed. After the starter broke we drove for 2000 kilometres, only switching off the ignition to pump gas once we'd secured a jump start.

Towards the end of the summer, we camped in Jasper National Park in Northern Alberta — a huge expanse of Rocky Mountain wilderness boasting abundant wildlife, glaciers and breathtaking mountains, perennially capped with snow. The aquamarine waters of Horseshoe Lake were still when I jumped from the cliff, some twenty-five metres above, and the slap of my impact echoed around the lake, causing Kev and other spectators on the shore to wince sympathetically. Stunned, the water closed over me, and long seconds passed as my body hung suspended underwater, while the first concentric waves raced to the shore.

Then I was forced upwards through swarms of bubbles and as air reached my lungs, pain exploded down my spine and coalesced in the lumbar region of my lower back. Equal volumes of water and air filled my mouth as my legs refused to kick. I flopped onto my back and it was clear I was not okay. Kev's friend, Trev, jumped from the cliff and his concerned face surfaced beside me.

'Are you alright Em?'

'No … No, I can't breathe, I can't see — I can hardly see,' I said as Trev helped me swim to the shore. Kev, on the other side of the lake, had waded in and supported between the two men, my eyes saw nothing but my bare feet on pine needles as we walked slowly through the forest to the carpark.

Trev drove fast to the hospital in Jasper and it still took almost fifteen minutes. Kev sat beside me in the back, my hand gripped his hard enough to turn my knuckles white.

'It's going to be okay, it's going to be okay,' he repeated gently as he stroked wet hair from my face with his free hand. But his eyes said otherwise. Numbness crept up my legs and every movement ignited the pain in my lower back and sent my stomach surging. Shapes swam across my vision and the hairs on my arms and legs stood erect as Kev quelled my sobs, mumbling words, lips touching my damp hair. Clad in bathers and wrapped in a towel, I stumbled through the sliding doors of the hospital, half carried by Kev and leaving footprints and puddles on the linoleum floor.

A nurse rushed towards me pushing a wheelchair. My torso and legs were strapped to a backboard and a cervical collar encircled my neck, preventing any movement except by my arms or eyes.

'Why do I need a backboard?' I'd asked the nurse.

'To prevent any further spinal damage,' she'd replied. 'After an injury like yours, the smallest movement can damage the spinal cord and could even result in paralysis. We need to find out how much damage has occurred.'

'Wait, what? A spinal injury? I don't have a spinal injury,' I said, 'I can't have a spinal injury.' The nurse was silent and beside me Kev squeezed my hand. 'Kev, I don't have a spinal injury, do I?' I was frantic. How could this happen?

A doctor appeared and began to lecture me on the dangers of cliff jumping as he examined me.

'Discounting spinal damage, there are many other dangers of cliff jumping,' he said, 'Including perforated ovaries, concussions and fractures. It is an incredibly stupid thing to do.' Noticing I was near tears, a nurse touched my inner forearm gently as I was wheeled into the x-ray theatre.

'Sometimes these things work out,' she said softly.

The x-ray image showed I had compressed my spine, but all visible vertebrae appeared undamaged. The problem was, one of my lumbar vertebrae was obscured in the image and the doctor couldn't tell if it was intact.

'I can't see one of your vertebrae clearly, so I'm sending you for a CT scan and I'll need to admit you until the results are reviewed,' he said.

'I don't have any travel insurance, it expired last month. How much will that cost?' I replied.

'Well, in that case I suppose if you don't move around too much and remain in bed, I guess I could release you. But you will need to call in two days for the results of the scan. And be aware that if the vertebrae is shattered, it could slice your spinal cord unless you're extremely careful,' he suggested reluctantly.

As I watched from the hospital wheelchair, Kev folded out the bed in the back of the van. I gingerly climbed up and lay down and Kev slowly drove back to Edmonton. Every time he drove over a bump the entire van rattled and shook and he looked back in concern as I cried out. Unable to climb stairs, I slept on a mattress in the lounge room. Kev slept beside me on an inflatable mattress so his movements wouldn't shake the mattress and cause me pain.

Two days later the nurse on the phone said that everything looked good when I rang for the results of the CT scan. It was as though something huge and terrifying had passed silently behind me.

* * *

The way I see the world and other people in it is changing. I notice a step here, a ramp there, a large, high curb over there. Suddenly, the three steps I easily hop up to collect our take-out dinner becomes something else to me — an insurmountable barrier. Do I really want to support businesses that are inaccessible to Kev? He wouldn't be able to simply jump in and grab the dinner without it being a huge mission. And suddenly disabled people are everywhere; not because the disabled population has boomed overnight but because, for the first time, I am noticing them — really noticing them. I meet the eyes of the middle-aged lady in the automatic wheelchair passing by me on the sidewalk, nod to the old man in the mobility scooter and smile at the young man with cerebral palsy walking with difficulty across the road. An entire sub-population that had been invisible to me is suddenly revealed, and I begin to understand how challenging life can be for some.

Outside of hospitals, hardly anything is designed with disabled people in mind: stairs, gaps, narrow doors, gravel, mud, fences and other barriers loom everywhere. Aisles are congested and narrow in stores, footpaths overgrown with vegetation, drivers blind to wheelchair users in parking lots, and high counters and pub tables leave wheelchair users staring at walls or crotches perched on high stools, enjoying cold beverages above their heads. It can be an unkind and dangerous world for a wheelchair-user and the new perspective opens my eyes.

Already struggling with anger over Kev's injury and the 'why us' conundrum, I find myself becoming more judgemental towards people I feel are wasting the abilities they possess. Walking along Broadway on my way to the hospital one morning, a young man slouches by the side of a building with his hat outstretched. He's a young, fit, walking man, possibly addicted to drugs or some other substance but physically whole, and his begging infuriates me.

'Excuse me, Miss, can you spare some change?' He asks as I pass and anger boils within me.

'Why don't you get a fucking job and you wouldn't need my change,' I snap.

'There are no jobs, no one will hire me,' he starts miserably.

'Bullshit,' I yell. 'You have everything! You are strong, you are young! My boyfriend can't walk and still he tries to work. You're wasting your life: the precious gift of a sound body. You don't even appreciate how lucky you are!'

I feel myself becoming hysterical. I'm not angry at the poor homeless man, I'm angry at life and the perceived injustice of Kev's injury.

'You are nothing but a FUCKING BUM!' The young man stares

at me in wide-eyed fear and I realise he's worried I might actually physically attack him. People are slowing down, staring at the crazy woman screaming at the homeless man. He doesn't even try and defend himself with a 'Chill the fuck out, you crazy bitch,' he just stares at me with huge, sad eyes and his hands held out in supplication. *Keep it together*, I tell myself as the man quickly collects his pile of change and swiftly walks down the footpath, glancing backwards several times to ensure I'm not following him.

That's it, I'm going psychotic. I'm completely and totally losing it. Whatever shred of rationality and reason I ever had has fled and in short order I will end up heavily sedated in a padded cell a few wards down from Kev. What is happening to me? Normally I am not crazy, I am calm and confident; well, at least I project that. But now I'm completely losing it. My carefully crafted facade is crumbling and I am broken.

Any perceived criticism of disabled people makes me livid and every time someone treats Kev in a patronising or condescending manner, which is often, my heart gallops and face burns red. Whenever someone acts thoughtlessly and slightly inconveniences him, such as stepping in front of the wheelchair, I'm outraged and completely snap.

'My dad was in a wheelchair and that really hurts,' says a father as his gangly adolescent pushes in front of Kev and is accidently rapped on the ankle by the footplate.

'Then you should teach your kid not to push in front of people in wheelchairs,' I snarl back. If I discover non-wheelchair-placard-displaying cars parked in disabled places, I want to smash their windscreens and demand the car be towed immediately as I rage like Godzilla, kicking tyres and swearing. If I happen to see someone pulling into a disabled space so they can just run into the store quickly I appear at their driver's window like an avenging Valkyrie, launching into a tirade of why they are the number-one asshole in all of Canada.

'I'll only be a minute,' the drivers protest.

'I don't care how long you'll be, that's not the fucking point; disabled parking spaces are here for a reason and you should appreciate the fact that you can walk half a block.' I take people acting like ignorant assholes extremely personally; everything is an affront to Kev and all he's been through and will go through. Whenever we go somewhere that is not wheelchair accessible I look around for someone to bitch at, even though in my previous blissful ignorance it would never have crossed my mind that a couple of steps may pose a huge problem for some people. I don't know who I am anymore.

As we leave the hospital more often, we come to realise that out-and-about in a wheelchair you attract a lot of attention. It doesn't matter if you are just going to shops for some milk or if you are a fire-eating street entertainer, still people stare.

'How dare they stare at you like you are some kind of a circus freak!' I rant furiously whenever someone allows their gaze to linger. The gawking little kids don't bother me: kids stare at everything and a guy in a wheelchair is more interesting than all of those boring walking people. It's when the parents or teenagers stare, that I glare back, simmering, as they watch slack-jawed and oblivious while Kev rolls up a curb or tries to go through a door.

Incredibly, while Kev and I ride the lift back to the ward with a woman and her toddler she says pointedly to the child,

'Look that man has wheels on his chair that looks like fun, doesn't it?'

'Yes,' replies Kev, leaning down to the child's level, 'and all you need to do to get one is drive a motorbike really, really fast.'

The staring bothers Kev less than it bothers me. He is a 'why would I worry about the things I can't change' kind of person. The most obvious answer to that question, coming from a woman who not only worries about but regularly rages against, those things she cannot change, is because they fucking piss me off.

* * *

On the spinal ward of Vancouver General, most patients are not looking towards home but look instead to G.F. Strong Rehabilitation Centre. From the first moment you arrive on the spinal ward, you hear about G.F. Strong Rehab Centre, British Columbia's largest rehabilitation centre, catering to patients with acquired brain injuries, spinal injuries, and neuromusculoskeletal arthritis amongst other things. It's the light at the end of the hospital tunnel — magical, amazing things happen at G.F.: people learn, heal and sometimes they even get better.

Kev whizzes around the spinal ward holding a wheelie after a month, eager to be punted over to G.F. and start on his recovery journey. But unfortunately, G.F. is just as crowded as Vancouver General and beds are not easy to come by. Six weeks pass from when Kev first arrived, broken and battered, to Vancouver General, to when a spot opens-up for him at G.F. Strong, and his parents come from Peachland to help make the transition. As Don makes a turn onto King Edward Ave, on the other side of the intersection, a man in a wheelchair attempts to wheel up the curb from the road and does not quite make it. He struggles then rolls back into traffic, struggles, rolls back into traffic and on the third attempt he makes it. I realise when he makes it up onto the footpath that I had been holding my breath and release it with a whoosh. *That is what Kev will be like*, I think.

PART II

REHAB

7

When two grizzly bears had first emerged from the trees on the other side of Kaslo Lake from where I lay in a tent, I thought they were cows. When it registered that they were grizzlies, I tried to stand up and nearly knocked our tent over.

'Em, fuck — relax!' Kev had hissed, pressing a canister of bear spray into my hand and pulling me back down onto the mattress. I'd never seen a grizzly before — never even been backpacking — before I met Kev. Camping as a kid involved Mum and Dad bashing the old land-cruiser into the bush somewhere and sleeping in the back, so the concept of hiking while carrying stuff, heavy stuff, was new. Consequently, Kev's pack was thrice as big as mine, which sometimes I didn't even bother to take. We had hiked to the lake the previous day, through high alpine fields afire with flowers of red, yellow and white, foxtail grasses and the soft, shaggy seedpods of chalice flowers that Kev used to brush my cheek. Shadowing the fields were the peaks of the Kootenay Mountains, upon which snow still clung in dirty patches. Marmots whistled and bugs orbited as his warm hand held mine. The night was cold, but we slept with just the fly-net on, watching the stars and feeling like the last people in the world.

* * *

'Well,' Don says, turning into the parking lot at G.F. Strong, 'we're here.'

Blinking, I bury thoughts of mountains and watch Kev, who has been waiting weeks for this, practically frame his face between outstretched palms on the window. Several faces peer down curiously from the windows of the four-level brick building and a messy snarl of wheelchair accessible buses, taxis and vans are parked haphazardly around the entrance: doors and trunks ajar in various stages of loading and unloading passengers. A crowd of beanie and sunglasses-wearing people in automatic wheelchairs, all tilted back to face the sun, line the pavement, each periodically reoriented during the course of the day like sunflowers following the sun's progress across the sky. A pall of cigarette smoke engulfs the group, drifting lazily from cigarettes attached to modified clamps, attached to braces, securely fastened onto wrists. As one, we nod shyly to the group and they watch us inquisitively as we enter G.F. Strong for the first time, full of anticipation, fear and the lingering nuclei of hope.

Wisely, I adhere to the advice of Vancouver General nurses to keep right in the hallways, as wheelchairs frequently barrel along the halls. I'm forced to leap askew as a young guy cannonballs around a corner, using the wall as a lever with one hand and missing me by me inches.

I'd heard rumours on the Vancouver General spinal ward that it's not uncommon for long time intravenous drug users to develop tumours on their spines resulting in paralysis, so there was potential for Kev to have a roommate who was not only dealing with becoming a quadriplegic or a paraplegic, but also heroin withdrawal, and if there is a time in your life when heroin may seem most appealing, shortly after a spinal injury surely must be it. So it is with great relief that I meet Kev's new roommate, an ageing, bearded hippy from the Gulf Islands, who became an incomplete quadriplegic as a result of a mountain bike accident sustained in the Whistler Mountain Bike Park, which seems to churn out quadriplegics faster than an assembly line.

The old hippy works as an air-cooled Volkswagen van mechanic and his side of the double room is crammed full of Volkswagen paraphernalia: small van models and posters of Kombis and Bugs are plastered to the walls. Kev is delighted. They immediately begin discussing techniques to convert the transmission of Kev's manual 77 Kombi to an automatic. Once Kev has had time to settle in and unpack his small bag of belongings and chat about vans for a bit, a nurse issues him with a daily timetable outlining his rehabilitation program and daily treatment schedule, organised into different coloured blocks of activities like a high school kid's daily timetable. Each day Kev has appointments with physios, occupational therapists, physiatrists and other medical personnel to enhance his abilities, manage his pain and spasticity levels and teach him how to live with his disability.

Kev is regularly consulted about his rehabilitation goals, which are initially 'to walk the hell out of here', but slowly become 'to be the best cripple I can be' and his treatment program is adjusted accordingly. He plans to regain his balance and learn how to sit upright without the use of his abdominal muscles; get back in his chair when he falls out; develop ways to move in and out of his wheelchair without using a transfer board; and an efficient technique of retrieving things that drop to the floor. He wants to learn to shower, dress, drive, swim, not to shit his pants, get back into the bush and most importantly, he wants to learn to ski again.

First on the physiotherapy agenda is regaining balance. Sitting on the elevated blue stretching mats in the physiotherapy gymnasium, Kev has his arms stretched out behind him and the physiotherapist asks him to bring them into his lap. It seems like such a simple request, but Kev teeters for a few moments then topples gracelessly onto his back. Learning to balance in a sitting position as a paraplegic, using only muscles above nipple height, is akin to balancing while standing on a Swiss ball. It can be done, but not without considerable effort. Kev's legs, hips and tummy are beyond his control and slide out beneath him, slamming him into the mat.

After a time, the sitting exercise evolves to clapping his hands, then holding arms outstretched and finally to catching a ball. The ball-catching exercise frustrates him by showing his frailty but as much as possible he has a pragmatic positivity and does not often wallow in the depths of self-pity, instead dealing with each additional challenge or setback with quiet dignity and resolve. And I love him for it.

8

You remember the people you meet in rehab forever. People who recover, and people who are worse off than you; the paras have the quads, the quads have the brain injury patients, and the brain injury patients have those who left Vancouver General via the service entrance in the basement.

The population of the spinal ward in G.F. is mostly young and predominantly male. It's full of men who have been injured riding motorbikes, driving, playing sports or doing any of the myriad of other dangerous things young men tend to do, blissfully unaware they are just one bad car wreck away from a vastly different life. There are also several women, one of whom had the misfortune to sustain a brain injury after tumbling over backwards on her bar stool while out drinking with friends, and another, broke her back after a fall on a cruise ship and, heavily medicated, she closes her eyes while talking, appearing to be asleep, then flings them open again and continues the conversation as if nothing untoward has happened; it's somewhat unnerving.

There are the three joint-rolling moochers, all young quadriplegics with a similar level of injury, C3 through C5, who mobbed Kev the day he arrived at G.F. with his long hair, red beard and hemp necklace because they saw joint rolling potential in his strong, thick hands and fully functional fingers. He is known as 'Fingers' and at least once a day one of the quads drops by Kev's room for him to roll them a joint. Across the hall is a tall, slight and charmingly polite road racing cyclist who became a C5 quadriplegic when an inattentive driver swerved into him, knocking him from his bike, breaking his neck and very nearly killing him. He constantly wears a Cook Islands ball cap to remind himself of his recent honeymoon to the South Pacific Island; a far happier time. Also on the ward, is a Ukrainian climber who spent twelve hours lying injured alone at the base of a cliff while his companion hiked out for help. He became a T6 paraplegic just like Kev.

At G.F., people have widely varying degrees of disability: from those with slight impairments to their gaits, to the more seriously disabled: seated in large automatic wheelchairs covered in medical paraphernalia with twisted, wasted limbs and mechanical sounding voices. In the cafeteria, I feel uncomfortable watching people being fed at mealtimes with their mouths hanging slack, food dribbling down their chins onto their large, adult sized bibs, and awkward when others yell or scream at thunderous volume. Ashamed, I try to hide it. But it is obvious because I have no peripheral vision and my eyes remain honed in on Kev at all times.

One afternoon as Kev and I eat lunch in the cafeteria, I meet a man who can see my thoughts and fears as clearly as if they are flashing on a neon sign above my head. He is a C2 quadriplegic since a diving accident on a hockey camp thirty-odd years ago, and works as a peer counsellor at G.F. He wheels up to me in his huge automatic wheelchair with bulky attached ventilator and says,

'Hi my name is Walt.'

'Hi,' I say.

'It's okay,' he says. 'I know the chair is scary, but I don't bite … much.'

I smile nervously but as he speaks I relax. I realise it is okay to be afraid. It's a normal reaction when everything is new and overwhelming, and I don't know whether to look, not look, or look while I'm pretending I'm not looking. I don't need to be afraid of disabled people because they are just like me, except a little hurt and — with the exception of crazy Australian girlfriends — they are unlikely to freak out at me if I show the remotest bit of interest in looking at them. I hadn't thought of everyone else in G.F. as being just like Kev. To be honest, I hadn't thought of Kev as disabled; I had thought he doesn't belong here with these people. He is not disabled, he is just hurt — and now I realise that everyone is just hurt to varying degrees. In the (slightly adapted) words of Shakespeare, 'Some people are born disabled, some people become disabled and some have disability thrust upon them.'

'You don't have a disability,' Walt says mockingly to Kev as he rolls away, 'I have a disability!' I think of Paul Hogan in *Crocodile Dundee* saying, 'That's not a knife, *this* is a knife,' and smile.

* * *

Wheelchair school makes up an integral part of Kev's rehabilitation program and, while fun, it's also very important because the world outside G.F. is not smooth, not all concrete and unfortunately soft mats do not cushion the inevitable falls. Glenn, one of the few male physiotherapists at G.F. and the wheelchair-skills teacher, looks like a male version of Pippi Longstocking, with red curly hair, freckles, pale bony limbs, brightly coloured unmatched socks, high top Converse sneakers and enthusiasm verging on mania. He's a wizard in a wheelchair, even without using his legs as a counterbalance. During wheelchair lessons, Glenn is exuberant, flamboyant and incredibly supportive, trying every manoeuvre he asks of his pupils and every so often he tumbles over backwards, sprawling onto the mats — to my secret pleasure.

'The wheelie is an essential skill for wheelchair users to learn,' says Glenn. 'It enables you to cruise down steep hills safely, hop over any small obstacles, such as gravel or sticks, and cover rough ground by lifting the small front casters while balancing on the larger back wheels.'

But most importantly, wheelies just look cool. Like being a kid watching an older kid zooming down the street on a rusted-out single speed bike, arms folded in a nonchalant manner, watching someone in a wheelchair hoon down a hill balanced on two wheels, thrills me a little. Mostly though, it makes Kev jealous and spurs him into bursts of frantic wheelie practice.

'Good work Kev,' says Glenn, 'how often do you overbalance these days?'

'Pretty often,' says Kev.

When the spills happen, they cause quite a commotion. Nothing quite moves a crowd like a person who has fallen out of their wheelchair; faster than a bunch of conservative Baptists trying to cover a topless woman, everyone tries desperately to put Kev back in his chair because seeing a guy lying sprawled on the ground next to an overturned wheelchair is just awkward. No one wants that. Eventually, after many potentially neck-breaking flips, Kev masters the wheelie, making life just a tiny bit easier.

Curb-hopping is the next trick Kev learns, a necessity because curb cut-aways are few and far between. The technique in a wheelchair is similar to the way curbs are handled on a bicycle: Kev hurtles at a concrete curb and at the last possible moment before smashing into the lip, he lifts the front wheels, popping into a wheelie, and pushes forward strongly. Ideally, the momentum carries him up and over the curb. Unfortunately, it is not an ideal world and all too often Kev is forcefully and powerfully ejected from his chair and lands with a knee-cracking thump on the up-thrown side of the curb with the wheelchair remaining below in the gutter. Due to the prevalence of ejections in the early days of curb-hopping, the skill is taught on soft gym mats which do not have the same consequences for failure.

After he graduates from the cushioning mats, Kev tackles the concrete curbs and I watch, cringing, from between spread fingers. Initially he falls with every attempt, dusts off his hands, then painstakingly climbs back up onto his feet into a crouching position and tries repeatedly to get back into his wheelchair on his own, until he slumps over, exhausted, with shaking arms and damp hair and reluctantly asks for my help in a small, defeated voice. Over time, he occasionally begins to sail up onto the curb like a teenager on a BMX and as his successes become more frequent, he becomes cocky and overconfident and once more is ejected disharmoniously. 'Check this out,' he'll say, charging at a curb that seems higher than the Berlin Wall and a slow involuntary groan escapes me.

By the time I ask, 'Kev do you really think that's a good idea?' He's kneeling on the curb with scraped palms and knees, an overturned wheelchair cupping his bottom and swearing like a drill-rig worker. I don't want to wrap him in cotton wool, and as much as it hurts me to watch him struggle I know the pain of seeing him give up, of watching his shoulders take on a defeated slump and his eyes acquire a passive kind of acceptance like a long-caged wild animal, will be much worse. So I choke back cautions when he does things I know he will fail at, or get hurt doing, because I know that one day, one day he will succeed. It is no more in my nature to baby him as it is in his to accept it.

Like all good schools, wheelchair school has field trips into the outside world. The world outside of wheelchair-friendly G.F. is a frightening place and some patients have barely left G.F. since their injury. On excursion days, a large wheelchair accessible bus pulls up outside the front door and trippers line up behind the lift, jostling to get on first. Since the lift only accommodates one wheelchair at a time, bus-boarding takes quite some time but eventually all the wheelchairs are fastened down with straps.

'Everyone ready?' Asks Glenn as we roar away with a line of happy faces smeared against the windows. Our destination is a nearby mall in search of escalators so Glenn can teach everyone how to use an escalator in a wheelchair. Looking for the escalators, Glenn, who is seated in a wheelchair for the excursion, wheels ahead of the main scrum and is waiting at the bottom of a double escalator when the rest of the group arrives and fans out around him.

'Okay, I am going to demonstrate how it's done first so make sure you can all see.' The group rearranges a little as Glenn confidently wheels up to the upward escalator, running his long skinny arms along the moving banister and latching on like a vacuum clamp. To my astonishment, the chair does not immediately tip over backwards and leave Glenn disorientated with a copiously bleeding head wound; instead he travels steadily up the escalator and wheels calmly off at the top. To descend, he wheels backwards towards the downward escalator, waiting until the chair is grabbed, then seizes the banisters with both hands, gliding elegantly down backwards while peering over his shoulder and spinning nimbly off at the bottom. It looks downright suicidal. But I am impressed — more than impressed: amazed.

'Who's next?'

'I'll have a go,' says cocky young paraplegic man with a lumbar injury. When the young man returns, Kev is keen to try it and I hurriedly suggest that perhaps we should wait until someone else tries; the idea of Glenn falling out and tumbling down the sharp corrugated stairs appeals to me much more than Kev with his barely healed surgical scar, spasticity and general fragility.

'I'll go next,' says Kev and, anti-climatically, he makes it both up and down the escalator, returning with the world's biggest shit-eating grin. A couple of other people go up and down but there is no carnage. No one falls spectacularly from their wheelchair and rolls screaming down the escalator, or is sucked into the moving mechanisms of the stairway. No one even stumbles awkwardly as I tend to do when dismounting an escalator. It is all very mundane. Well, mundane if you call a large group of wheelchair users going up and down an escalator mundane. Most people have never seen one person in a wheelchair using an escalator, let alone a dozen or so, and hence it does not take long for security to arrive. Apparently, the mall is not too keen on having a bunch of wheelchair users learn how to use a potentially dangerous instrument on their property. They mention something about liability costs, and so after a tense discussion with Glenn, we are asked to move along.

9

Leaving Kev in Edmonton was harder than I had thought it would be. My visa was expiring and a job teaching snowboarding was waiting for me in Breckenridge, Colorado. I was on a plane to Denver when I found the letter he wrote to me:

To my darling Emma, if I were a poet I would write you a sonnet to make a nation weep; if I were a sculptor I would carve your beauty for the ages; if I were a painter I would create a masterpiece around you; if I could spell, this would be easier; but I am just me and you will have to imagine how you make me feel. I wish I could be those things and show you what you already know: I love you.

A blond curl had been sticky-taped next to the poem with: *to remember me by* scrawled next to it. Prickles tore my throat and had the plane not been airborne I'd have tried to get off.

Time always seemed to be running out. We had time here and

time there but we were often just waiting to be parted again. After Breckenridge, the Canadian Government approved my second visa application and I returned to Canada. Kev and I spent the summer together before I left to get work in the ski town of Fernie, British Columbia. We travelled together to Queenstown in New Zealand, where Kev was a ski instructor and I worked on the lifts, and afterwards, I flew to Australia and Kev to Canada. Saying goodbye was heartbreaking. I could not let go of him as shakes gripped my body. All our visa options had been exhausted and it was difficult to see a way to remain together. I wanted to go back to university and study geology and Kev had his final year of geophysics to complete. Ten months passed before he arrived at my house in Melbourne, dragging his mountain bike in a huge cardboard box, an eighty-litre backpack slung across his shoulder, and an ample red beard framing his tremendous smile. He spent four months hanging out in Melbourne, riding his bike, climbing with my cousin, and spending hours at the Victoria Market haggling with old men over vegetables, before he was notified of winning a prestigious graduate scholarship to study avalanches using geophysical equipment in the mountains of British Columbia. I couldn't ask him to stay. It was his dream, the perfect merging of passion and practicality: getting paid to ski tour. I decided to continue my geology degree in Canada so we could be together and so, in September 2003, we applied for a common-law visa that would enable me to live and study in Canada. *Finally,* I thought, two months before the accident, arriving in Vancouver with a permanent resident visa stapled into my passport, *our separation and visa problems are over and our life together is about to start.*

* * *

At G.F., patients are actively encouraged to go out, explore, socialise and live their lives in as normal a manner as possible. Consequently, being in G.F. feels like freedom compared to Vancouver General;

it feels like the difference between high school and university. No one constantly looks over your shoulder and checks up on you. The first night Kev, Alex and I go out drinking since Kev's accident, we find ourselves at a bar around the corner from my apartment that presents live flamenco dancing shows each night. We are all quite drunk when a middle-aged woman suddenly begins dancing in the middle of the small stage and to me, in that moment, she is beautiful. Her long dark hair is tied back from her round face with a red sash, large pendulous breasts are amply displayed in a low-cut blouse and a soft tummy strains against her tight black skirt. But her chin is lifted and her nose is proud. She thrusts out her full chest and stomps as though putting out a fire, trilling throatily all the while to the frantic strumming of her accompanying guitarist. 'Whoa,' I breathe, as my body tingles, finally understanding the power of self-confidence. The woman has rhythm. She doesn't care if we think she's sexy or not, because she knows she's sexy. To hell with Hollywood starlets, I want to be her!

After walking Kev back to G.F., I make my way back to my apartment passing a 'women only' sex shop called Honey and I duck inside. I have only been into a few sex shops before: sleazy ones, staffed by fat balding men with horn-rimmed glasses and thick wet lips, or ageing, inappropriately dressed ex-strippers. Honey is a lovely surprise because it is run by women, for women, stocking tasteful items such as sensuous massage oils, delicate sexy lingerie and elegant feathers, candles and books, among other items.

'Hello,' says the attractive lady behind the counter, raising her eyes from her book 'If you have any questions, please let me know.' I browse the shop for some time, smelling oils, caressing soft lingerie fabric and flicking through the many books. Eventually I buy Kev a beautiful Indian silk-bound copy of the Kama Sutra (which unfortunately does not have a wheelchair section). Perusing the book, I think of the flamenco dancer and her blatant sex appeal and of her fluid, languid movements and dark, sultry eyes. To her, I assumed, sex was like a fine red wine and had only improved with age. However, these days, to me, sex feels like a foreign country: fraught with fear and misunderstanding and disaster.

'Why do you want to have sex with me?' Kev asks. 'My legs are disgusting, it's creepy and weird.' He cannot accept that I want to have sex with him and I cannot accept that he wants to have sex at all.

'Well why do you even want to have sex with me? Can you even feel it with your dulled sensation?' I ask, on the verge of tears. 'I'm hurting you.'

'No, it's not you … my back just hurts all the time. Of course I like it … it feels different but still great.'

I am so conscious of every expression that crosses his face, and assume I've caused every grimace.

'Should I stop? Are you sure you're okay?'

'Yes, yes I'm fine.' But he is not fine. His back aches constantly and the spasms rip through him torturously. He's hurt and fragile and less able to roll about than before. Sex feels like something I am doing to him instead of something we are doing together. We are at odds, acting like nervous, awkward virgins, unsure of how to please each other and at the same time, so desperate to please.

'That part of my life is over,' Kev had said melodramatically three days after his injury and, at the time, I felt that too. The first time we had sex after Kev's injury was when he was still a patient in Vancouver General and was visiting my apartment. He attained an erection and we had quick, awkward sex, with me terrified of hurting him. As we lay together on my bed, Kev suddenly began to urinate and, stricken, he grabbed his shirt and bunched it over his penis to stop the flow. Traumatised, we barely spoke of it. Still, we didn't want to acknowledge things had changed in our sex life, but simply mourn what we thought was lost forever.

With time, Kev learnt an effective system to manage his bladder to prevent such mishaps, but the incident burned deep and it took a while before we had sex again. G.F. offers sexual health information and we are given numerous pamphlets demonstrating positions suitable for a recently injured paraplegic man and his partner, and patients are encouraged to experiment with sex as soon as they feel physically able. On the spinal ward is a room that is set up essentially as a hotel room, with a double bed and bathroom, known as the Living Room. Patients book a stay accompanied by their partners, giving them a glimpse of how life will be when they go home but with the safety-net of nurses just a call-bell away. Between the Living Room and visits to my apartment, we snatch moments of intimacy and trying, yet failing, to take mishaps less seriously and laughing instead of crying. The nurses tell us to keep trying, that it is early days, and with ingenuity, modification and practice, sex can again be great.

* * *

As summer fades to fall, the days remain warm and sunny but the mornings feel chilly, the trees turn crispy and yellow, and the wind has a frigid bite. Winter is near. Although Vancouver does not get the piles and piles of snow that Calgary or Edmonton endure, the overbearing greyness and complete absence of sunlight makes spending a winter there a grim prospect. Furthermore, this will be the first winter since Kev was two that he won't ski and it pains him more than I can imagine. One day we will think of our seasons spent together — of hiking through deep snow for fresh tracks in New Zealand, drinking beers in the sun in Colorado and tree skiing impossibly deep powder in British Columbia — without choking back tears of loss, but not quite yet.

Tacked to the board beside Kev's bed are photographs of happier times and cards emblazoned with inspiring sayings I'd pinned there to make the room feel warmer. One picture particularly pulls me, causing my diaphragm to spasm a little each time my eyes light up on it. Taken the previous year at a campground on Stradbroke Island off the coast of Brisbane, Kev, XXXX beer in hand, sits on a blanket outside our small orange tent — open so I can see a strawberry lip balm lying on my sleeping bag — books, bags and dinner dishes spill out beside him and a large Malibu surfboard rests on a patch of bare dirt alongside the tent. Quizzically, he looks directly at the camera. And it feels like a punch.

To me, the photo represents everything we have lost. How do you go camping when you need a white sterile box packed with stuff that can't get dirty and about half an hour just to take a piss? How do you wheel around dirt, sleep on a crappy one-centimetre-thick sleeping pad without pressure sores and transfer to and from the ground, or pick up the Leatherman when it falls beside a campfire? How the fuck do you camp in a wheelchair?

I didn't think camping was possible until Kev's sister Jos sent me a link to a website called Crip College. Started by a guy in Calgary who broke his back snowboarding in the mid-nineties, it chronicled his recovery, provided informed practical advice and showed pictures of him camping, skiing and sailing. I clicked obsessively through the blog: a guy in a wheelchair, camping — really?

With Kev still struggling to learn basic, everyday skills and unable to get back into his chair, it becomes clear he also has much to learn that cannot be taught in a rehabilitation hospital — things that to us are crucial. We need to get away. Away from hospitals, rehab centres, anxious parents and wheelchair accessible taxis that don't stop even though the driver saw us, and then when they do stop, having drivers blurt things like, 'I'd rather be dead than in a wheelchair.'

We need to reclaim our life together and go where memories do not haunt us like restless ghosts nipping our bourgeoning confidence with visions of the past viewed though rose-tinted glasses. Neither of us wants the disability to change our relationship, and although we have no idea what life in a wheelchair will be like, together we had travelled and hiked and camped, and we intend to do that once again. For the sake of our relationship, we need to figure out how.

The thought of a completely new country with no support is too overwhelming right now, and as Kev still hasn't seen much of my home county, Australia, it seems like the best choice. With my family in Melbourne, that is the logical starting point but where to after that? Australia is a vast country and there are lots of places to visit. I sit on the hard, plastic-covered hospital bed in Kev's room, staring at a full-sized map of Australia spread out on the table between us and, hesitantly, begin to outline the entire perimeter of the country in a thick black texta: west from Melbourne through the mighty Australian outback — *with a man on whom the hospital doors will have barely closed* punctuates my anxiety. Once the trail on the map has been set, we can't refuse to take it and honestly, I'm afraid. Neither Kev nor I think we will actually do it — or, more accurately, that we *can* actually do it. We don't really know what we can do these days, when even a trip out to a new restaurant without calamity is a huge accomplishment. The room does not seem to have enough air and we feel as if we are constantly struggling for breath. The air has been recirculated and rebreathed so many times that it is exhausted, tired air; tired like the people breathing it. We feel that backing down from any challenge is surrendering to the disability and we cannot accept other people setting their limitations on Kev. He has to prove his independence and, paradoxically, at this point he needs me to do it.

'Okay … we are going to Australia and we'll go around it together,' I say with false heartiness. 'It will be fun.'

Kev smiles and squeezes my hand. He is nervous, too. We are running away from everything and every step takes us further away from G.F. and towards something akin to hope.

10

Kev's rehab is progressing well. He long ago mastered the wheelie, his balance and strength have improved and finally the time has come for him to think about moving out of G.F. to make room for someone else. After six weeks living at G.F., Kev is discharged but remains a physiotherapy outpatient five days a week. We spend several days staying at the Holiday Inn on Broadway waiting for a vacancy at Millennium Place, the transitional housing subsidised by BC Housing and run in part by the BC Paraplegic Society, that will be our home for the six weeks before we fly to Australia in late November.

During our hotel stay, Kev develops a severe urinary tract infection (UTI), which is common in spinal injury patients due to changes in the way the bladder voids. Some people have spasmodic bladders that spontaneously empty when full, like a teetering bucket under a tap, while others require an intermittent catheter to void the bladder, which otherwise would remain tightly sealed causing long-term complications. Kev lies somewhere in between: his bladder voids spontaneously but sometimes fails to empty completely and the use of an intermittent catheter is required to remove stagnant urine. But catheters can also be a vector delivering bacteria into the bladder where it multiplies, resulting in a UTI complete with fever chills, increased spasms, nausea, headaches and generally feeling crappy. The infections can be very serious if untreated and spread to the kidneys, potentially causing permanent kidney damage. A condom catheter, distinct from an intermittent catheter, attaches to the penis with an adhesive paste, connects to a hose that runs into a one-litre bag strapped to the leg and is used when the bladder spontaneously voids.

During his first severe UTI, Kev is prescribed Ciprofloxin, the most commonly used and most effective drug, and something to which Kev is violently allergic. After taking a tablet, angry red hives erupt from his skin and his lips pout, plump and botoxed. As I am helping him into the bathtub for a dousing in calamine lotion, he loses his balance, flails backwards into the tub and before I can catch him, cracks the back of his skull with a dull thud on the tap, while flipping his wheelchair over with one powerfully spasming foot. Stunned, I look at Kev — naked, crumpled and splotchy with hives, still grasping the shower curtain, now ripped free of several rings, rubbing the back of his head and swearing — and I giggle. Like most inappropriate laughter, I can't help myself. It seems so absurd and, in a way, ridiculously comical. Laughing, I'm as helpless as Kev. But he does not have an episode of autonomic dysreflexia; it seems that, with the exception of the one instance soon after his injury, autonomic dysreflexia is not something that will trouble him.

We stay in the Holiday Inn for almost two weeks before an apartment becomes vacant at Millennium Place, where the spacious units are all accessible or adaptable to some degree, with low benches and cupboards, space underneath the sink for knees and feet and no danger of bumping into furniture or getting jammed in corners and hallways. The bathroom is huge and empty like a gym shower. It is so wheelchair accessible I begin to get back problems. Everything is placed at an awkward level for a person standing up — great for Kev, not so great for me.

There are no cupboards for storage in the bathroom so that Kev can get his legs under the sink to wash his hands and brush his teeth, and in the kitchen, all the useful stuff like cups, glasses and plates are on the bottom level of cupboards so I have to crouch down to get them. I feel like Alice in Wonderland after she took the blue pill. But for Kev, Millennium is magic; a little sense of independence, a snippet of the future outside hospital — of a life that can be lived normally, happily, easily.

* * *

At G.F., wheelchair salesmen literally have a captive audience; patients cannot get away unless they have purchased or loaned a wheelchair from somewhere. The salesmen court the patients, hawking their brands and merchandise by offering it up for trial periods. Kev tries out a few 'loaner' chairs and chooses a titanium framed 'Quickie Ti-lite' wheelchair. Once decided on the chair, the process of fitting man to chair begins. Currently, his bum is being measured by the wheelchair salesman, much as a tailor measures for a suit. The wheelchair salesman looks grumpy. He doesn't hum as he works; he doesn't even smile. Apparently, he's having a crappy day. As usual, Kev flips up into a wheelie and his shoulders move back and forth to retain the balance.

'Man, that is such a newbie trick: no one who's been in a wheelchair for a while spends all the time in a wheelie,' growls the salesman as he writes Kev's hip width on an order form. Kev's front casters crash to the ground and the salesman leans down to measure the distance from Kev's feet to his knees.

With a bum-size right on the border between an eighteen inch and a seventeen-inch-wide wheelchair, Kev can't decide which to get. His generous ski-bum bottom is slowly wasting away but at the moment it's still a tight squeeze into the seventeen inch. An entire inch narrower makes a big difference when you are trying to jam through narrow wheelchair inaccessible doors and hallways, but pressure sores are scary and can be caused by jamming into too-tight wheelchairs. Luckily for him, he has sensation which could alert him to the formation of a pressure sore, so finally he decides he will shoehorn himself into the seventeen-inch chair and hope that his bum keeps shrinking.

* * *

Two weeks before Kev and I are due to leave for Australia, a field trip to the Vancouver international airport is organised through G.F. The only person on the trip with Kev, me and our guide, is an elderly lady who sustained a spinal injury on a cruise ship. As we are slowly getting off the bus, a young guy in a wheelchair with his bag on his lap wheels in to the terminal *on his own!* We gawk like yokels.

'Did you see that guy?' I ask, poking Kev in the shoulder, 'He's going on a plane.' To Kev and me, it seems inconceivable that Kev will be able to take trips alone someday. The guy flinches under our wide-mouthed stare, waving nervously as he hurries into the terminal. He is no doubt used to many people expecting little from him simply because he is in a wheelchair, but he likely does not expect an 'you are amazing because you can go out without a minder' viewpoint from another disabled guy and his girlfriend. It is a hard feeling to reconcile when you think that your life has been irredeemably ruined and then slowly come to the realisation that perhaps, perhaps it hasn't.

Disabled people doing stuff independently — even basic, everyday stuff — impresses us, and weeks earlier Kev and I had watched wide eyed from the window of Kev's room at G.F. as a woman wheeled to her car, transferred in, took her chair apart and drove away.

'That is so cool, I need to learn how to do that,' said Kev and I agreed. I'm not sure how I had expected that she would get into the car; common sense dictates that of course she knows how to get in and out of her car. If she didn't, she wouldn't be driving around — unless of course she is driving around with two large, Swedish men packed snugly into her trunk that leap out to help her back into her seat each time she stops. Which, for all I knew, is how disabled people got in and out of cars. I had no idea of how wheels come off with quick-release connections, or that some chairs can be folded tighter than origami into absurdly small spaces, or that wheelchairs are ridiculously light — like a high-end mountain bikes that can be lifted in one hand. Wheelchairs to me had always been huge, clunky, impossibly heavy and cumbersome things, not the over-engineered, fancy chairs that are now available. There is a ton of stuff made and designed for people in wheelchairs, useful, cool stuff, which Kev and I are only just discovering.

We are leaving for Australia in a few days and our housemate from Kelowna, Bec, has come down to Vancouver to visit. To celebrate the end of Kev's official rehab and our impending trip, the three of us go out drinking, finding ourselves drunk and emotional in a deserted piano bar late on a dreary Tuesday evening. Kev wheels up to the pianist with a request, and the pianist launches into a hearty rendition of 'Leaving on a jet plane.' On the notes of the song, I am carried far away to a crowded, dirty street in Kuala Lumpur. I am sweaty, dusty and drunk, sitting in a street-side bar listening to a busker serenade me with the same song. Kev and I had stopped over in Malaysia on our way to do a ski season in New Zealand, our first real trip together, and it is a fitting song for the occasion of our new adventure. As Bec leaves the following morning, she places a small red Buddha in my hand.

'It is for tranquillity,' she says, closing my fingers over the round tummy. I smile, thinking that perhaps one the size of the huge reclining Buddha in Thailand might do the trick.

Kev's wheelchair still hasn't arrived and we are leaving in two days. 'It's not going to arrive in time and you're going to have to take the crappy old hospital chair. How am I going to pack that monster? You need to ring the wheelchair salesman and hassle him!' I fret.

'It'll be here, stop stressing out.'

With the exception of the wheelchair, our clothes and medical equipment has been packed into several large heavy bags, and oversized equipment piled in a heap near the door includes an off-road set of wheelchair wheels and a raised toilet seat.

Thankfully, the wheelchair arrives on the last possible day and Don and Diane arrive to help us pack up. Don fussily packs our luggage into the back of the car as though he's playing Tetris, and insists upon lowering the air suspension of the car to make Kev's transfer fractionally lower, then drives us to the airport and helps me carry in the bags.

Kev, his parents and I stand quietly in the queue to the ticket counter, watching the other passengers and repeatedly checking our watches.

'Now, do you have your passport?' Asks Diane.

'Yes, Mum,' replies Kev.

'What about Moira and Gordon's address in case you and Em are separated?'

'Yes, Mum.'

'And you'll call us when you get there?'

'Yes, Mum.'

They are hesitant to leave. After the scare of almost losing their son they don't want to let him out of their sight again lest something else catastrophic befalls him; the battle for independence Kev waged as a teenager has suddenly flared again. Don and Diane are understandably anxious about the trip and it will take some time for Kev to assert his capability again: he is their baby and they treat him accordingly.

Shuffling forward, we eventually reach the front of the line and I say to the young hostess at the check-in desk, 'We need seats that are easy to get into, perhaps the bulkhead or emergency exit seats,' I add hopefully.

'Disabled people can't sit at the emergency exit seats,' she replies matter-of-factly. 'If there is a disabled person sitting to the exit door, other passengers would be blocked from exiting the plane if there was an emergency.'

'What?' I cry, outraged. 'What if there IS a crash, how will Kev get out in time, if you put him in the back of the plane, like a great hunk of deadweight?'

I can hear my voice rising and then I feel Kev put his hand on my forearm and gently say, 'Em it's okay. I am a roadblock; I will have people trampling me and tripping over me if we crash but I will latch on to the biggest strongest looking guy around and refuse to let go, so he will either have to beat off a cripple — which is very bad karma — or drag me out like a parasite. Not to mention if the plane goes down, we are all more than likely stuffed anyway.'

Somewhat mollified, I glare at the hostess with her *let the cripples burn* attitude as she selects our seats, depressingly far from any of the emergency exits. After protracted, teary farewells, we enter the customs hall feeling ever so light.

As the doors to the customs hall sigh shut behind us we are finally alone. For the first time in over four months there is no one just around the corner about to pop in and make sure that everyone is okay; no one in the airport has any idea how difficult the past few months have been for us. We are normal again. Now, if something goes wrong, it is up to us to deal with it — which is both exciting and incredibly nerve-racking. We feel like teenagers tasting the first sweet taste of independence. It has been a long, hard, four months, but we are going somewhere!

Kev and I present ourselves to the immaculately groomed girl at the departure gate. We are flying with Cathay Pacific with a stopover in Hong Kong to allow Kev to stretch out and take a shit — a routine he is trying to train his body into. We are both paranoid he will shit his pants on the plane because as his body still adjusts to his injury it's not uncommon. The stewardess calls Kev and I for pre-boarding and he transfers into the tiny aisle chair at the door of the plane, and three tiny, highly made up, high-heel-wearing Asian hostesses manoeuvre him, with difficulty, onto the plane. His wheelchair is whisked away by a grubby, jumpsuit-wearing man with earmuffs.

Kev throws his cushion onto his seat and shuffles his way across, much to the surprise and amusement of the three pretty hostesses. He settles into his aisle seat and I throw all of our stuff into the overhead compartments and nod to a large, middle-aged businessman, who gives Kev an impromptu lap dance as he takes the window seat. Once in his seat, Kev does not move for the remainder of the flight, draining his urinal leg bag into an empty Coke bottle, and I worry that someone will report that I'm going to the bathroom carrying bottles of yellow liquid and could presumably be assembling a complicated chemical bomb.

I ask him at least once every ten minutes, 'Are you okay? What does that look mean? Are you in pain?'

'I am not in pain,' he says, clearly lying, and surreptitiously gulping pain medication, and trying to move around as much as possible when sitting, paralysed, on an aeroplane.

My belt clicks closed and as Kev takes my hand, I hope this trip makes us happier. I hope it is not a terrible disaster that wrenches us further apart.

PART III

AUSTRALIA

11

Two days after leaving Canada, Kev and I arrive in Melbourne, staggering out of the arrival gates at Tullamarine International Airport, tired, grumpy and with the inexplicably upset tummies frequently acquired on transcontinental flights. Mum runs when she sees us, too anxious to wait until we have come out of the arrival passageway and, almost crying, she meets us halfway, enfolding us by turn in long-sustained hugs.

'How was the flight? It's so good to see you!' Delighted, she can't stop smiling, showing the large gap between her two front teeth. Short, no-nonsense, steel-coloured hair frames her face: a dependable face flushed by excitement and accentuated by a red sleeveless shirt. Her arms and shoulders are thick and strong from gardening and farm work and she grabs my trolley, expertly manoeuvring it forward with hands almost as big and roughly calloused as Kev's; hands that never failed to open a tightly sealed jar, yet were delicate enough to extract even the most recalcitrant splinter.

'Dad is waiting outside, he doesn't want to walk too far,' says Mum, leading us to Dad who is leaning against a pillar with crutches tucked securely under his arms and his weight emphatically on his right foot. Tendinitis of his ankle has led to the crutches and he totters around wearing Mum's high heels because the elevation reduces the pain. Of average height, Dad is skinny, with fine, almost dainty, features and abundant, white, game show host hair, styled from his high forehead in a forward swoop. As usual, he wears blue Hard Yakka shorts from which his long skinny legs poke like matchsticks and his shirt reads *I see dead people* — a joke presumably funny only to other pathologists.

'Good to see you, Floss,' says Dad, shuffling his crutches around and giving me a one-armed hug.

'Kev, great to see you too,' he grabs Kev's hand, shakes wildly and repeatedly pats his shoulder.

I squint against the blinding sun as I step from the terminal. Skin is everywhere: bare shoulders, short skirts, midriff tops, and cleavage. The overabundance of flesh is shocking after months of layering, heavy jackets, thick woollen pants and sturdy boots.

It feels good to be home. A weight has fallen from my shoulders and I stand taller. Seeing Kev in a wheelchair must have been a shock for Mum and Dad, having not seen him since the previous year. They had missed the whole hospital ordeal; I had refused Mum's offer to fly to Vancouver shortly after Kev's admittance, suggesting instead that the money be spent on my ticket home. It is still a shock for me when I see him from a distance, wheeling instead of walking. I still dream of Kev walking; my subconscious denies the injury.

I lean forward and breathe the dry Australian air as we cruise down the Tullamarine Freeway, relishing the site of eucalypt trees, the sun and the trams, still accustoming myself to being on the left side of the road after so long in North America. I hadn't realised how much I missed the sun, living in perpetually rainy Vancouver. Nothing heals the spirit like sunshine — even tepid Canadian sunshine through triple glazed windows rejuvenates, but nothing compared to the hole-in-the-ozone-layer sunshine of Australia.

Exhausted but wired, I suggest lunch on Errol Street in North Melbourne before Kev and I settle into the wheelchair accessible hotel room Mum and Dad booked for us. Afterwards, Kev and I decide to walk the few blocks to the hotel with Mum while Dad drives the car with our luggage. We reach a large section of footpath that a construction crew has dug into a messy, uneven swath of mud and Kev, jetlagged and tired, manages well until he reaches a curb above which the cement has been removed, leaving only soft dirt.

'Do you need a hand?' I ask hesitantly and he replies with more confidence than his ability merits,

'No thanks, I will be fine.' Smiling reassuringly at Mum, I stand back to watch as Kev charges the curb and at the last minute pops into a wheelie. The front casters of the wheelchair are sucked into the viscous mud and Kev's forward momentum stops suddenly. In slow motion, he crumples, tumbling face first into the mud, grunting half in surprise and half in resignation. Horrified, Mum gives a strangled sort of cry, and reaches out, catching nothing. I close my eyes for a long instant. Cars are slowing down, the workmen downing tools and running, pedestrians gawking, cyclists swerving: everyone wants Kev back in his chair and no one more than Mum. We are a scene and Mum hates scenes.

Hauled back into his chair, Kev calmly laughs off the fall but it was clearly not the impression he had wanted to project for his mother-in-law. She had not seen 'sick–weak' Kev during the hospital and rehab period and since we had arrived he had been acting as if nothing had changed. But now it was obvious that it had. Knowing that Kev can fall from his wheelchair as easily as Humpty Dumpty from the wall, that no seat belts or safety bars keep him in, worries Mum and she now looks at Kev with the same overly concerned, anxious glances as his own mother — just the stifling concern he had hoped to escape. To be fair, he's a Gumby in a chair: a newb who has no idea what he's doing. I look at him with the same motherly concern, only my thoughts and emotions play less vividly across my face and, somewhat accustomed over the past four months to scooping Kev back into his chair, the fall rattles me less.

Mum and Dad had recently returned from a year-long trip to the UK and are renting an apartment while they look for something to buy. However, the apartment is up a flight of stairs so a wheelchair accessible hotel room was deemed the best solution for now. 'Wheelchair accessible' is a very generous term to apply to the room we are shown to at the local hotel. A seventeen-inch wheelchair can, if correctly aligned, get through the door and into the bathroom — where the shoddily installed support bars fall off the wall as soon as Kev applies pressure — but only after bumping up a sizeable step. And if a fire breaks out, Kev will have to cautiously negotiate around unnecessary furniture and will be burnt to death long before he reaches the door.

The alley leading into Mum and Dad's apartment is under construction, the council repaving the lane from concrete back into cobblestone to give it a period charm that the tourists love. The cobblestones mean walking along a fifty-metre alley takes about twenty-five minutes — longer if Kev falls out — and fighting a recurrent bladder infection, he tires easily. At one end of the alley are the cobblestones and about fifteen metres past Mum and Dad's apartment a snarl of construction equipment, digging tools and traffic cones marks the transition to the passé bitumen alley. Only one of the ancient monasteries precariously perched high atop a jagged mountain somewhere in the Himalayas could be considered more wheelchair hostile than Mum and Dad's place.

So Kev and I eat dinner with Mum and Dad in their garage; plates balanced on knees and beers leaving wet circles in the dust on the concrete floor, listening to the regular thumping from the washing machine as it completes its spin cycle, and the engine sounds and swearing from the auto detailing shop on the opposite side of the lane. Cars travelling too fast frequently swing into the detailing shop, driven by men in blue overalls with loud voices, while other men stand smoking and watching us.

When a neighbour's large white Alsatian lifts a leg on the garage wall and narrowly misses Kev's beer, he decides to give the steep wooden stairs a try, his legs straightening in spasms as he claws for the railing before he's pulled down by the weight of his flexing legs.

'Once you get up the stairs, the rest of the apartment is on one level,' Mum assures him.

Kev climbs the stairs more frequently and after a couple of days we move in.

The local pool where I lifeguarded years before has a disabled changing room and showers that Kev uses. He swam once during his time in G.F., hoping he would be able to do it — that swimming would not have changed and he would wheel into the pool and immediately begin swimming laps with impeccable coordination. But it didn't work like that. He had changed into his bathers and wheeled out on to the brightly lit pool deck where I was waiting to help him into a swimming wheelchair — essentially a waterproof, upright wheelbarrow — and I wheeled him backwards down the ramp bracing the weight of the chair against my leg. Neoprene floats were strapped around his chest and legs, his scar was jagged and red: an angry zip up his back. The water lifted him out of the wheelchair, spinning him like a log as he struggled to keep his head above the water. Once again, it was back to the basics. He floated on his back as I cradled his head.

The sun is huge and bright and shines with an alarming ferocity on our pale bodies as we bob in the pool. With the neoprene straps, Kev floats confidently and, after time, I stop shadowing him and swim myself. The past several months of pain and hurt seem to float away with water, the sun warm on my back and the smell of the nearby dog food factory on the wind. We swim most days in order for Kev to use the change room, and with practice, Kev's balance improves and he becomes a strong and efficient swimmer.

We spend a night out in Brunswick Street with my friend Monica and her husband Tim, who upon hearing our plans to travel around Australia excitedly asks if he could travel with us through Western Australia and the Territory, so we make tentative plans to meet in Perth. As we make our way back to North Melbourne along the darkened streets and through the campus of The University of Melbourne — a walk we made many times together the previous year — I stroll beside his wheelchair and it strikes me: this is normal life. Had the injury not occurred, nothing would be different at this point: we would still be making our way back to North Melbourne together. The simple act of doing a terribly normal thing together feels beautiful.

* * *

If Kev and I plan to make it around the entire perimeter of Australia, we need a car; a solid, dependable car. After looking through the classifieds in the newspaper and the Trading Post, Kev arranges an inspection of a Toyota Hilux truck. Dad has offered to come along to help with inspections because he knows about cars and what to look underneath them for, whereas I would need a big sign reading 'this is bad, it will cost you a lot of money', to know whether I am buying a lemon.

'G'day. The name's Rob,' bellows the owner of the Hilux, ambling from his house wearing a singlet, a cigarette in one hand and sausage roll in the other. 'The wife is making me sell her,' he says, gesturing to the Hilux as Kev and Dad arrange their respective mobility devices. 'For the bike,' he adds nodding to the garage. His eyes slide to Dad, hitting and poking at stuff under the car with his crutches, then back to Kev.

'We are planning on driving around Australia, so we're looking for a dependable car,' Kev says, and between alternating bites from the sausage roll and drags from his cigarette, Rob launches into how he and his wife have been everywhere in this car — everywhere! I have visions of a chain-smoking Rob driving it around Australia in the heat and humidity, wearing his blue singlet with hairy shoulders and pale, flabby arms exposed, oozing sweat into the ultra-absorbent sheepskin seat covers on the front seats and I don't want it. It smells like goat: like Rob.

But, Kev writes a cheque and suddenly we become the proud (and not so proud) owners of a well-used 1998 red Hilux Surf. It has been five years since I've driven for any extended period of time. I've always hated driving; I am one of the slow drivers that make frequent car-driving-people go completely insane — the hair-pulling-out inducing, peptic ulcer causing type of driver, who drives at — or (heaven forbid) even occasionally below — the speed limit. Nonetheless, as I find myself stuffing ownership papers into the glove compartment, it occurs to me that the Hilux has to get back to North Melbourne in some way. Kev can't drive it because there are no hand controls and Dad is already driving his car. Looks like I'll be driving. Shit, I should have brought Mum. I didn't think we would be buying a car today; today was just for looking.

Perched forward in my seat, back straight and eyes darting from the road to the rear-view mirror, I'm going thirty in a sixty-kilometre residential zone when suddenly from a steep side street a scruffy kid on a bike flashes in front of the car. I slam on the brakes and Kev and I are thrown forward, and the scruffy kid and I meet eyes, wide and terrified. He has fallen from his bike in shock and as I sit breathing rapidly, he picks it up and scurries away. He is gone before I realise I want to take him home so I can tell his mother how he was almost killed. It takes a minute before I can continue and I hope it isn't an omen.

Crawling along the four lane Monash Freeway back into

Melbourne, Kev keeps up a constant stream of, 'good job, you're doing so well, you can merge now, well done, turn off your indicator.' By the time we arrive at Mum and Dad's place, I've isolated the epicentre of the goat smell as the sheepskin covers and, wrenching them off, I throw them with disgust into Mum's top loading washing machine, where they partially disintegrate, strings of blue wool sloughing off everywhere like little blue maggots. I replace the slightly damp seat covers and the car smells like wet sheep.

* * *

The bladder infection Kev has been fighting for several days has worsened. The infections have been fairly constant since his indwelling catheter was replaced by intermittent catheterisation a few weeks after his injury. Sometimes the infections can be beaten back by drinking copious volumes of water or forcing down glasses of cranberry juice and avoiding the sugary foods bacteria love; then the urine loses the characteristic smell, spasms calm and it looks like the infection has passed. But then it returns.

Usually all it takes is Kev forgetting to drink enough water, or getting a bit run down by lack of sleep, or overdoing things, or else forgetting to take alkalising tablets or drink cranberry juice. It doesn't take much before the smouldering infection becomes an inferno. Antibiotics are used when all the other methods fail and the infection begins to spread, first to the kidneys, then to the testes — swelling them to grotesque proportions — and then to the blood. At that stage things become serious. Kev is allergic to Ciprofloxacin and there are not many heavy duty antibiotics able to knock out a well-established infection. All it will take is one antibiotic resistant superbug to kill him. But we are not thinking about that. We are thinking antibiotics fix infections; put a square block in a square hole. But Dad knows sometimes the hole is triangular for which square blocks are useless.

Kev has retreated to the spare room, lying shirtless on the single bed, heated from within by his fever. I am in and out, emptying vomit buckets and catheter bags, filling up camel backs of water and cups with cranberry juice, dropping alkalising tablets into tall glasses of water causing them to fizz and spit explosively. It is a vicious circle: the vomiting dehydrates him, which further worsens the infection, causing more nausea and then more vomiting.

I close the sliding doors each time I pass through and Dad cranes his neck to see what condition Kev is in.

'I'm fine, Gord,' wafts weakly through the doors. 'I started my medication yesterday and it should kick in any minute.'

Dad, seeming so old, wise and assured looks at me. 'This is not a game; he can die from blood poisoning.' Why is he being so serious? It's just a bladder infection — they happen all the time, not a big deal right?

'It's under control Dad, these infections happen a lot,' I say with more confidence than I feel.

He looks at me from under heavy brows in disapproval tinged with disappointment. Dad, who'd let me walk around with a broken arm for an entire week because he didn't think it was too serious, who could never be fooled into giving a day home from school, who more than once conducted minor surgery on himself and used true-blue livestock ointment on his wounds, was telling me this was reckless.

'If this happens again, I'm calling an ambulance and he is going to hospital,' he hisses just out of Kev's earshot. I agree. Dad wants him in hospital but stubbornly Kev holds out, placing his faith in the antibiotics, and so my parents and I sit in silence looking at the crack in the sliding doors and listening to Kev vomit and groan and burn.

Within a few hours, his temperature drops and I help him to shakily sit up on the bed supported by many pillows. Having barely eaten in two days he's hungry and slurps cautiously at broth. Dad enters and delivers a stern lecture, Kev nodding at appropriate times, reluctant to admit how vulnerable he is and grasping at the illusion of control he has with antibiotics. He has spent the last four months in hospitals, the last thing he wants to do is return there even when it's clear that he really needs to. Kev wants to be better so badly, he wants to be strong again, not someone who is known by name in the emergency room, that he pushes his body and sometimes he pushes it too far. I don't want to fail Kev and decisions he resists, sometimes need to be made. The antibiotics worked this time; Kev has been lucky. Next time he may not be so lucky, warns Dad.

12

When empty, the Hilux appears cavernous compared to Mum and Dad's little Ford Focus. Lists have been written and rewritten, hastily annotated with notes, scribbles and addresses and phone numbers of all the shops we intend to visit. Our stockpile of supplies needs to last for at least a couple of weeks — the longer the better — because the specialised medical supplies Kev requires will be difficult to find outside of the major cities.

Kev and I drive out to a medical supply store in Collingwood, to purchase large quantities of condom catheters, intermittent catheters, leg bags, cleaning sprays and to try and get some hand controls for the car. Strolling the aisles, I am swayed by manufactures' claims of *best cream for pressure sores* and *most pressure relieving material,* because I'm terrified of Kev getting pressure sores and having half of his bottom removed, necessitating an ass implant.

We are both paranoid about pressure sores because just before Kev left G.F., Christopher Reeve had unexpectedly died, sending ripples of anxiety through the spinal wing. All the recently disabled people were curious to understand why he, someone with the best medical care money could buy, had died relatively young. So, one of the doctors put together a presentation entitled 'What killed Christopher Reeve?' It was the biggest crowd I'd seen at any of the G.F. lectures and, arriving late, Kev and I squeezed in up the back. Christopher Reeve had been a hero to many disabled people. He'd raised awareness and lots of money, lobbied for stem cell research, was good-looking and successful, so when he died, it touched me much more than the death of a movie star usually does. His paralysis made him seem more human. The doctor presenting the lecture first described how Christopher Reeve broke his neck in a 1995 equestrian accident and then detailed his accomplishments since, which were many.

Christopher Reeve was a busy guy. That, apparently, was the problem. Working demanding hours and remaining in his chair for long periods, his body became worn down and more susceptible to pressure sores. Once a pressure sore establishes, it is a very difficult and time-consuming process for it to heal — especially if it becomes open and infected. The doctor's tone was reassuring as he told his horrified audience that with the correct precautions, and prompt attention to any red spots, the gruesome images of weeping sores projected on the wall behind him would not happen to anyone in the room.

The talk reminded me of the Transport Accident Commission ads televised in Australia and used by driving safety courses worldwide: a happy couple, laughing as they drive, are suddenly flattened by a speeding cement truck, or a little kid chasing a ball is abruptly mowed down by a mother distracted by her screaming baby; then a monotonous voice intones, 'drink drive, bloody idiot', or 'speed kills'. The ads feel like a punch in the face, and so did the

Christopher Reeve lecture. *Pressure sores are bad, very bad*, is the lesson Kev and I learnt from it. The longer you are in a wheelchair, the less susceptible you become to pressure sores because your skin grows tougher, but I imagine it takes longer than a few months.

My basket overflows with skin creams and I pick up a sort of strap-on butt pad and wave it at Kev. His glare compels me to gently replace it. The young salesman helping us decide on hand controls for the car also uses a wheelchair, and is even a professional wheelchair basketball player.

'I have this brand set up on my car,' he says, holding up the type of controls we intend to buy, 'I can show you if you'd like.' Strong, fit and quick, he drops down the large step out the front door instead of going around and down the ramp. Kev follows him. Kev is not strong, not fit and not quick, but weak, healing and inexperienced, and he is rudely ejected from his chair. He falls onto the concrete at the feet of the young salesman. Acutely aware of the salesman's gaze, Kev slowly tries to get into his chair, each time falling to the ground, then eventually, grudgingly, asks for my help and I grab the back of his pants and drag him into his chair.

The salesman turns, wheels towards the street, and drops the high curb into a cobblestone gutter to cross busy Smith Street, glancing back at Kev. Again, Kev falls, cutting his hand open on a piece of broken glass and narrowly avoiding sprawling into the path of oncoming traffic. Kev has not explained how recently his accident has occurred, and the salesman watches pityingly as I haul Kev back into his chair for the second time. The salesman has mastered his chair and can do things that at this point Kev can only dream of, and he wants to learn from, and impress, the salesman. It stirs up conflicting emotions: disappointment and embarrassment because Kev is not as capable as the salesman, but also hope, because one day he will be.

'This is it,' declares the salesman proudly and I'm surprised by how much of a complete bomb his car is. So far, all the wheelchair accessible vehicles I have seen are spacious vans, kept scrupulously clean and full of spare wheelchair parts, motorised lifts and ramps. Seeing his hopeless disaster of a car with the hand controls, which are little more than golf clubs duct-taped to the pedals, is encouraging. He is just an ordinary young guy with a crappy car, who just happens to be in a wheelchair. Kev buys the hand controls and many boxes of medical crap, then we head back into the snarl of traffic to complete the list.

Trooping from camping shop to camping shop, we buy tools, camping and accommodation guides, maps, the Lonely Planet guidebook, a plastic chair for Kev's showers, several plastic boxes to label and fill with list stuff, books, a cigarette lighter plug-in fridge, a screw-on stove top and propane bottle, lantern, several huge plastic water jugs and a new terry towelling hat for Kev to wipe the rivers of sweat from his face. Kev buys sandals for his feet, that are now red and peeling with psoriasis, his toenails protruding upward like ships sinking in quicksand. He hopes the sunlight will help them.

Over the next few days, I sign up and receive a mobile phone that promises extensive coverage in remote areas. I join the RACV (Royal Automotive Club of Victoria), pay through the nose for really good car insurance and extend Kev's travel insurance. Mechanics check over the Hilux, installing reinforced handles on the passenger side so that Kev can pull himself up, examine the spare tyre and carefully top up the windshield fluid. I cram a bulging toolbox under the front seat and meticulously clean and vacuum every inch of the car. I buy spices, sauces and take half of Mum's canned food, packing it neatly in the food box when I think she isn't looking.

Kev has antibiotics for diarrhoea and for UTIs, he has spasm medication, extra spasm medication, pain drugs, neuropathic pain drugs, prescriptions, spare prescriptions, drugs to make you high, drugs to make you sleep and drugs to make your body sleep but your mind race. The designated medical box is like Hunter S. Thompson's lunch box.

Packed away in the pile are plastic mattress protectors stolen from Vancouver General, white wipes, catheters, more catheters, stick on condom catheters by the box load, gloves and several cases of lubricant. Kev adds a book titled *Australia's Deadliest Animals,* the point apparently being that he can identify the deadliest snakes and spiders from the simply creepy and unpleasant ones. During a trial pack, the cavernous space in the car is reduced to enough space for an extra person, a wheelchair and a couple of bags. Kev drove me around in his Kombi to his favourite places in beautiful Western Canada, carried all the heavy stuff so we could backpack into incredible spots, pointed out all the landforms, trees and wildlife, what to touch, what not to touch and made me feel safe. He had shown me his country, and now I am going to show him mine.

Mum and Dad watch the hurried preparations with interest and tolerantly pretend not to notice as I plunder their home and garage for anything remotely useful. As the heaping pile of trip equipment grows and grows in a corner of the garage, the trip becomes more of a concrete reality, and while Kev's excitement builds, I worry I'm forgetting something crucial and lifesaving.

Obsessively arranging the contents of the medical box from smallest to largest, Mum says suddenly, 'Remember when you first arrived you asked if I wanted to go with you to Perth? Well I've been thinking, and it would be a good idea if I came with you. Dad and I are a bit concerned about Kev getting sick and the pressure on you.'

'Ok, that'd be great. Would you fly back from Perth, then?'

'Yes. I'll book a ticket back for late January. A month should be long enough to reach Perth, right?'

'Sounds good. Thanks, Mum.'

She is convinced Kev is going to die in the desert somewhere and that I'm going to die trying to save him. So now we are three.

13

Kev has named the car Yota. Personally, I don't think cars should be called anything except 'You Stupid Bastard' when they don't start, but Kev is ridiculously pleased with the Hilux and insists on constantly praising it and saying how great 'Yota' is. A thick vein, that I was until this moment completely unaware of, throbs rhythmically in my forehead. I stick the little red Buddha Bec gave me on the dashboard with Blu Tack and there he sits: fat, jolly and enlightened, bestowing benevolence on all. Yota bulges with so much stuff that it prevents me from seeing out the back window, increasing my aversion to driving. Yet, Mum insists on bringing a camping chair, and being a crappy, cheap, non-folding one, it takes up an inordinate amount of room, making packing even more difficult.

On Christmas morning, Kev, Mum, Dad and I open our presents over a leisurely breakfast, before a big lunch with all the relatives at my aunt and uncle's house; only my brother, who lives in Colorado, is missing. After consuming great volumes of food and receiving mediocre presents, Christmas is suddenly over and we leave early to finish last-minute packing before the morning.

After breakfast, Kev heaves himself into the passenger seat and I accidentally poke Mum in the neck with a wheel as I jam it in.

'Ow, that hurt!'

'Well there would be more room if you didn't have to bring your camping chair.' I answer sweetly, and she gives me a look.

Excited yet filled with trepidation, I pull Yota slowly out of Mum and Dad's street, feeling as though there should be some sort of elemental acknowledgement of our first step — a lightning strike, crashing thunder, or, at the very least, a mariachi band, maybe with some doves released — but all we have is Dad, standing outside the garage in his blue dressing gown and slippers, eating a bowl of cereal with one hand and waving a crutch at us in farewell with the other.

Westward we travel, around Port Phillip Bay to Geelong and meet the coast at Torquay: the start of the Great Ocean Road. I'm still getting used to driving, and navigating through traffic is stressful, but thankfully the roads are fairly empty due to it being Boxing Day. Nonetheless, I pull over every five minutes to let cars roar pass.

The Great Ocean Road is one of the most scenic drives in Victoria, stretching along the south-eastern coast from Torquay to Warrnambool, encompassing stunning views of the ocean and coastline. I spend the entire time staring obsessively at the strip of dark blue bitumen laid out in front of me. Each time I manage to pry my eyes from the road and steal a glance at the ocean, an oncoming car or caravan demands my attention and my heart hammers like a pneumatic drill.

Boxing Day is a very popular time for camping because school kids are on holidays, so all the best camp grounds are booked solid. Consequently, as I hadn't thought to book ahead, we camp in a paddock at Johanna Beach in the Otways and feel fortunate to get it. The only facilities are basic pit toilets and a patch of wild long grass to set up our tents on, with all the other disorganised people who didn't book campsites in advance. Risking the potential of gusting ocean winds, we set up the tents on the side of the car closest to the beach so we can admire the panoramic view of the ocean.

My fear of pressure sores led me to put considerable thought into Kev's camping bed, ensuring adequate padding to prevent development of red spots or tender areas that precede sores. Consisting of a full-length Therm-a-Rest mattress with a plastic covered memory foam overlay, lush sheepskin rug (to prevent sticking to the plastic cover protecting the absorbent Tempur overlay) and crowned with my childhood farmyard animals sheet, Kev's camping bed is more comfortable than the majority of hotel beds. In contrast, my bed is a basic Therm-a-Rest barely wide enough for my shoulders. It lacks a sheepskin rug or sheet and I must peel myself off every time I roll over. I lie well below Kev's luxurious bed on my crappy mattress, simmering in sullen resentment.

That night the wind screams as gale force gusts and nearly horizontal rain buffets and pummels the tents. Our tent performs well and holds itself together admirably while Kev and I cower inside. However, Mum's tent sucks. When morning finally comes, I wake early or, more correctly, emerge from my tent early, as I have been lying awake listening to the wind moaning all night, and peer in on Mum, still tucked into her sleeping bag.

'How was your night?'

'Oh, not too bad; I could have done without the tent brushing into my face though. It was pretty windy.'

Flattened by the wind, the side of the tent stroked Mum's cheek all night, and whenever she touched the walls, water blossomed there like a gushing wound through gauze.

The sky hangs low, grey and threatening. My muscles ache, my stomach growls, my purple hands are tucked into the pockets of a fleece jacket and Mum has a beanie pulled down over her ears.

'I thought it was bloody summer,' I gripe.

'Where are the clothes I left hanging on the bonnet to dry?' Mum asks, discovering to her horror they have mostly vanished, and anything remaining is much wetter than before.

'Some breakfast will help,' says Kev, rifling through the camping box. 'Where are the matches, Em?'

'I dunno, in the box I assume.'

'Nope.'

'What! Let me see.' I tear through the car and it doesn't take long for me to realise we've forgotten a few essential things, such as matches and water: we have eighty litres of air in our plastic water tanks so we can't actually do any cooking, drinking or eating. There will be no hot tea or warm steaming oatmeal to warm our bellies and comfort us after a night of misery. My mood darkens. The euphoria of our departure has long worn off and I wish I was sitting in the kitchen in North Melbourne eating toast smothered in honey and sipping Earl Grey tea from a piping hot cup. Instead I start packing up. It takes over half an hour to wrestle the tents down, the gusting wind threatens to rip them away and hurl them to Antarctica and, almost seeing them skip and dance across the angry grey ocean, my grip tightens.

Struggling to wheel in the sandy soil, long grass chokes the front casters of Kev's wheelchair and he functions mostly as a convenient table to place tent pegs, bags and other tools upon, occasionally offering encouragement when Mum and I appear to be losing the battle of the tents. Finally, the tents are down, everything is packed and, after Kev climbs in, I artfully pack his chair then thump heavily into the driver's seat as the wind continues to knead Yota furiously. Turning the key yields only a strained, strangled whine and Kev and I exchange a heavy, panicked look. Urgently, I try again and again but Yota stubbornly refuses to start. It then dawns upon me with a hot, prickly feeling that the fridge has been plugged into the cigarette lighter all night. Unbelievably, it's completely drained the battery.

'Shit! Shit! Shit!' I smash the steering wheel in frustration and Kev and Mum are silent. I have a flashback to Rob telling Kev, 'This baby has two batteries and it's fantastic for camping, just fantastic!' The goddamn lying bastard!

Two scruffy young guys driving a rusted-out Kingswood from the adjoining campsite drift over when I flip our bonnet up. As constant as the law of thermodynamics is the law of opening your bonnet. It seems to attract every man within a few miles' radius to your car so they can peer knowingly, quizzically or mournfully (depending on the circumstances) into the bowels of your vehicle, and offer advice, helpful or not, on your predicament. In this particular instance, it is clear our battery has been drained — 'out of juice' is the way the blond-mulleted kid put it morosely. Mullet carefully reverses across the grass and hooks up the Kingswood to Yota and I stand back expectantly to watch as the Kingwood gets Yota moving, but when Mullet tries to restart the Kingwood, nothing happens; absolutely nothing. It is a stunning anticlimax. The Kingswood begins to emit the same strangled whine we heard from Yota, as if it had just been infected with some sort of virulent car flu.

'Sorry, don't know what's wrong with it.' Mullet unplugs the Kingswood and backs dejectedly back to his campsite. There is nothing quite as emasculating to a young man who is into cars as failing at something as simple as a jump-start. I climb back into the driver's seat to think.

'Would you like some orange juice Em? It's nice and cold from being in the battery-draining fridge all night,' offers Kev glibly but I am too pissed off to laugh. Jabbing at my phone, I find I can't get a connection on the phone I specifically bought for the extensive coverage.

Reluctantly, I accept that I need to find a landline somewhere and slog several kilometres back down the dusty track towards several farmhouses we passed on the drive in, angrily swatting the few resilient flies attempting to crawl up my nose and suck my eye juices. A cloud of dust turns into a rusty old ute full of hay, and a friendly farmer and three dogs poke their heads out of the driver's window when it pulls up beside me. I climb in and a black-and-white dog settles itself on my lap. Sitting in the ute with the affable farmer and his dogs, I quietly question the wisdom of our journey. I hate being the one who has to sort stuff; I want to be the one sitting in the car drinking cold orange juice, goddamn it.

I joined the RACV the previous week in case of car breakdown and have been an official member for only four days before needing roadside assistance.

'I've been a RACV member for twenty-four years and have never needed roadside assistance,' Mum had said from the back seat with a touch of prissiness as I climbed from Yota.

'Yeah, but how many times have you rung Dad saying "come get me", "change my tire" or "bring me some petrol"' I'd snapped back, slamming the door.

The polite voice on the phone tells me a mechanic will be there as soon as possible and, with the farmer's assistance, I tell them where exactly 'there' is. After a soothing cup of tea provided by the farmer's lovely wife, I walk back to the car to tell Kev and Mum that the RACV is on the way. The mechanic wears overalls and asks automotive questions I can't answer, but carries functional jumper cables and knows how to use them. Yota is chugging within five minutes. The young guys with the Kingswood come over when they see the RACV arrive, as apparently, the Kingswood has also broken down — probably due to the battery draining in the attempt to get us started. After both cars are revving contentedly, the mechanic takes off and I follow close behind.

Kev is feeling unwell, weak and nauseous and as I drive into the town of Warrnambool he vomits violently into a jar of mixed nuts. We check into a nondescript motel, complete with adjoining double rooms and a menu you need to fill out the night before so breakfast appears in a box beside the door. Again, Kev has a UTI that has become systemic. He's shaking, sweating and vomiting with a high fever and constant uncontrollable chills. Mum, understandably, is incredibly anxious. She fires worried looks at Kev through the connecting door as he lies, fetid, in a tangled mess of sheets while she paces the room, snaking her hands around each other, making hushed calls to Dad and, snapping that Kev will die if we continue. In my other ear, I have Kev telling me weakly through bouts of vomiting that he is okay, that he does not need to go to hospital, that the antibiotics are going to work. He started a course of antibiotics from his rapidly depleting stockpile and does not appear to be getting any worse. I don't know what to do; I am not sure we will be able to go on. I don't want to put Kev in danger but I don't want to give up either.

Frustrated and fighting, Kev says, 'You should go around Australia with someone else … someone not disabled. I will be a burden.' I can't cope with this. I can't cope with the stress of organisation and then reassure him he's not a burden when it is clear to a blind man he is. It is a crushing realisation that the trip may be over before it's even begun. If he has not made a big improvement by tomorrow, I'm going to have to take him to hospital and then back to North Melbourne.

What the hell am I doing? Am I completely insane? I'm taking a recently disabled guy with serious health issues, who is only just learning how to live life in a wheelchair, into the Australian outback. What if we break down and have to walk for help — or rather, *I* have to walk for help? He could die! More importantly, I could die! So many potential dangers: the murderous stifling heat, the bugs, germs, the world's most deadly snakes and spiders, dirt getting into Kev's sterile cathetering process sparking an antibiotic resistant bladder infection. A psychopath could kill us and bury us in the desert somewhere, Kev could be bitten by forty-five snakes and not feel a thing, he could brush against a deadly jellyfish while swimming or lose a limb to a great white, or worse still, a crocodile could seize us by the head while we sleep soundly in our tent. I have to put it all out of my mind or I am going to hyperventilate. There are so many ways things could go wrong — spectacularly, catastrophically wrong. I feel flattened, stressed and overwhelmed. I am lost.

14

By morning, Kev's fever has broken, his eyes are clear and focused, and while he still feels nauseous and weak, he is definitely on the mend.

'How do you feel? Do you want to keep going or should we head back to North Melbourne?' I ask as he struggles into his wheelchair.

'I'm okay to keep going.'

Onwards, we decide, to Mum's chagrin.

The following day we drive north-west towards the volcanic landscape of Mt Eccles national park, assuming all the campsites will be booked and planning for a picnic and walk. The park contains many interesting geological features such as lava flows, lava caves, scoria cones and crater lakes and after one year of geology at university, I've become a painful 'expert' on all things geological.

Amazingly, Mt Eccles has vacant campsites and, even more incredibly, disabled toilet facilities in the campground with *hot* showers, which seem positively lush after Johanna Beach.

'Who votes to camp here for the night?' I ask and Kev enthusiastically nods.

'Whatever you two want to do is fine by me,' says Mum.

Our campsite is beautifully peaceful, surrounded by fragrant gum trees, crawling with koalas and colourful birds and with kangaroos and wallabies hopping serenely by. It is picture perfect Australian bush, until Mum starts to inflate her air mattress with the cigarette plug pump, and the sound of the little compressor echoes through the campsite and sends birds to screeching flight.

'More tea, Mum?'

A kettle bought in Warrnambool whistles on the stove — far more efficient at boiling tea than the previously used saucepan — and I'm so delighted with it I make many cups of tea just because I can.

'Oh, just one more.' Mum really likes tea and drinks it like water. Anytime is an appropriate time for tea. When we leave somewhere, Mum has a 'last cuppa' and when we arrive the first thing she does is put the kettle on. Whenever she has a cup of tea she says 'aahhhhhhh' on a slow exhale after each sip from the pink plastic cup as if injecting herself with a slow release form of heroin, her pinkie extended like she's drinking from fine English porcelain.

'Ahhhh,' she says again, and I feel a flash of irritation. 'Ahhhh, yummy-cuppa-tea,' all one word.

After dinner, Kev and I slowly amble up to a viewpoint of Mt Eccles and a beautiful groundwater-fed crater lake while Mum cleans away the dinner dishes. As I sit in Kev's lap, we watch the sunset together in silent contentment listening to a soundtrack of roaring koalas and screeching cockatoos. Sitting together in the middle of the Australian bush, feeling the warmth of the day disappear with the sunlight and watching the still, dark lake, is poignant for us; a good moment.

'Are you sure you're up to continuing Kev? I'm worried you're pushing yourself too hard too soon — expecting too much from a body that's still healing. You're always so tired and sore. Lots of people are still in rehab at this stage and you're camping on the other side of the world.'

In constant pain, his spasms relentlessly vibrate him and bladder infections pummel him, one after another, and he functions through stubborn will, refusing my help when possible, forcing me to watch him struggle as huge malevolent hands crush my chest.

'I just feel guilty because I can't carry anything and help you the way I'd like to. At least if I push myself … even if I don't achieve much … I feel that I'm doing the best that I can. It's hard for me to watch how difficult this is for you, but I'm doing okay right now.'

He rubs my thigh with his rough calloused palm and we decide to go on.

I wake in the middle of the night to the almightily racket of possums fighting and smashing through the food box. After packing everything in the car the way I should have done in the first place, I spend the night chasing them from the campsite, scattered with remnants of spilled food. The sound of possums fighting is a blood curdling, bone chilling yowling, not unlike a woman screaming, and it unnerves me for the rest of the night. I've been away from Australia for too long: forgotten about possums. When camping in Canada, every scrap of food and anything even remotely resembling food (such as deodorant or toothpaste) has to be packed tightly in a bear-proof cache, or hung high in a tree, far from your campsite, lest an unpleasant visitor appear in the dark of night. A possum is no comparison to a grizzly bear, but I had still been lazy and should have remembered how diabolical possums are. I hear them marauding through our campsite for the millionth time and, swearing, I throw both of Kev's sandals at their bright beady eyes to his sleepy protests.

When morning comes, I boil the kettle for Kev's coffee and tea for Mum and me while Kev remains in bed, mustering strength for his morning routine.

'Morning.'

'Morning … Thanks.'

I hand him the strong, sweet coffee he uses to wash down his medication, and he pulls himself into a sitting position, un-zipping his sleeping bag and sitting for a moment, reacquainting himself with this new position. Nothing happens very quickly. He pulls on his pants, tucking his night drainage bag down the front, slips a shirt over his head and shoulders and shuffles forward, lifting his feet out of the tent to where his wheelchair is stored in the vestibule. His feet, reeking of rotting meat, are pushed into sandals that no longer seem new. The vestibule flaps open and Kev pushes his wheelchair back, shuffles forward further, bum crowding feet, twisting his body so he sits perpendicular to the wheelchair and tries repeatedly to pull himself into his chair. Eventually he says, 'Uh Em, could you give me a hand into my chair?'

I carry the padded toilet seat and the blue bucket containing a day drainage bag, wrapped in a plastic bag, a urinal bottle, cleaning solution, lube and catheters and follow Kev into the bathroom. His transfers are still wobbly; generally there are no bars, just a toilet-roll holder to grab for, and falls are not uncommon. I jam the raised toilet seat on to the bowl and stand in front of Kev as he slowly transfers up onto the seat, teetering slightly as my heart sprints.

'Give me a yell when you're done,' I say, carefully closing the door. Later, he transfers back into his chair and I carry the bucket and the toilet seat back to the car, returning with the plastic lawn chair used for showers, into which he transfers. After he showers, I help him back into his wheelchair, pull on his pants as he leans forward, place the towel and dirty clothes on his lap, and carry the chair back to the car as he slowly wheels.

With the time it takes, it is amazing that we go any distance at all. Mum is impatient and rises at daybreak; it's more a race than trip for her. Kev takes so long that most of the morning is spent waiting for him and he recognises impatience in my eyes, understanding I want to chuck him in the car like a sack of coal. Each time we stop, I pull up, park, unclip, get out, open the back and unpack the wheels, frame and cushion, fitting them all together while trying to avoid the frame smashing into my shins, or leaving a smear of dirty oil on my pants, and wheel the chair to Kev. I brace it against my leg while he slowly lifts one, and then the other, foot from the car, drops into the chair and carefully places his feet on the footplate. I grab his backpack then reach in for anything he has forgotten. Cities have been built faster.

'The roads are pretty quiet around here,' says Kev.

'Yeah, so?'

'I'd like to try out my hand controls and see what they're like to drive with.' Mum, wrestling her mattress into its bag, looks up sharply. For Kev, climbing into the driver's seat using a handle held in place by two small screws presents a greater challenge than the passenger seat, equipped with a reinforced support bar. Clawing for a handhold, spasms force his legs straight, almost as if he were trying to stand, toppling the chair over and sending me scrabbling to help as he clings from the seatbelt, then drags himself into the car stomach first. Not the most auspicious start. The hand controls are pretty basic: long sticks with clamps on one end, attach onto the brake and the accelerator, and a small knob attaches to the steering wheel, allowing Kev to steer with one hand. Apparently, the knobs are very popular with long distance truck drivers because they enable the driver to make wide, swinging turns with only one hand. The other hand is presumably used for smoking a cigarette or gobbling methamphetamines. Consequently, the spinner-knobs are highly illegal if you do not have a medical condition requiring the use of one.

Kev adjusts the mirrors, moves the seat back and carefully ties his feet underneath the seat with a belt to prevent the spasms from kicking the pedals. 'Okay here we go,' he turns the ignition key, pushes the accelerator stick and Yota jerks forward, bunny hops for a while, then shudders to a stop. Steering with the spinner-knob and pressing the pedals at the same time requires some juggling at first because in order to press the brake, Kev has to release the accelerator and, because the setup is not rigid, there is a slight lag between wanting to break and actually braking. If Kev needs to indicate while accelerating, decelerating, honking or turning on the wipers, he runs out of hands and has to release the steering wheel for a second or two and Mum, sitting in the back seat drumming a tattoo into the back of my seat, completely freaks out.

Trying for indifference Kev says, 'I remember an old guy at G.F. told me driving with your hands becomes second nature, and that he drinks coffee and answers his mobile phone while driving now.' Mum is not reassured and we finally make it into town, sodden with sweat. After a brief tour of the town, I leap into the driver's seat and we all sit somewhat more comfortably.

Blasting through Portland, we camp in a crowded caravan park in Nelson on the Victorian–South Australian border. Once we have the tents up on our patch of well-trodden grass, I screw the hotplate onto the propane bottle, flip the gas open and hastily flick on my lighter, anxious to get dinner on. The hotplate immediately bursts into blue–orange flames that shoot alarmingly to the neck of the bottle where the hotplate is cross-threaded and gas escapes rapidly.

'Holy shit, it is going to blow! Run! Run!' I yell in alarm, backing and tripping away from the flaming canister.

'Aaaahhh, run!' Mum panics, and we knock over the food box, camping equipment and our drinks as we mill and flounder about trying to decide whether to throw the canister away from our campsite or just run like hell towards the river. Focused on our impending doom, we don't notice Kev wheeling slowly and purposefully through the deep sand towards the impending fireball, picking up the Leatherman I had dropped. Using the Leatherman, he reaches through the fire, losing most of the ample hair on his hands, turns the valve to closed and the fiery gas ball splutters and dies. Disaster averted, Mum and I both look down like chastised children, ashamed of our cowardice as Kev pointedly glares at us and needlessly lectures me on the danger of cross-threading the hotplate.

West into South Australia, we pass through Mt Gambier, hugging the coastline, and as we approach Kingston, a huge, red crustacean of nightmare proportions appears in front of us.

'What the hell is that?' Asks Kev.

'That is the "Big Lobster of Kingston SA, and his name is Larry",' replies Mum, reading from the guidebook. "'Larry shapes up at seventeen metres high and weighs in at about four tonnes.'"

In Australia, there is an unusual cultural fascination with 'big' things: huge, roadside attractions, which are often a very, very large version of a mundane item or animal. Australia's big things include a ram (Wagin, WA), a banana (Coffs Harbour, NSW), an earthworm (Bass, Vic), a crocodile (Normanton, QLD) and, most famously, a pineapple (Woombye, QLD). Larry the Big Lobster is lesser known, doesn't have a restaurant in its tail, can't snap his pinchers or flick his tail, and you can't even climb on it: lame.

We spend New Year's Eve camping in Coorong National Park: a long, narrow stretch of lagoons, white sand dunes and dry salt lakes separated from the Southern Ocean by a peninsular. About 150 kilometres south of Adelaide, it's famous as an important sanctuary for pelicans and other wildlife. The area is unique due to the interaction of fresh water from groundwater and the Murray River, and saline water from the ocean. Desolate and windy, with the smell of seaweed and dead crab on the air, the campsite does not endear itself to me but, completely deserted, it's eerily beautiful in that particular way harsh unforgiving places are: beautiful and terrifying at the same time.

I have to get up and pee during the night, and as I stand outside the tent watching the lights on the distant shore, a cool wind caresses my face. The night is as clear as thin ice and a billion stars sparkle and gleam above me. My lungs fill with air and as I feel it flow throughout my entire body, I see a glimpse of the future and it looks okay.

15

Mum is tense, but then again Mum is always tense — fluctuating above and below a baseline level of tenseness depending on how lost we get (above) or how much alcohol she has consumed (below). Mum's tension elicits an opposite effect in me; if Mum is stressed to breaking point I actively try to be so laid back I'm almost comatose — at least externally. I don't have to worry or be the one to say 'I can't do this'; Mum has that covered. I am too obstinate to admit that anything is too much, or that I can go too far. I think Kev and I can do anything but in reality, we simply can't. Kev is vulnerable. He is fragile because life in a wheelchair is very new and his body has taken a beating over the past few months. Fortunately, we have Mum to prevent us from doing anything too stupid or dangerous.

Mum researches and prepares for her trips, organising every aspect of her travels well in advance, carries a dossier the size of a phone book crammed with hotel names and addresses, bus lines, taxi companies, itineraries, alternate itineraries, emergency contacts and so forth. Whereas, if I have insurance, I feel I am super-ultra-sorted. I am a disorganised, leave it to the last minute, it will all be good, type of traveller. We are like Steve Martin and John Candy in the old movie *Planes, Trains and Automobiles* and sadly, I am the obnoxious John Candy. Travelling with Kev and me is not how Mum likes to travel: camping instead of quaint hotels with hard, floral-patterned antique couches, sitting in the back even though she gets car sick, and not knowing what town we're going to sleep in, let alone the name and star-rating of the hotel. We eat at crappy restaurants serving food that is plentiful and filling instead of trendy and unpronounceable. Out of her element, she is stoic. But friction is beginning to show. While I love and appreciate Mum for coming, she isn't the easiest person to travel with and tempers are short.

Kev is familiar with Mum's anxieties and at times plays on them for his own amusement. Slowly, we are running out of petrol. Kev claims he wants to see how long it takes after the red light comes on until the tank runs dry in case we need to test it; but I have my suspicions it's a passive-aggressive way of venting his frustration at Mum, because travelling with his mother-in-law is no man's dream vacation. Mum is really worried — way above baseline tense. She peers at the petrol gauge every fifteen seconds, lurching from the back seat and shooting furtive glances at the gauges as if they have changed in the last few seconds. We pass another petrol station and Mum watches it go by longingly until it vanishes in the distance. Yota begins to cough and lurch and Mum starts to emit a similar keening, whining noise.

'Stop being a dick,' I snap to Kev. 'I am filling up the tank.'

From the petrol station onwards, continuous suburbia becomes the city of Adelaide: capital of South Australia. Slower, sleepier and more relaxed than Melbourne or Sydney, Adelaide feels more like a large country town than a city of over a million people.

Leisurely exploring the city, lazing by the River Torrens, poking into shops and having long decadent cafe lunches involving scones and jam, I relax somewhat. We are all enjoying staying in a hotel and the luxury of having a bathroom attached to our bedroom instead of a long walk away. The slow pace feels restful after packing and driving each day, and gives us time to recover from the first week of our travels. The break is good for Kev, the high lift into the Hilux, onto unsteady toilets and up and down from the ground has caused pain to flare in his shoulder — pain which concerns us both.

It feels like the three of us have been travelling forever, but on the map we have barely gone any distance at all, Australia is so unimaginably big. North of Adelaide, through the picturesque Clare Valley, we reach Orroroo, a small farming town near the Flinders Ranges, where the passage of time appears to have ceased in the sixties. The Commercial Hotel on Second Street looks as if it hasn't changed in fifty years: counter teas are advertised and specials are written on a chalk board out the front, beside benches where old people meet to gossip, laugh and watch the empty street.

A friend of Kev's parents, Anne, grew up in Orroroo and, being the good Irish Catholic family that they are, Anne has about ten siblings one of whom, Simon, still lives at home running the vast family farm. Simon's about forty, stocky and quintessentially rural, with a ruddy face, extreme friendliness and charming colloquialisms peppering his speech. He manages a huge sheep, cattle and grain farm in some of the harshest country I have ever seen with a sunny optimism which beggars belief. How he can be so grateful, so content, so happy, amazes me; most people would be bitching and moaning about the crappy, never-ending drought, the rising rates the bank charges on their loans and the falling wool prices, but Simon is unfailingly cheerful.

Simon's parents, Norelle and Tom, remind me of Mum's parents, Nana and Chester, who together ran a 1000 acre mixed farm and horse riding school in country Victoria. Norelle is tiny and compact, all bustling efficiency and 'have you had enough to eat love', while Tom is large and introverted, slouched in a big armchair in front of the TV, giving off 'don't bother me kid' vibes; they have been married forever. With Tom having suffered a stroke, Norelle cares for him — fussing over him during meal times and dedicating her days to his comfort — in between helping Simon run the farm, chasing rabbits from her veggie patch and yelling at the dogs for getting into the chook house. She is quite a woman.

After we have settled in to the big, old farmhouse with the welcoming kitchen and wide covered veranda, Simon gives us a tour of the farm in his battered Falcon, leaping and shuddering through the rocky potholed paddocks, threatening to set the long grass alight with the drooping exhaust pipe. Over the brown paddocks we go, passing skinny, naked sheep fleeing en-masse, startling a healthy red fox from cover and sending numerous fat rabbits racing — legacies from homesick Britons. Between the dry, ancient windmill and the rusted galvanised iron water tanks, hollow and empty, Simon follows the orange clay track up the hillside where the view can be admired. Pink galahs and sulphur-crested cockatoos shriek across the sky in clusters, and Simon watches them through narrowed eyes. He waves his arm, encompassing all the eye can see — brown dusty paddock after brown dusty paddock — describing what has been planted where, which paddock has the best feed, and which, in his opinion, is the most beautiful. I don't have the heart to tell him they all look equally grim to me. While he admits the farm does not look its best, he shakes his head and chuckles that it certainly doesn't look its worst, either.

After surveying the sheep farm, we arrive at the neighbour's farm, and he puts on a shearing exhibition for the 'city folk.' The farmer is weathered by the elements, encrusted with grime and sweat, yet unbeknownst to him, my mother could likely have caught, flipped and shorn the sheep before he had even picked up his blade. Having spent countless hours in shearing sheds, Mum and I pretend to be impressed. However, Kev is as giddy as a groupie at a Rolling Stones concert.

I trail behind Simon as he carries out his daily chores: feeding the sheep dogs, checking the animals, fixing the fences, feeding the sheep, and countless other tasks. Up at dawn and in bed later than me, it's a hard lifestyle, but he says he would have it no other way and I am strangely envious of his simple needs. Country people say that the land gets into your blood. And I believe it does. Even after living in the city for many years, I still miss seeing the stars at night. I miss hearing frogs outside my window, I miss the smell of the eucalypts after rain, of putting my face against a horse's damp neck and feeding a newborn lamb from a warm bottle on a chilly August morning. I miss the country.

Watching Norelle with Tom is humbling for me. In her generation, forever meant forever and people were less likely to leave their partners when the relationship became inconvenient. Of course, no one ever knows the intricacies of other people's relationships, but I can see love in her eyes and gratitude in his. My impatience and frustration with Kev and the difficulties due to his injury seem vapid when faced with something huge like dealing with a brain-injured partner. I hadn't had much to do with any of the brain-injured patients in G.F. — I'd occasionally see one guy, super ripped, lifting weights continuously in the gym and mumbling to himself, 'I can't remember … did I work my biceps?' And another young man, a gangland shooting victim, eyes rolled up in his head, pushed around in a wheelchair by his kid sister. But I couldn't imagine what it was like, not really.

* * *

Something is wrong with our car. I know this because Simon has spent several hours (and at least five coolers) underneath it peering into its innards and a pool of viscous oil rapidly expands on the concrete around him, creeping along the cracks and collecting in depressions. The car wouldn't start a couple of times, stressing Mum out, so Simon offered to check it out.

'What's the problem?' I ask, looking down at his feet sticking out from under the front of the car.

'Hard to tell,' say the feet. 'I will get me mate Macko over 'ere to have a gander.' Despite their valiant efforts, Simon and Macko are unable to determine the nebulous malaise that seems to plague Yota, whereas I know exactly what the problem is.

'It's a piece of shit,' I say to Kev.

'Nooo,' he counters defensively. 'It's an older car, they sometimes need some work. It will be fine.'

'Whatever,' I humph and give Yota a vicious kick in the front left tyre. While Simon is dismantling our white elephant, he loans us his car to drive to the Flinders Ranges — harsh, rolling, country but truly lovely; the country of poems and of Bushmen's songs.

On the way back, we stop at the Orroroo pub to pick up some coolers for Simon to show our appreciation for his generous hospitality. I open the door to the pub crammed with rowdy, rough-looking local men, and all heads immediately swivel towards Kev and me. I feel like a gunslinger entering a Wild West Saloon. Under the unwavering, unapologetic gaze of the entire room, we approach the bar with Kev squeezing past bar stools that squeal along the floor. A grizzled old man propping up the bar nudges the barman and says, 'They're gunna ask for some fancy drink you won't know how to make, mate!' There is loud cackling all round. The surreal Wild West feeling intensifies and I feel uncomfortable.

'I would like a six pack of peach coolers,' I stammer.

'What, like Simo drinks?' The barman demands, at once assuming that not only do I know 'Simo' but also what Simo drinks.

'Actually yes, they are for Simo — we're friends of his,' I hasten to mention.

'You're friends of Simo?' The barman hollers. 'Oh well that's great, we thought you were just some city wankers.' *A city wanker*, I muse paying for the coolers. That's what I have been reduced to now. I grew up in the country and I think of myself as a country kid at heart and I thought I was connecting with the rural folks because I was one of them. But apparently not. It hurts my feelings more than a little.

16

The term Nullarbor can be translated from Latin as meaning 'no trees' (*nullus arbor*) which is a pretty apt description of the flat, arid, treeless expanse of limestone plateau, stretching all the way from Ceduna in South Australia to Norseman in Western Australia; a distance of approximately 2000 kilometres. Nothing but red sand, scabby little salt-tolerant bushes, the occasional big red kangaroo lying in the shade of a gnarled, stunted tree and innumerable wedge-tailed eagles eating road kill mashed by the thundering road trains that drive the Eyre Highway night and day. Despite the scorched earth appearance of the landscape and the scarcity of anything remotely hospitable to sheltering and nurturing life, there is a stunning abundance of life on the plain; almost 800 vascular plants, over 50 mammals, nearly 250 bird species, about 80 reptiles and 1 frog: the incredible desert trilling frog, able to spend years living burrowed safely underground surviving on stored moisture in its skin and yearning for the few short weeks when the rains arrive and it can breed rapidly and somewhat desperately. Several settlements are scattered across the plain, but they are few and far between. It takes a special type of person to live on the isolated, barren, Nullarbor without going completely mad.

The explorer Edward John Eyre made the first European crossing of the Nullarbor in 1841, with the assistance of Wylie, an aboriginal 'guide'. Eyre is reported in Henry Kingsley's *Eyre's March* to have described the plain as, 'a hideous anomaly, a blot on the face of nature, and the sort of place one gets into in bad dreams'. The early Australian explorers were a mad lot: embarking on journeys into the most unimaginably inhospitable country populated by some of the world's most dangerous snakes and spiders, and more often than not would never be heard from again, simply vanishing into the desert. The myth of the great inland sea of Australia propelled many a heat-struck explorer forward. It was something every explorer yearned to discover. Mountains were given charming names, such as Mt Disappointment (Victoria), when the expected sea was not visible from the peak. Disappointment would have been a slight understatement if I had toiled for weeks, if not months, through rough, dangerous country almost dying of thirst, heatstroke, or animal attack and had not found what I expected and so dearly wanted; I would be more than *disappointed*: Mt Complete and Utter Devastation, Mt Soul-Crushing Sadness, Mt Ever-So-Weary-Heartbreak are just a few that come to mind.

Yota's air conditioning has broken, now cooling us as much as a hairdryer. Within the confines of the car it is so horribly, terribly hot. I feel like I am baking within a tin oven and opening the window just lets in more hot air that blows in my face like monstrous dragon's breath. As I sit whining while Yota churns up the miles, I think of Edward John Eyre and his lack of air conditioning, shelter and most importantly water, and I feel weak, pampered and soft. The heat is murderous and so is my mood.

'Fucking Rob, I am going to personally smash his face in when

I get back to Melbourne.' That's if his piece of crap car doesn't fall to pieces before then! I glance at Kev sitting beside me. His face shines red and sweaty and I can see dampness at his temple. He is hot too. Whatever, I am hotter. In a futile attempt to cool myself, I set up a system whereby I can sip water from a camel-back that hangs from the reinforced handle, and have Kev periodically spray the mister and wave a battery powered fan near my face. It doesn't help with cooling anything much, let alone my temper.

A 'wicked' campervan painted with pot-smoking rock and roll fraggles crawls along the highway at about forty kilometres per hour, and even our diesel four-wheel drive flashes by it. Yota doesn't flash by much, unless it's stationary, and both Mum and Kev sit straighter in their seats, craning their necks to watch the campervan vanish quickly behind, checking whether it's on fire or missing a wheel or something. Everyone notices that I have actually passed someone.

The Nullarbor Plain ends in a southern direction when it drops abruptly into the ocean at the Nullarbor Cliffs — huge limestone cliffs plunging into the Great Australian Bight and known locally as the Bunda Cliffs. They are breathtaking. It feels like standing on the edge of the world. You could almost believe the earth is flat, that it is possible to fall off, after seeing cliffs such as these. They appear un-ending, vanishing into a point far into the distance; no fences, no guard rails, and no elderly vest-wearing volunteers to tell me to mind my step and keep back from the edge, just the almost vertical cliffs plummeting some 100 metres into the swirling ocean below. With one step I can be happily admiring the view and with the next, speeding to my watery doom. It is both unnerving and liberating in a nanny state country like Australia, where one can barely cross the road without a lollipop lady holding your hand. The beauty of the cliffs is almost worth the hours and hours of boring driving it has taken to reach them. If they were somewhat closer to civilisation they would be crawling with tourists and hawkers selling miniature figures, but as it is Mum, Kev, and I have them completely to ourselves.

The Eyre Highway is a single-lane highway, and etiquette demands that drivers raise at least one finger in greeting to the occupants of oncoming traffic. Almost everyone observes this particular social nuance, so Kev feels obliged to also waggle a finger or two when we meet another car head on. It becomes a bit of a problem because constant pressure is required to maintain acceleration and to prevent the car from veering. So he drives with one hand on the spinner-knob and one hand on the accelerator and to wave, Kev briefly releases the steering wheel and Yota swerves slightly; Mum — hunched in the back seat with a clenched jaw and nails clicking together, sending spasms of irritation up my spine — almost leaps into my lap in panic. I am grimly pleased when the oncoming drivers pass us with steely gazes, jaws set and eyes cold.

'Look at the galahs,' Mum says as several pink parrots are flushed from roadside scrub.

'Actually, those are pink cockatoos not galahs,' I reply.

'A pink cockatoo? Hah I don't think so,' she snorts dismissively. 'I've never even heard of a pink cockatoo.'

'No, really, they are cockatoos.'

Mum raises her eyebrows and purses her lips in a downward, disapproving frown, insinuating with a single glance that not only am I a complete ignoramus, but also, that she is far above debating rudimentary bird identification with such ignoramuses. My blood pressure climbs.

Finally, after two days, the desert falls behind and the town of Norseman appears. It feels like re-entering the world.

'Oh, thank God,' sighs Mum as the first scattered buildings come into view. Crossing the Nullarbor is like a brief excursion to Mars, a monochromatic landscape; my eye becomes so accustomed to reds, oranges and browns that finally seeing green on the horizon shocks. Life returns to normal, only it is so far away from other Australian cities. An entire civilisation here that is just so far away it is easy to forget it exists. Perth, one of the most isolated cities in the world, is closer to Jakarta in Indonesia than Sydney.

17

Driving south from Norseman, we pass many glistening salt pans — scalded white depressions where the natural salts in the rock have risen to the surface with the groundwater table, providing stark evidence of Western Australia's struggle with dry land and irrigation salinity.

Reaching the coast, I check my email at an Esperance internet café, googling pink cockatoo and then pettily copying the Wikipedia definition into my diary.

'Huh,' Mum says later when I triumphantly show her, as if it isn't a big deal that I am right and she is WRONG! Sometimes I forget how old I actually am.

Protected by an inlet and turquoise waters gently dissolving onto the white sands, Twilight Beach in Esperance is one of the most beautiful beaches in Western Australia. Soft birds flutter in my stomach as Kev slowly ploughs through the sand, hypersensitive to the curious stares of onlookers. He is intent upon swimming at the beach for the first time. The ice cream man leaves his yellow van and follows us down to the shore, shaking his head from side to side and saying, 'What are you doing young man?' as if Kev is completely bonkers and in the process of the slowest, lamest suicide attempt ever.

I feel like the Pied Piper with a trail of gawkers and yokels instead of rats, and each asks at least three times whether they can push him and I snap, 'Look, we are fine okay. Thanks for the offers but we don't need any help and as soon as we do, we'll make sure to ask you.' I just want them to leave us alone, to go the hell away; why does it have to be such a huge public production? We are just going to the beach for Christ's sake! Kev is not a public spectacle as much as a public spectacular. Finally, he reaches the water's edge and the crowd retreats a few metres to watch.

Kev falls heavily onto the sand within reach of the small waves gently folding onto the shore, drags himself backwards into the ocean where unfamiliar waves twist and turn his lower body at will. This is not like swimming in the ramp-equipped rehabilitation swimming pool in Vancouver. The waves seize his lower body and frustratingly, toss him about like a buoy in a storm. Seeing his struggles, I grab him by the neck of his wetsuit and drag him into deeper water where he is fully buoyant and swimming becomes easier. Finding his balance, he strokes out further and deeper, towards an island several hundred metres from shore. Mum sits watching from the beach with the last of the gawkers, wearing her bathers, sunglasses, a hat and half a bottle of sunscreen.

We swim happily together in the tranquil blue waters. Floating on his back, Kev is quite stable and he swims backwards like an otter eating a fish. It was a tremendous struggle to wheel through the deep sand, humiliating to have feeble, elderly people offer to push him and it stings his pride and dignity to be such a source of entertainment. Nonetheless, the swim makes Kev feel more like his old self; in the water there is no wheelchair and the disability is less limiting.

Getting back to the car presents a challenge and we recruit four guys to help, three young surfer bums and a rotund middle-aged man. Two guys drag from the front and the other two push from behind. It would be immeasurably easier if they simply picked the chair up and carried him, but instead, they strain and push a 180 pound wheelchair through deep, soft sand. Obviously, a wheelchair is not designed to go through deep, soft sand so it is extremely arduous: akin to pushing a ride-on lawnmower over a sand dune. Not an enviable job. After about two metres the older man is bent over with his hands on his knees, gasping and sweating, and appears to be in eminent danger of a cardiac arrest.

'Just need a quick breather guys, I'm not as fit as I used to be,' he says every few steps, but finally they make it.

'Jesus what a mission,' says Kev, mortified, and then smiles. 'But wasn't that awesome!'

* * *

That night, I ring Dad and mention I have arranged to go on a boat cruise the following morning.

'Is Moira going?' He asks incredulously.

'Yes,' I reply, 'she thinks she will be okay because apparently it is not too rough.'

Dad chuckles wickedly. 'Have fun; it will be a complete disaster. Moi will be sick for sure.'

As Kev, Mum and I board the boat the next morning, a busload of intellectually disabled people are helped on by a group of concerned, fussy helpers. One of the helpers starts to push Kev towards the gang-plank, and says, 'Come along love, we'll get you all sorted in a jiffy.'

'Let go, I don't need sorting and I'm perfectly capable of getting onto the boat by myself,' snaps Kev. The old helper could not have been more astonished if Kev had suddenly stood up and slapped her hard in the face, and it reminds me of a Dickens quote from *David Copperfield*: Try not to associate bodily defects with mental, my good friend, except for a solid reason. Unfortunately, many people equate physical handicaps with mental handicaps and are exquisitely patronising to Kev, speaking to him as if he is a slow child or a slightly demented, dangerously unpredictable mental patient that requires soothing tones, pastel colours and lots of hand patting and shoulder squeezing; most of the time though, they speak to me like Kev is not even there at all: 'Does he need some help?' is a common question I get when standing directly next to Kev. 'Erm, I don't know, maybe ask him yourself,' seems a pretty obvious reply from me.

As the boat slowly chugs out into the open ocean, the waves steadily increase in size and the boat begins to lurch from side to side; Mum takes on a decidedly greenish tinge. Suddenly, the water becomes really rough. Kev, Mum, and I remain on the deck because the bus group is crammed into the cabin and Kev refuses to enter. He holds onto a waist-high guard rail — made of two rails with ample room for a person or a wheelchair to fall through — and I stand behind, stabilising him.

'Oooohhhh,' groans Mum, slumping miserably on one of the benches, each wave causing her to visibly cringe. As the buffeting waves toss the boat, pitching it from side to side, Mum's nausea worsens and she sinks slowly to the deck, lying spread-eagled to prevent rolling around. Other passengers step gingerly over her and bump her body as waves slap the far side of the boat.

'Mum! Mum are you okay?' Mum weakly flaps her hand in assent and whimpers pitifully. 'Just don't pass out Mum, okay?'

With every crashing wave, Kev becomes airborne. All four wheels leave the deck then crash down alarmingly. I keep one hand on the railing to steady myself and the other on the back of Kev's chair, my knees jamming the chair against the railing to prevent him from tipping over and sprawling down the listing deck, through the gap in the guard rail and into the grey, heaving waters below. He has a death grip on the railing and I can see his fingers, white through the spray mist obscuring my glasses. Yet he is grinning. He is grinning like a slightly demented, dangerously unpredictable mental patient. What the hell is he grinning at? Is he going to fling himself into the ocean?

'Fun huh,' he yells over the wind and surging seas, over the groans of my mortally seasick mother, and the yells of the group inside.

*   *   *

We head down to the affably named Lucky Bay in Cape Le Grand National Park, south-east of Esperance. Pulling in I notice the 'rock and roll' fraggle van parked in the parking lot and setting up the tent, I chat to the two young hippies it belongs to. Dreadlocked siblings in their twenties from Auckland, the brother informs me that it has taken them five days to cross the Nullarbor.

'Our car keeps overheating so we have to drive at thirty kilometres per hour, and the piece of crap is costing us $35 a day,' he whines.

'Oh possum,' I want to say, 'my piece of crap cost me $14,000.'

I am lulled to sleep by the sound of the waves crashing into the sand and feel relaxed for the first time in a long, long time. The rhythmic rushing surge, eddy and ebb sounds fill my ears with comfort and I sleep as though medicated. The following day, Kev and I swim out into the rough ocean off the beach and large waves pummel him as he battles his way through the surf, smashed back four metres for every five he advances. Feeling strange sensations in his feet, he constantly turns to check everything is okay, and we are about forty metres from the shore when he yells,

'Em, Em can you come over here?' Thinking he is in trouble I swim rapidly to him. 'Can you check that there is nothing attached to my feet?' He says flipping over onto his back.

'So,' I say, 'if you think there's a shark or something attached to your foot you call me over instead of telling me to swim for it, thanks. I can't see anything. It must've just been a weird feeling.'

The days pass quickly as I swim with Kev, walk along the beach poking into rock pools and explore the area surrounding Lucky Bay. Mum combs the beach for interesting shells and reads under the same tree each day, slurping milky tea, and Kev swims or lies on the beach for hours. Before we realise, it's time to move on.

Packing our belongings into the car, I notice ants dropping out of a tree onto the bonnet, marching across to the windshield in an unbroken line and disappearing down a crack under the hood. *How neat*, I think, *they're making an ant bridge to get themselves from the tree onto our bonnet*, and forget about them as we roar out of Lucky Bay. Driving from Denmark, we indulge Mum and stop at lots of the little galleries and pottery studios for which the south-west region of WA is famous, eating a genteel afternoon tea of scones with jam and cream in a lovely little teahouse at Nornalup. An ominously loud crunching, spronging noise from behind the car startles me, as I am backing out of the parking lot.

'What the —?' I leap out to see Kev's right wheelchair wheel trapped under the wheel of Yota, the ludicrously expensive wheelchair wheel warped and the push-rim flush against the tyre.

'Shit, this is going to be expensive and a pain in the ass to fix.' Getting back in the car I am defensive, as clearly it is not my fault that I forgot to put the wheel in the car and backed over it. Kev changes to the big knobby mountain bike wheels at our next stop, which make the chair too wide to fit through standard doorways.

It is too late to camp when Mum, Kev, and I finally arrive at Margaret River. Being the weekend and a popular getaway for the inhabitants of Perth, Margaret River is jammed with holidaymakers. Weekends mean nothing to me; I barely notice when they come and go, except that it becomes more inconvenient because banks are closed and everything is busy. At the only motel with vacancies we can find, the wheelchair room is already booked and Kev can't fit into the bathroom of the non-wheelchair room with his big off-road wheels.

'Well, we are going to have to stay here anyway,' says Mum, 'surely Kev can figure something out.' An uncomfortable stand-off ensures.

'No, I am not staying somewhere that I can't fit into the bathroom. We'll have to find something else.' Kev says from the passenger seat.

Mum and I walk into every motel in town with no success. We are all tired, hungry, cranky and sick of each other. No one relishes the idea of driving onwards.

'There is nowhere else, we have to stay here!' Mum looks like having a heart attack if no solution appears, so Kev sulkily agrees to drag himself into the bathroom on his bottom. My tolerance spent, I dream of waiting till Mum and Kev get out of the car, locking the doors, and pretending I am sleeping. 'Right, this can be my bed,' she puts her bag on the bed closest to the door. 'I will go and get some tea, are you both okay with chips and dim sims?' Tummies growling, Kev and I nod. By the time Mum gets back with the food, she's relaxed, I've relaxed and so has Kev. He puts on the skinny wheels, conveniently flattened on one side giving him at least an extra inch or two clearance, so he can squeeze into the bathroom.

'I am a burden,' he had said while Mum was gone and, exhausted, I said nothing.

* * *

We have a couple of days in Perth before Mum needs to catch her flight back to Melbourne and are staying in a downtown hotel room so small that the wheelchair can only go forwards or backwards. Kev barely squeezes through the doors in his off-road wheels, but the location is convenient. Walking the many paths and parks of around the city, signs of development and wealth are everywhere —

a product of Western Australia's booming resource industries.

On Mum's last night in Perth, she offers to buy dinner at an upmarket restaurant. Pink and giggly from sipping wine all night, she sheds no tears at the end of camping as we fondly rehash our trip. Kev fumbles in his lap, hand down his pants, a concentrated expression on his face. Looking away, I pretend nothing is amiss. Whenever a look of concern crosses Kev's face, I panic, assuming his condom catheter has failed and he has wet himself again. The nurses at G.F. recommended a particular brand, but he can't find them in Australia so has to experiment with different brands and accidents are frequent. My nerves on a razorback, Kev catches my eye and gestures accident; self-conscious, he prefers me not to tell Mum, and every time an accident occurs I make up another complicated lie. I lie about why Kev and I take so long in the mornings, why Kev has to leave places at times, and why I need to do laundry yet again. And the lies create tension.

Back in our room, humiliation and frustration darken his face, which crumples inward. 'I fucking hate my life! What is the point anymore?' He says angrily, his mouth a twisted smile as if his life is an unpleasant joke. 'I can handle not being able to walk; I am just so sick of all this other shit as well.'

The infections, the spasms, the pain and the embarrassing accidents are a kick in the guts after a fist in the teeth. 'Why do you want to be with me?' He'd demanded in Adelaide after a similar accident, and all I could say was 'because I love you'. He doesn't want to keep going. It is too hard — on me, on him, and for him to watch me struggle. Too much fighting, too much crying; so many apologies that they start to lose their meaning. All those inspiration books are full of shit. This isn't fun, I don't have a warm sense of accomplishment at the end of each day, just an empty place. I sit on the bed, my hands cupping his, trying to explain to him I know how he feels when he watches me struggle to lift something heavy, something that he would have done before. The same feeling of constriction, of a stick catching in my throat, overcomes me at times like these; times I want to help him but am powerless to do so. I can pretend to know how he feels only as much as he can pretend to know how I do. As much as I say it is okay, sometimes it is just not okay. Sometimes I can't deal with it either.

'You're being ridiculous,' Kev had said to me the previous year as he carried an overflowing jug of my warm urine outside to dump in our outhouse as my face glowed with shame and apologies tripped over thank you's.

I was recovering from knee surgery and couldn't make it to the toilet at the bottom of the garden so Kev insisted I pee in the jug, brushing aside my protests. It felt horrifying to me that the one man I wanted to appear sexy and desirable to, would end up covered in my pee if he didn't step very carefully on his way through the darkened yard. I wasn't the type of girl who pretended I didn't go to the bathroom, but there were certain things I wanted to keep separate and I made a few struggling steps towards the toilet before falling in agony against him.

'Em, come on, how are you going to get up the steps if you can't even make it out to the toilet?' I collapsed into frustrated whimpers and Kev carried me back to bed.

He had helped me bathe in the ancient claw-foot tub that took up most of the shed that sufficed as a bathroom. Gently peeling off my clothes, adding bubble bath when he ran the water and bringing the heater from inside to try and keep me warm, he played blues on the stereo, lit a candle on the sink and opened the window so the heady smell of the flowering jasmine carpeting the fence wafted in. He had taken care of me, pushing me around in a wheelchair when a visit to the zoo became too much, and even though my injury was temporary, I was envious as he leapt up steps with ease, ran and rode his bike.

It had given me a tiny insight into how difficult things must be for Kev.

* * *

Returning to the car after dropping Mum off at the airport, I notice she's left her camp chair in the back, regardless of my complaints. *Goddamn it*, I angrily shove the stupid chair aside, causing a cascading avalanche of junk to tumble down, further incensing me.

Before leaving Perth and heading up the north coast towards Broome, Kev and I need to get Yota's air conditioning fixed, do some wheelchair repairs, restock his medical equipment and buy a bunch of tasty food — the sort Mum doesn't like. Fixing the crushed wheelchair wheel Kev still gamely uses — careening down hills in spurts when the flat side meets his fingers and he cannot grip — tops the list. After spending the morning ringing around, Kev finds an aluminium fabricator in the industrial section of Freemantle (Freeo) willing to try and fix the smashed wheel. The aluminium fabricator is a bright and cheery fellow of advancing age, and claims he will have us going in a jiffy; a 'jiffy' being four hours on Western Australian time, apparently. While we are waiting, Kev rings some medical suppliers and arranges for condom catheters to be sent to Broome, because by then supplies will be running low. After the fabricator's attention, the wheel looks remarkably undamaged and has a new coat of black paint thrown in for free.

The fabricator's reasonable price puts me in high spirits as I climb back into the car, reflexively brushing an ant from my hand and pulling the door closed. Another ant scurries across my arm and a third disappears up the inside of my shorts. *What the hell? Did I leave something sweet out?* Looking around, our car is full of ants. There are fucking ants everywhere; crawling across the windscreen, roof, seat, doors and steering wheel. My driving is dangerously erratic as I watch the hurried crawling of ants instead of the road ahead of me — I am going cause an accident swatting ants. This is intolerable.

'Ah, what's up with all these ants?' I ask, pulling over at a car park in Freeo, and Kev shrugs in reply. Pulling everything from the car and piling it in the adjacent parking stall in a great messy heap, I peer into the empty car and ants crawl around everywhere.

'Fuck,' I swear softly, flipping up the back seat and ants explode. I have found the mother lode. Big ants, little ants and ant eggs as far as the eye can see. There is a bloody great ant nest *in our car*.

'Coooool,' says Kev, poking his head through the open door.

'You have got to be kidding me,' I say, watching the ants in horrified fascination. 'Kev, you watch our stuff while I run to the shops for some ant killer.' I storm down the street for chemicals, insecticides and other poisons to rid the car of ants and any other as yet undiscovered vermin, and return with bulging bags of ant-killing sprays and insect bombs.

'Okay move back a bit, a bit more, alright good.' I tell Kev as I unleash a bottle of Raid on the nest and watch as the majority of ants convulse, and the few lucky enough to escape the initial onslaught scramble desperately for cover. My stomach swirling and head pulsing, I watch macabrely, unsure whether my squeamishness is due to the agony of inflicting death and destruction on a living civilisation, or the fact I'm using Raid in a confined space.

Kev and I go for lunch while the Raid does its grim duty. After lunch, we return but still ants crawl weakly and piteously through the car — considerably less post-Raid, but still enough to piss me off. To the big guns — or, more precisely, bombs: insect bombs, in fact, claiming to kill all crawling insects for up to three months. The label is frighteningly intense, advising me to use it in a four-metre-by-four-metre room at least (not a two-metre-by-one-point-five-metre Hilux cab). I pull out the pin, chuck the bomb in the car anyway — quickly, like a live grenade — slam the door and watch anxiously as the grey cloud engulfs Yota from within, rapidly obscuring my view of the cab.

'Shit,' I remember that I left my purse in the console and wrench open the door, fumbling through the toxic haze to grab it. The cloud starts to seep out of the cracks between the doors and windows and looks as though Yota is slowly smouldering, likely to burst into flames at any minute. A bystander is going to call the fire brigade leaving me to explain what the hell I am doing.

'Let's go for a walk or something,' suggests Kev, 'I don't really want to hang around here breathing in toxic fumes.'

'I can't leave! I need to watch the car.' So I loiter just beyond the haze of the noxious grey cloud, biting my fingernails and wishing it was over. The bomb, as promised, kills everything and when the smoke finally clears I sweep the ants from the car, the small curled bodies resembling spilt poppy seeds, reeking of chemicals. I can still smell it, heavy in the air like a mist, and I'm convinced it will give me cancer.

PART IV

DUE NORTH

18

Before leaving Melbourne, Kev and I arranged to meet my old friend Monica's husband Tim in Scarborough, a beachside suburb of Perth, so he can travel with us up the north-west coast and down to Alice Springs for the next six weeks or so. He is keen to explore the west coast and for me, now Mum has left, having another person around in case Kev gets sick or we break down is comforting. In his late twenties, tall, pale and skinny with a sharp-featured, heart-shaped face and heavy black eyebrows, Tim, from London, looks stereotypically English. Inquisitive, adventurous and fun, everything is '*excellent*' to him.

'Hey Guys,' says Tim happily, jamming his pack and five multicoloured juggling batons into the void created by the removal of Mum's case, and climbing nimbly into the cramped backseat. 'Just so you know I have loads of pot — loads!' Kev and I meet eyes in the rear-view mirror; *it is the dawn of a new era.* The era of Mum worrying about us and getting up early is over, the era of getting wasted and sleeping in is about to begin. As Kev takes my hand, I smile.

We camp for the night at Jurien Bay, about 200 kilometres north of Perth. Remarkably more stable than Mum's and requiring far less drama, theatrical sighs, and mumbled 'buggers' during assembly, Tim's tent almost assembles itself so within no time we're ready to find the local pub — smoky, rowdy, and crammed with sweaty middle aged men wearing singlets. Tim, Kev and I spend our first evening together as a new threesome gaily chatting to the singlets and drinking much beer. A good first night for us, coming from the alcohol-soaked environment of a ski resort.

Travelling north from Jurien Bay to Geraldton, the last sizeable town for a while, we hit the grocery shop and fill the food box with enough food to hopefully make it to Exmouth. Tim floats around the store wearing a ludicrously bright full-brimmed hat from Ecuador that screams *I am a tourist come and hassle me* and Kev carefully reads all the labels on the food items instead of grabbing familiar-looking packaging like a local. They could not look less like the sun-baked locals of Geraldton and together they fill the cart with ridiculous, expensive, impulse items that I promptly remove.

'I'm buying a fishing rod. I've always wanted to learn how to fish but I never really got the chance growing up in the city and all,' says Tim. Not content with buying the first rod and reel he comes across, Tim yearns for the perfect set, tailored to his very hands. Hours later, after visiting every fishing store in Geraldton (of which there are a remarkable amount) he buys a red fishing rod, on special, and two greyish packets of horrid, stinky, frozen, squishy stuff — possibly prawns or squid — for his bait. With the fishing equipment jammed in the back of the truck, we are finally ready to leave. Pulling out of the parking lot, Tim starts rearranging everything in the back of the car trying to gain access to the fridge. I watch him in the rear-view mirror rummaging around in the fridge, unpacking the cheese, the fruit and the juice and when he crams the stinky, squishy bait into the void he created at the bottom of the fridge, I slam on the brakes and swerve to a stop.

'Get that out of there NOW!' I yell hysterically.

'What?' He asks innocently.

'The bait! The fucking vile stinking bait! Get it out of the fridge and away from the food now.'

'But it needs to be frozen,' Tim pleads. 'It will go off if it isn't in the fridge.'

'I don't care: there will be no bait in my fridge, you'll have to go and find something else.'

Reluctantly climbing out of the car, he looks around despondently, as if expecting a solution to magically appear from nowhere and starts walking past the pier back to the closest fishing store. About fifteen minutes later he returns beaming.

'Look what I found on the pier,' he says, holding a pink bucket crusted with old bait and blood and smelling like a fish rendering plant up for our admiration. 'It's someone else's bait bucket.'

My stomach heaves.

'Someone just left it there,' he enthuses. Well fancy-fucking that! The bucket is not exactly what I had in mind when I said *find a solution*. It comes with its own personal swarm of flies and for some reason I find the pink bucket flies more disgusting than regular flies, shuddering in revulsion whenever one lands upon my skin. The bucket stinks. I hate things that stink. I imagine I can smell it from the driver's seat and as Tim winds down the back window to jam it in I simultaneously wind down my window.

We head for Kalbarri, one of the premier windsurfing places on the planet — unsurprising considering the force and consistency of the wind. Scrub and gnarled stunted trees, twisted, shaped and buffeted by the wind, disguise the beachfront campground from where we watch the windsurfers and kiteboarders flip and dance across the waves in the late afternoon sunshine. Copious amounts of old fluorescent windsurfing junk, drying clothes and dilapidated campervans litter the sites, full of Euro surf trash squatting in the campground, avoiding the thirty-day limit by moving out once a month and returning the following day. Many long-haired, semi-naked European men wander past, peering at us like prospectors watching a stranger wander into town. Somewhat miraculously, we find an empty camp site and pull in gratefully. Opening the flip-down back door, the pink bucket tumbles down the mountain of equipment and onto the ground by my feet and I look with horror at the brown smear left on my pillow against which it had lain. Blood swirls from my face and I completely and utterly freak out.

'What the fuck Tim? Look at my fucking pillow it's covered in horrid horridness!' My body jangles with adrenaline as though he has personally threatened me and, breathing like a woman in childbirth, I walk in pointless, upset, little circles, twining my hands together.

'It's not too bad,' says Tim, smudging the smear with a tissue.

'Not too bad! Not too bad! Are you insane?' My voice approaches frequencies heard by bats.

'Rightio, I'll have that pillow: I don't care.'

'Fine! Good.'

The smeared pillow becomes Tim's pillow. After ranting neurotically about how the pink bucket should be tied to the outside of the car with baling twine, with time and adequate huffy indignation, I calm.

The prickly-looking shrubs offer some protection from the wind but still gusts sneak in, snatching papers from our hands and hats from our heads, tossing them playfully into the darkening sky as we scramble after them. Having become lazy with tent anchoring, tonight looks like a full-peg-bag night. We eat watching the pink and purple sunset blaze spectacularly over the Indian Ocean, silhouetting graceful acrobats speeding across the water and screaming gulls diving through the sky. A couple of tanned guys wearing low-slung board shorts barely supported by their skinny shanks stand by as their friend scrubs sand from his board under the water tap. The muscles in his brown back jump as he caresses the smooth surface of the board, stretching his long, muscled arms up and down rhythmically to brush the last few grains away. Unkempt blond hair falls across his face and salty stubble coats his chin. He laughs easily at whatever his friends are saying, pausing to flick water in their direction, and once finished, slings the board onto the roof of a dilapidated old campervan covered in stickers with clothes, underpants and food wrappers spilling out of the rusted doors.

I am staring. Worse, I am drooling. When he drives past us and nods, flashing us a grin, my stomach slowly somersaults and by the time I raise my hand in return, he's but a rapidly dissipating cloud of red dust. Kev notices me checking out the surfer and looks away quickly. His confidence is still in pieces. He had been a man who never knew the fever of jealousy; assured in the fact that I loved him and wanted to be with him, he felt no insecurity even when I lived with a bunch of young Aussie guys in the resort party town in Fernie for a ski season. We had both been young and strong and fit, equals in the relationship, but now something has changed and our relationship is unbalanced for a time.

Hurt, frail and emotionally reeling, he needs me more than before, for both my physical ability and my emotional support. Where before he would have laughed at my attraction to the surfer bum and maybe teased me a little, now it hurts and worries him, sparking a desperate fear that I am going to leave him for a man who can lift and carry, hike and bike, surf and ski, and have sex standing up against the dusty back of a crappy, sticker-covered campervan. He hides the vulnerability well but from the occasional unguarded comment and look I know it is there; a little crack or spore of doubt has entered our relationship.

He feels that now he is somehow less of a man — two thirds

less to be exact, and why would any woman want one third of a man when she could enjoy a fully functional whole? And deep in a hidden place, lurking like a vile parasite, is the conviction that he will ultimately be alone.

Weeks earlier, in the midst of a horrible and drawn-out fight in our Millennium Place lounge room, Kev had smashed a cup against the wall as he shouted, red-faced and angry. 'This happened to ME not to you.'

'It affects me, so it fucking well happened to me too,' I spat back.

'Why don't you just go? I know you want to, and maybe I want you to as well so at least your life won't be ruined too. I have to deal with this; I am the one who has to be alone.'

'I am just fucking sick of it, sick of everything,' I said, flopping down, defeated, onto the couch. I had flirted with the idea of leaving him during rehab and the dark, fight-cluttered days in Millennium Place, but it was never really a concrete plan, more an abstract thought — the way exhausted, overwrought mothers wish they could place their newborns in reed baskets, watching as they sail away down the river. I loved him: I didn't want to leave him, not really. I just wanted things to be easier.

But Kev was convinced it was just a matter of time and internally steeling himself against the inevitable. The sad look he gave me reminded me that nothing had been resolved; we had of course made up, made assurances we were not sure we could keep and let the matter drop, but it was still there: a dam hastily and shoddily patched up on the verge of bursting. With time, Kev's confidence will return as his ability and independence grow. It is so easy to forget how recent his injury is — barely six months have passed since his spine was severed. But at this stage, he worries he will rely on me forever.

Wind peppered with stinging sand drives us inside Tim's tent and he lights a small pipe. Filled with smoke, the tent reminds me of a Native American tepee during whatever ceremony it is where everyone smokes loads of pot. The pipe is lit again and again, smoke burns my eyes and, coughing uncontrollably, I stumble out of the tent. A couple of hairy guys walking past stare at me struggling to breathe as clouds of thick blue smoke balloon out behind me, and they nod in a slow, knowing manner. The pot helps Kev's spasticity, eases his constant pain and relaxes him, but most of the time it makes me comically paranoid. 'What is that?' I ask incessantly, 'It's the cops isn't it, come to arrest me for smoking a joint?'

It amuses Kev and Tim no end and they tease me gently until I become so paranoid that it is not even funny for them anymore and they backtrack desperately to calm me. Sleep comes slowly. Truncheon-wielding policeman shake our tent and lights explode behind my closed eyelids, all the while Kev whispers, 'You will be okay Baby, you just had a bit too much,' as he strokes the hair from my forehead.

North of Kalbarri lies the Peron Peninsula, stretching into World Heritage listed Shark Bay Marine Park, home of the stromatolites: black, knobby-ish humps that to the untrained observer look decidedly like rocks but to a geologist, stromatolites are like Galapagos finches to an evolutionary biologist. Similar fossilised algal mats have been discovered in sediments ranging back to 3.4 billion years old, one of the earliest records of life.

As I turn from the north-west coastal highway, passing a huge sign proclaiming the Shark Bay World Heritage Area, my excitement grows and I drive faster. At Hamelin Pool, modern examples of the ancient stromatolites exist, equivalent to — but admittedly nowhere near as cool — as a living, breathing dinosaur. Tim and Kev feign polite interest as long as it means a break from the car, a pee stop and hopefully a snack bar well stocked with frosty drinks. They joke that the most interesting thing we've come across all day is rocks: bloody boring rocks in the middle of nowhere.

Pulling into the Hamelin car park, I grab my hat and leap out to assemble Kev's chair and a wall of heat flattens me; diabolical, malicious heat — a full body assault after the air-conditioned comfort of Yota. No liquid shade to cling to or creep from patch to patch, the sun hammers relentlessly, crushing and frying us like three eggs on a black bonnet.

'Fuuuucking hot,' sighs Tim, and Kev and I wearily nod.

There are just a couple of buildings, a few shacks and a path leading down to a boardwalk built over the stromatolite mats. The absence of kitschy souvenir stalls, hot-dog vans, bright billboards and pushy crowds of impatient tourists feels like a cool breeze.

'Anyway, stromatolites are not rocks,' I lecture, a tad boorishly, on the path down to the boardwalk. 'They are organo-sedimentary structures made by microorganisms trapping and binding sediment together, that eventually form little domes.'

'Look like rocks,' says Kev as the boardwalk out over the water comes into view.

I have to agree; the 'rocks' are visible for up to tens of meters out into the bay and from the boardwalk nothing (with the exception of the informative signs) hints to the fact the rocks are actually alive. Looking down at the stromatolite mats, peculiarly linear grooves cut in to the domes catch my attention, which, unbelievably, are wagon tracks; the oldest form of life, exquisite, unique, irreplaceable, stomped by horses and cattle and scarred by vehicles. How typically human. Previously, Hamelin Bay was a small port and countless wagons were driven over the stromatolites to deliver goods to the waiting ships, resulting in deep cuts scarred across the domes, looking as raw and fresh as if they had been made only yesterday, but requiring thousands of years to heal.

After touching the water surrounding the stromatolites, it becomes clear why they only occur in several regions in the world. It is hot and hyper-saline: my skin feels almost greasy after touching it. Not an environment hospitable to life.

Feeling strangely deflated after the stromatolites, I climb back into Yota and onwards to Denham, the western-most town in Australia. A pleasant coastal town with a nice beach, seaside caravan park, shop, pub and evidently not too much else, Denham has an easy, restful feel and after pitching the tents on the side of the concrete pad serving as a camp site, Tim, Kev, and I head to the pub.

From the front, the Denham pub could be an old lawn-bowls meeting house circa 1950, with a few outside tables, umbrellas and garden lanterns scattered outside. Like many old pubs, it boasts a dark and gloomy interior with grimy, smoke-encrusted windows and a peculiar smell unique to drinking establishments of a certain age: the smoky, slightly sweet smell of beer-soaked mats and bulging ash trays.

As I order our beers, some local guys at the bar lift their chins in greeting, 'How ya goin' love?'

'Not bad, yourself?' I reply, and we strike up a conversation. Mostly cattle workers and one gregarious roo shooter, the men appear to consume beer in heroic proportions, gulping huge mouthfuls the way a kid drinks chocolate milk. Each man is tanned and cured, skin etched by sun and wind, crow's feet wrinkles crawl down their cheeks as they smile or squint to light another cigarette. Roo Shooter wears a stained, blue singlet stretched over his hairy chest and improbably broad shoulders, giving him a top-heavy, triangular appearance. His face is baked red by the sun: clearly a man who works outdoors. An accumulation of several weeks' worth of dirt and grease clings to him, and 'bad' cannot describe the way he smells. But he is quite friendly and very excited to be talking to someone new for a change, particularly a woman, and he stretches himself along the bar in my direction.

From his obvious need to be constantly talking to someone, I get the distinct impression that Roo Shooter spends a lot of time alone in the bush with just his 'roo dog' for company.

'I've just got back to town,' he informs me, 'been out collecting … got quite a few this time — some big ones too. Now I just gotta figure out what to spend my money on.' I don't ask what a windfall in the roo shooting business is because honestly, I don't want to get into any more details than I'm already being subjected to. Tim saunters over and leans with both of his hands against the bar, rocks backwards on his heels and looks Roo Shooter up and down.

'Well, you are quite broad, aren't you? I think you would probably beat me in an arm wrestle.'

I stifle a giggle as Roo Shooter looks at Tim, who likely weighs less than half of his considerable bulk, as if Tim has just proposed a Devonshire scone-baking competition, and remarks derisively,

'Yeah, I reckon mate,' as if the concept is a personal insult.

'So, what do you do for a living, something outside I presume?' Asks Tim, launching Roo Shooter into an obviously well-rehearsed description of the solitary hunter's lifestyle that makes the career sound as exciting, dangerous and sexy as Indiana Jones'. Tim and I are regaled with stories of how he 'destroyed the fuckers' (in regards to kangaroos), told of his many guns, his amazing marksmanship, and how generally manly you have to be to be a roo shooter — whence he looks pointedly at Tim. Tim nods as he listens to explanations about what the roo carcasses are used for, what tastes best and worst, and raises his thick black eyebrows at the many charming pet-names Roo Shooter has given various parts of the kangaroo, using synonyms from the female anatomy. Spent, Roo Shooter takes a tremendous gulp of beer and waits for me to throw myself at his feet.

By this time, Kev has joined us at the bar wondering what's taking so long to bring over the beers.

'How ya goin'?' Roo Shooter shakes hands with Kev roughly and I can see him thinking *what the hell does this guy do for a living?*

The black paint so carefully applied in Freeo has flaked off the wheel's rims and coats Kev's hands in a layer of toxic grime. Every time Kev touches the rims to push, his calloused hands become dirtier and dirtier as the paint creeps into the deep crevices, cracks and sores, dying them even darker. From my henna days, I learnt hands absorb dye excellently and Kev can scrub his hands all day like Lady Macbeth and still they will be black. Kev's arms have become strong and brown, forearms thick and knotted with ropey cords of muscle that can be traced running into his heavily slabbed shoulders; the type of strength that only comes from using them as legs. I unconsciously compare other men's arms and hands to Kev's strong, battered ones capable of incredible tenderness. Soft, pampered, naked hands lack the brute appeal of Kev's hairy mitts. I trace my fingers along a prominent vein running along the back of his hand as I pass his pint down. Roo Shooter catches the gesture and shifts his gaze from me to Kev and then back again. The pub fills up. Everywhere, sunburnt people laugh and drink, most of the men wear Akubra hats and women are few.

Roo Shooter peers at Kev, 'Are you a hunter?'

I snort into my beer imaging Kev, a crippled hippy, out hunting kangaroos for a living.

'No, I'd be hard-put to catch road kill these days,' and Roo Shooter in turn snorts loudly into his beer and says,

'All you need is a big gun, mate'. We could have been in any rural pub in any country of the world and heard a similar sentiment.

19

North-west of Denham, the entire Peron Peninsula has been converted to François Peron National Park: a stunning, arid scrubland blanketed in red sand and fringed by impossibly turquoise waters. François Peron National Park and the Peron Peninsula exclude many of the feral animal species that plague Australia, with help from the Project Eden initiative started in the nineties, which involves the removal of feral animals including goats, cattle, sheep, cats and foxes. The program has virtually eliminated foxes on the peninsular but cats, mice and rabbits persist. The native populations have benefited and I hope to see the shy and beautiful Bilby.

I insist on taking all eighty litres of water, terrified of breaking down on the sand track and being discovered as desiccated skeletons months from now, sitting in the shade of Yota after drinking all the windshield-washer fluid in desperation. Heaving the jugs into the back, I'm aware that both Tim and Kev think I'm being excessively paranoid.

Except for the southern-most area near the Peron Homestead, once a working sheep station, the park can only be accessed by four-wheel drive 'tracks' and I feel very hard-core as I deflate our tyres. The road unfurls as an endless strip of red sand through arid acacia scrubland, barely more than a clearing, that pulls and wrenches the steering, causing Yota to lurch from side to side — more akin to skiing than driving. We skid and slip for miles and miles and I come mere centimetres from impaling Yota on an ancient fence post, when I briefly lose control.

The cyan water glitters from the beach, made all the more dazzling by the contrast to the red sand and parched bush. The ocean looks as if it should be lapping the shores of a white sandy beach covered in palm trees, where tourists lounge under huge multicoloured umbrellas, drinking complicated cocktails filled with fruit, instead of the red deserted shores of dry, unforgiving country. Hot, isolated and brutally windy, the beach is completely ours. Kev and I snorkel in the choppy waters while Tim fishes obsessively with his new rod. In the back of my mind lurks the thought that if anyone is attacked by a shark, bitten by a snake or I roll the car, it will be a tremendous mission to get to medical aid. I hate being the responsible one. I jealously watch Kev and Tim carelessly play in the water. I have officially become Steve Martin to Tim's John Candy.

Tim hooks a couple of parrot fish and is so ridiculously pleased because they're the first fish he has *ever* caught. Many photographs are taken of the glorious hunter posing with his prize, which is slightly longer than my hand's width. Tim gently puts the fish in the blue bathroom bucket, half full of water, and they swirl slowly around the bottom, tails constantly catching on the side of the bucket, pulling them sideways. The larger one starts to float ominously on its back, fins flapping desperately to right itself, then swims sideways in the bucket for some time before death. My stomach shrinks in on itself.

A capital letter sign screams 'Stonefish found in area, can cause excruciating pain and death' and I worry about Kev dragging himself bum first over one.

'That doesn't sound too pleasant,' says Tim glibly.

'No, it will be really bad. Kev, you need to make sure you don't plough into a stonefish resting on the sea floor.' All kinds of nasty, bitey, stingy things dig themselves little burrows in the sand and wait for an unsuspecting paraplegic to haul his bottom over them. And Kev's bottom is fragile, no longer the large, generous bottom of a ski bum; for the first time in his life, it is bony. Dragging a bony bottom susceptible to skin breakdowns over lurking landmines such as stonefish, stingrays, crabs or sea snakes, concerns me. However, Tim is not concerned and ploughs Kev a track with his feet, shuffling his toes through the sand to scare 'the lurking nasties' away.

'Maybe I should let you go first Kev, a stonefish sting is meant to be excruciatingly painful — at least you probably won't really feel it,' he says cheerfully.

'Thanks mate,' Kev replies drolly.

Kev and Tim lack the innate fear of brightly coloured things most Australians possess. They want to touch and poke blue-spotted stingrays, thinking how pretty they look instead of a huge flashing warning sign: 'I'm dangerous, don't touch me!' The plenitude of organisms that can potentially kill them slowly and painfully both fascinates and horrifies them. I tease Kev about his ignorance of Australian wildlife and he gently reminds me about the bears and my conviction that they would climb up the front of the Volkswagen van and drag me screaming to my death. I palm the book of the reptiles and amphibians of Australia, packed on the unlikely occasion we need to identify a snake or spider that has just bitten us: to decide whether to panic or whether to *really* panic. I take perverse pleasure in the abundance of dangerous, deadly animals in Australia.

'What is the deadliest snake in Australia?' Asks Kev.

'That would probably be the mainland taipan: "the size of the taipan and the potency of its venom make it the most deadly of the land snakes", I read.

'Just how big is big?' He asks.

'It can grow up to four metres.'

'Holy shit,' he whistles softly. 'And it is the most potent of the land snakes — just what does that say about the sea snakes? Are they more potent?'

I flip to the sea snake section. "'Stokes sea snake: one of the world's largest, bulkiest and potentially, most dangerous", I read. 'If provoked it will bite savagely, discharging its large venom glands with a chewing motion or a series of rapid bites.'

'Ugh, is it present in these waters?' asks Tim

'Yes,' I say, with my own savage venom.

As Tim drives back along the track, we become bogged. I climb out to push while the wheels spin furiously in the red sand and Tim and Kev sit in the front seat. After I get a face full of sand, Tim grunts in exertion behind the car and I spin the wheels in futility from the front seat. He appears at my window, sunglasses on top of his head, temple damp from sweat, and with hands on his hips he sighs,

'We need wood.' Looking around, the trees are all scrubby acacia bushes that barely reach our shoulders; wood to prop the wheels out of the sand is decidedly hard to come by in François Peron National Park. It takes us ages to carefully scavenge enough sticks, to stuff in the hole and regain traction. Finally, Yota heaves out of the hole, then barely half an hour later, Tim almost flips the car twenty metres from the bitumen.

'Tim, get in the back,' I snap. 'You can't drive anymore.' He morosely climbs back into his back-seat hollow. For a moment, I think he's going to start kicking the back of my chair.

Back at camp, we sink into chairs with barbecued fish on our laps and cold beers in our hands, as the heat of the day's sunburn glows on our faces. Kev sits on a large pillow while his cushion dries from his swim. The inflatable roho cushion he generally uses as an alternative has broken, likely due to over-inflation. The loss of it hurts. He had gotten used to using it when he sits on the ground for extended periods, during his showers, and in the car; now he has to start doing weight shifts every thirty seconds or so when sitting on something hard to prevent a pressure sore developing. Luckily, Kev has feeling in his bottom. He cannot distinguish hot from cold, or sharp from dull, but he can tell 'bad' from 'not bad'. When a part of his lower body feels 'bad' he worries almost as much as me.

It has been a good day and we retire with full tummies and high spirits.

Monkey Mia, about twenty kilometres from Denham, is famous due to the dolphins that have been regularly coming into a protected little bay for over forty years. They arrive so reliably that an entire dolphin-watching industry has sprouted around them and the waters off Monkey Mia are deemed a marine park. Rangers staff the area and ensure tourists don't try to grab the dolphins, feed them beer, injure them, or anything else tourists are liable to do when drunk and unsupervised. I am buying our over-priced tickets from a slender ranger when she notices Kev sitting at the base of the stairs and gushes excitedly that the ranger's station has a beach wheelchair.

'It is especially for people in wheelchairs to get down to the water to see the dolphins,' she looks expectantly at us, 'I'll send someone to bring it 'round.' She disappears before I have a chance to reply.

'I guess you're getting a beach wheelchair Kev,' I yell down to him.

'Great,' he mutters.

The huge beach wheelchair looks more like a small tractor than a wheelchair. The seat is lost amongst the foot-wide wheels and appears to weigh approximately as much as a baby elephant. Reluctant to use the wheelchair, Kev feels obliged because the overly helpful park ranger has already enlisted a couple of guys to help bring it out for him. So, shooting me a resigned look, he half-heartedly transfers into it. And his spasms go ballistic. His legs flex, his knees lock and his entire lower body shakes uncontrollably as though he is experiencing a seizure. Kev leans forward, grasping onto his legs to prevent an abdominal spasm throwing him backwards, and the wheelchair pushers stand around helplessly, wondering if they should try and subdue Kev's legs into a bent position with brute force. One brawny guy looks likely to break Kev's femur until Kev snaps at him to let go. Eventually, the spasms calm and I can almost feel a collective sigh of relief from the onlookers.

Once seated in the gigantic wheelchair, Kev has no control over the direction he goes because it lacks push rims — a moot point anyway considering Kev's arms would need be a couple of feet longer to even reach push rims. It requires four men to push the chair through the deep sand and they are no nubile eunuchs: huffing, wheezing and grunting in effort, making Kev feel like a great fat boat anchor as the chair ploughs its way across the sand leaving tracks a hummer would be proud of.

The spectacle of Kev reaching the water attracts more attention than the dolphins, with kids skipping alongside as though he were a float in a parade, and every second person commenting on how great it is 'that you are getting out.' Kev looks at me in distress and humiliation as I follow his wide wake. He really feels disabled. He thinks everyone is staring at him, which pretty much everyone is — open-mouthed in some cases. Watching him lose another little piece of his dignity upsets me and although I know these people are only trying to help, it makes it worse. Kev would have made it to the dolphins eventually — inching his way along, push by tiny push — but the site of a person in a wheelchair wheeling through sand makes people feel uncomfortable and spurs the same desperate urge to help them with which activists replace beached whales in the ocean. People want them at their destination and stare surreptitiously thinking 'Has he made it? Has he made it? Oh man, he still has ten metres to go.'

The men push the chair into the water, depositing Kev directly in front of the woman feeding fish from a bucket to the waiting dolphins. On the upside for Kev, he gets to see the dolphins up close without kids and punk teenagers pushing in front. Tim and I crane our necks from the back of the tourist scrum standing on tippy-toes and looking at the back of people's heads, glimpsing the occasional fin, tail or splash.

* * *

A tiny, idyllic town with a few shops and houses, two campgrounds, a pub and a population of less than 200, Coral Bay would be the perfect location for a television soapie such as *SeaChange*. Australia's largest fringing reef, the Ningaloo, lies just offshore and, unlike the Great Barrier Reef, it is so close that you can swim to it. The ocean abounds with life and beauty in stark contrast to the parched, wilted countryside where everything struggles to grow. Coral Bay sees humpback whales in the winter months and offers amazing scenery and creatures just offshore frolicking on the reef year-round. But the whale sharks are the star attractions. Migrating along the coast between March and mid-July, the largest recorded individual is twelve metres long, their beautiful spotted appearance and docile nature make them ideal for snorkelers and divers to swim alongside and occasionally catch a ride. As filter-feeding sharks, they don't pose a danger to people, although unconfirmed reports of careless divers almost being sucked up exist.

We check in to the cheaper of the two campgrounds on the main street of town and find our dusty campsite opposite the bathroom block. Tim assembles his tent and Kev helps me set up ours. As time passes and his recovery progresses, Kev is able to help more and I hope for a future where he can do all the setting up when we camp; something that would be made easier if we didn't always camp in deep, soft sand. The two tents are almost touching, jostling for the premium shady area underneath the one tree. The grass tries valiantly to sprout from the sand but mostly consists of scratchy, mangy patches where the odd stalks reaching weakly towards the sky, are encouraged by sprinklers dragged from spot to spot, soaking an area in its annual rainfall within minutes. Although rain generally is not burning hot. I make the mistake of walking through a sprinkler in an attempt to cool off, yelping with pain as sixty-degree water scalds my leg.

Coral Bay depends on deep groundwater for its water supply and wells have been sunk to depths exceeding 850 metres, explaining the water temperature, and the brief time spent falling from the sprinkler, allows it to cool sufficiently as to not kill all the meagre grass. Even a shower offers no relief; hot water flows from the cold tap and leaves me feeling sweaty, salty and prickly. No cold water can be found anywhere, except in the fridge of the store, where it is a sumptuous luxury. Unfortunately, with all the beer crowding our fridge there is no room for water.

The Coral Bay campground, like many campgrounds, has a separate disabled toilet if you ask for a key during check-in, and, like in most other campgrounds, the Coral Bay disabled toilet is forgotten in the weekly cleaning schedule. A thick layer of sand covers the floor and enough insects to initiate Biosphere 3 thrive. But accessible toilets are not to be sneered at in the outback. Curiously, campgrounds tend to offer more disabled bathroom facilities than motels, even if they are poor for wheeling. To access the bathroom, Kev wheels across the sand and up a small embankment, progress is excruciatingly slow: wheelie, push, and stop. Wheelie, push, stop. He moves about ten centimetres with each wheelie and push, then ploughs a furrow into the sand and abruptly stops. A slow, torturous crawl and, carrying the bathroom bucket and toilet seat, I stifle impatience.

The beach yawns at the end of the main street, and consolidation by vehicle traffic has made the sand smooth, firm and easy to access in a wheelchair. Kev wheels over the hard sand and straight into the water, which is quite shallow for a fair distance, meaning Kev has to wheel through water until it becomes deep enough for buoyancy, then crawl over the scattered coral, potential cone shells, crabs and stonefish on his stomach till he can swim. I wait for him to yell in pain or see blood blossom from his stomach. Once in the deep water, Kev swims happily and more strongly than before. Each day brings improvements in his capabilities.

Lounging in the shallow water, Tim lazily flips onto his back and floats, staring up at the wide blue expanse above him musing, 'There is a man in an office somewhere dreaming about being where I am right now … I know because I used to be him.'

I think about his statement for a moment; somewhere, someone is dreaming of being right here, right now: jealous of where I am and what I am doing.

'You know,' he continues, 'when I was at the sugar factory, I literally counted the days until I could travel again and soon, it will be over and I will have another crap job.' He continues on about his days at the factory and I zone him out, focusing on the fact that someone could be jealous of me now. It feels good. It seemed inconceivable five months ago that anyone could be jealous of Kev and my life ever again.

After wheeling in and out of the water a few times, Kev's wheelchair begins to fill with water and I hear it sloshing around as he wheels about the campsite. Kev chose the wheelchair specifically because the frame is made of titanium and less susceptible to rust, but when the bolts holding all the components together begin to rust away, it becomes evident that many non-titanium steel bolts were substituted to cut costs, and the ability to withstand frequent immersion in salt water, was clearly not a priority for the manufacturer. Completely corroded in place, the steel bolts can no longer be unscrewed and will require drilling out at some later date.

'Hopefully the chair lasts until we return to Melbourne and I can use your Dad's tools and garage to try and fix it. I just hope nothing crucial will break because replacements will be really hard to find out here,' says Kev. 'Maybe if it all rusts and seizes together nothing will fall off.'

We wander about Coral Bay searching for a dive company for Tim and a snorkel tour for Kev and me to get out on the Ningaloo reef. When I mention Kev's wheelchair to Bushy from the snorkel company, he replies a breezy 'no worries,' and adds that Kev needs to be down at the dock early so that Bushy can help him onto the boat before the rest of the tourists arrive. The other passengers are the usual lot of European — predominantly British backpackers — with a couple of Americans, one other Aussie guy and an exceptionally tanned young woman wearing a black bikini with amazing breasts, who no one on the boat, especially Bushy, can take their eyes off.

'So, we can find: manta rays, whale sharks and most importantly tiger sharks, by maintaining constant radio contact with a spotter aeroplane up there,' explains Bushy, pointing to a comforting little speck in the blue sky. 'The pilot relays the information to me, and so if I say you should get the hell out of the water, you bloody well better listen.'

I spot a few manta rays, or large dark blobs, in the distance, which speed away as soon as we jump in — which is the closest we get to them. Then the pilot radios an end to swimming due to proximity of tiger sharks.

'Out of the water,' bellows Bushy and everyone climbs over each other to get out.

In high spirits, Kev and I laugh about the day on the patio of the Coral Bay pub, waving to a couple of backpackers from the boat, and begin to feel 'normal' again instead of sick and sad and different. Scarred by everything we have been through together, we needed some small measure of happiness like today. A day playing on a boat in a beautiful setting cannot make us forget how difficult the past few months have been, or how hard the ensuing months and years will be, but it certainly helps.

I'm lying in the tent reading when Tim rushes into the campsite, knocking stuff over in his haste and excitement while grasping the tail of a sizeable black-tipped reef shark in one hand and his fishing equipment in the other.

'Look, look I caught a shark!' He cries in delight, holding it up for my admiration. I poke my head out of the tent as he lays the shark on the tailgate of the Hilux, which serves as our food preparation area.

'Holy crap mate, that's awesome,' says Kev.

'Do you guys know what to do with it?' Tim asks.

'Umm no, I've never caught a bloody great shark before — they don't exactly frequent the inland creeks I used to fish in.' Tim flies down to the general store to consult with the locals, and returns bursting with knowledge.

'Apparently,' he professes, 'I should have bled the shark when I first caught it because you need to get rid of all the blood or it tastes gross.' I silently hand him my Leatherman and he disappears to start the bleeding and gutting process. Most chip shops use shark (flake) to make fish and chips, so I whip up some batter using a bottle of Boags and a cup of flour and slice up potatoes into paper-thin chips. The huge fillets Tim hands me are dipped in the batter and thrown in the pan, and shortly, the wonderful aroma of fish and chips surrounds us.

'Smells good,' says Tim, and we each grab a cold beer from the fridge, clink our bottles together, and tuck into the best fish and chips I've ever had.

20

After stocking up on food and water in Exmouth, we head to Neds Campground in Cape Range National Park. I set up the tent on the hot red sand beside a couple of sad little trees on the opposite side of the campsite to Tim, stringing the green tarp between the trees so it drapes in front of our tent like a shroud. Considering Kev does not rise before 9am, when the sun hangs high in the sky, the tent heats rapidly. Unpacking the car, I feel the tips of my ears and the sensitive skin of my hair-part burning because I can't find my goddamn hat. I feel like an ant under a magnifying glass and keep looking up at the sky, much as an ant would I suppose, thinking *why? What have I done to you?*

Ned's Campground has several small scrubby trees, the only shade to be seen for miles and miles of harsh rocky rangeland and, consequently, also has all the roos for miles, which bring with them all the ticks for miles. Everywhere I look I see ticks: crawling creepily, unsteadily but monotonously and purposefully through the sand towards our bare flesh. I loathe ticks. They instil the same level of panic as a leech, the same, 'get it off, get it off' feeling. We examine them with horrified fascination, poking them with leaves and sticks, from which they tumble off drunkenly, and triumphantly show each other ticks attached to various parts of our bodies. As I toss the sleeping bags into the tent, I notice a tick crawling lazily across Kev's mattress. I hit it with a sandal but on it crawls. I hit it again and on it crawls. I begin swatting desperately at it with the sandal as it inches closer and closer to me but it simply will not die. Eventually, breathing rapidly, and feeling my heart beating strongly in my chest, I smash it with a full Nalgene bottle of water and smear it across the mattress.

The tourist brochures I picked up in Exmouth claim the best time to visit Cape Range National Park is from April to September, and that walks during the summer are not recommended. It's February; the absolute height of summer. And hot. Dreadfully hot — shockingly hot. I find myself looking around and marvelling at the abundance of life when no fresh water can be seen. None: not a single drop. I can't remember the last time I saw a dam or a flowing stream.

The heat is blistering and all encompassing; the kind of heat generated by a sauna. A red prickly rash develops where my thighs rub together, my skin is flushed and itchy and body hairs are hypersensitive. Whenever a slight breeze springs up promising some relief, it delivers a storm of red, gritty dust, which invades ears, eyes and mouths, coating us in fine dusty sand. I constantly feel grains in my mouth and taste it in my food: a little extra unwanted seasoning. Sand fastens to my sticky skin, clogs my sunscreen and my limbs scrape each other as though emery boards. Swimming simply replaces sand with salt, pulling the skin tight against my cheekbones and scalp. Sweat dribbles down my spine pooling in the small of my back and my glasses constantly slip from my face as perspiration beads a moustache on my upper lip. I feel sick from the heat. I can hardly move. The heat amplifies gravity, pressing down upon me, and walking feels as if I am walking through waist-deep water.

The stifling heat really affects Kev, sucking the energy from him like a leech. He has never done well in the heat, even before his injury. When we travelled to hot countries, a conga line of water vendors trailed him as he oozed sweat, but since the accident, his sensitivity to heat has worsened. He sweats above his injury, face flushed and moist, but at mid-chest level the sweating ceases; a damp, matted line of chest hair marks his injury level. Poor temperature regulation makes him a prime candidate for heat exhaustion.

After unpacking the car, I tip long-overdue laundry from the bucket into the ocean, letting the waves churn the clothes and sheets around like the world's largest washing machine, mashing them into the sand. I have no soap so there is no real cleaning: only diluting. The sweaty, salty smell of us is replaced with the salty, slightly fishy smell of the ocean — and of course more sand, which grates against my bare skin like a rough woollen coat.

I hang the sodden laundry in the trees behind our tent to dry, twisting sleeves around twigs and tying the corners of the bed sheets in knots around the branches to prevent them from landing in the red dust below. I have to work quickly as the tree crawls with ants; horrible, aggressive, vicious ants, which dart onto my fingers if I linger too long in one place, biting, and frighteningly, racing up my arm. I have read about desert ants that live in a symbiotic relationship with certain trees and fiercely protect their tree from predators in return for some sap and a place to live. These ants could well have a similar relationship with this tree, because they protect it with a ferocity rivalled only by a Confederate American protecting his right to bear arms. The ants surge forth onto my laundry, conquering new territory for their tree, and a brief battle is fought and lost. I retreat to tend my bites and find a stick to poke my washing onto the ground, where the ants mill angrily, then eventually, swarm back up the tree. Sighing, I pick up the washing puddled in the sand and wander back to the beach.

Tim carefully unpacks his fishing equipment and sets off over the dunes to the beach. Surprisingly, he is back within fifteen minutes. 'Check out what I caught,' he exclaims proudly, holding up a large, yellowish fish covered with small, blue spots.

The fish looks like some type of exotic reef fish that could be seen swimming in aquariums amongst sea turtles and stingrays. I flick through my discount-bin fish book to identify it.

'I think it's a Spangled Emperor. Apparently they taste awesome … and, most importantly, are not poisonous.'

'Excellent,' says Tim, laying his fish on the picnic table like a gladiator, then rushing back to the beach to try and catch another. His enthusiasm is infectious and I'm smiling as I fry up the fish for Spangled Emperor pasta, a welcome change from curry. We eat slowly, relishing the delicate flavour of the fish, which couldn't be fresher.

After cleaning up the dinner mess, Kev rolls a large joint. Since the sun disappeared in a radiant blaze about an hour ago the temperature has dropped quickly, and we huddle in the small pool of light supplied by the camp lantern. Darkness stretches out around us forever. Insects converge on the light, batting against the cover noisily. Languishing in Mum's camp chair that I've come to love, I admire the still, clear night and dig my toes into the warm sand. Tim flits around the lit margin of the campsite, shining his torch on 'beasties' such as huge black ants marching purposefully in a line — probably directly into my tent — a crab, a larger crab and a small brown wallaby staring at Tim with huge liquid eyes reflected by the torchlight.

'Em,' yells Tim, 'check it out.' He holds the torch on the wallaby, acting as though he's David Attenborough and the wallaby is the endangered white rhino.

'What?' I rise unsteadily, feeling way too stoned, and follow Tim as he creeps theatrically towards the wallaby, repeatedly shushing me in an exaggerated whisper. Giggling, we lurch at it and it vanishes into the inky darkness. We follow the tracks through the sand, around the grass mounds and tussocks, over the dunes and down onto the beach where we hear the waves gently fall onto shore. Headlamps were forgotten in our haste and the torch beam is slight and wavering, intensifying the darkness surrounding us; a small oasis of light in a black desert below a moonless sky festooned with stars. We huddle closer together and I unconsciously try to wrest control of the torch from Tim. Everyone is slightly afraid of the dark, consciously or unconsciously; fear of the dark is primal, hardwired into our psyche. *There are monsters in the darkness*, our biology tells us.

Waves softly slap the beach and my eyes strain to distinguish the white foamy waterline through the blue–black darkness. Staggering closer to the water, several crabs skitter through the gloom just beyond the circle of light and, seizing the torch, I shine it along the beach. As far as I can see, crabs, skittish of the light, scatter and dance in the frothy waves.

'Wow, Tim look,' I exhale, delighted. It is akin to finding fairies in your garden: something magical.

'This is so cool,' says Tim as we watch the crabs frolicking, the bolder ones acting aggressively, mock charging us and clicking their pinchers menacingly, causing us to both shriek and leap panicked back up the beach.

With the total absence of ambient light, the stars glitter like pyrite and tension slumps from the back of my neck. Weightless, I breathe, 'I'm going to get Kev, he'll love this.'

As I walk back into camp, Kev sits stonily at the picnic table, glaring angrily as I approach. 'Where the hell have you been?'

'What?'

'You were gone for ages!' He accuses. 'Where have you been?'

I am confused: I'd been gone barely ten minutes.

'We saw some crabs over at the beach. They are so awesome! Come and see.'

'I don't want to see the fucking crabs,' he snaps. 'You just left and I didn't know where you went.'

'I just went down to the beach … You're angry at me because I walked over the dunes?' I ask incredulously. 'What, are you jealous that I can walk out and see the crabs? Should I not go just because you can't?'

Doubled over, his forearms rest on his thighs and his breathing is short and forced.

'I am not jealous of you,' he shouts, as tears and mucus plough tracks through the constant cinnamon-coloured dust on his face, 'I'm jealous of Tim! I want to walk through the dunes with you! I want to walk down on the beach with you! I want to be the one who is laughing and giggling with you, stoned in the dunes … and when you walked away with Tim … I was so fucking jealous I couldn't breathe. I wanted to smash his face in!'

I stand shocked as he clenches and unclenches his fists, refusing to meet my eyes, looking instead at a patch of sand.

'What, now you think there is something going on between me and Tim?' I retort defensively.

'No, of course not, not when I think about it rationally … but I kept on having visions of you and Tim together and it made me freak out.'

'I am not into Tim: not now, not ever. I was thinking about you the entire time — how much you'd like it and trying to figure out how you could get down there — and now you're having a go at me. I came back for you!'

'And do you think I like sitting here alone waiting for you to come back? Sitting here waiting for you to figure out how to move me — do you think I like being carried around like a fucking anchor?'

'Oh, and do you think I like carrying it?' I scream back, regretting it immediately.

'So now I am a burden, a fucking cripple, and I can't do anything. At least admit it. Why don't you go around Australia with Tim? You'll have more fun.'

'I don't want to go with Tim. I want to go with you.'

We both burst into hurt, angry tears and then eventually, exhausted, and tired of fighting — tired of crying — we reach an uneasy truce; the issues not really resolved but dormant like a quiescent volcano. We can pretend to be happy and occasionally fool ourselves into thinking that we might actually be happy, but we aren't happy, not yet; it's still too soon, too fresh and too raw. Watching me do something fun that he longs to do is difficult enough as he adjusts to certain limitations, but watching me do something fun with Tim is especially hard. Stoned and alone, listening to Tim and me laugh as we crept through the sand dunes, Kev felt replaced.

When night falls the next evening, we follow the road down onto the beach. I'm desperate for Kev to enjoy it and every wheelie-push-stop and furrow through the sand I dance around him like his own personal cheerleader. I keep up a constant string of, 'it's fun … it will be really cool … you're nearly there' as if trying to convince myself that it will be fun, that it will make him happy — it will make us both happy, right? Along the beach, the crabs are out in force and Kev laughs as Tim runs towards them and then yelps as they brandish their claws at him.

'Let's go skinny dipping,' yells Tim, running towards the water shedding his clothes, and the happiness spell cracks. Kev doesn't want to go skinny dipping; he feels too self-conscious of his condom catheter and leg bag, and the time, pain and effort involved in disrobing and transferring to the ground, means that Tim and I will be swimming in the darkness for at least half an hour.

'I don't want to go either,' I say, standing behind Kev. But I do. And I want Kev to go too. I want him to have confidence and not to worry about the fucking bag: it is irrelevant, serving a purpose but not changing who he is. Since when can a bag change Kev from someone who skinny dips to someone who doesn't? A screw press grips my chest, and rubbing Kev's back, I choke down hysterical, angry, frustrated tears. I want to hit things. I want to throw, break and smash things the way I feel my life has been smashed, broken and thrown into scary alien territory where I don't belong and don't know how to behave.

We return to camp in near silence, both sniffling quietly, too lost in our own melancholy thoughts to notice the vibrant stars overwhelm an eggshell sliver of moon. Almost touching on the narrow path, my arm brushes his shoulder occasionally, but the distance between us feels immense and insurmountable.

21

Turquoise Bay, sheltered by the fringing Ningaloo Reef, shines a striking blue-green true to its name. Tim, a friendly young park ranger and I drag Kev over the dunes and down the steep, sandy embankment to the rocky shoreline, banishing the thought of the return voyage, sans ranger, from our minds.

'There's a strong rip in this bay,' the floppy haired ranger cheerfully tells us, 'and if you're not really careful you can be sucked out beyond the reef.' He makes a popping gesture akin to a cork coming out of a champagne bottle, then happily waving, he climbs back over the sand dune, not the slightest bit concerned that he has just dragged a disabled man into a potentially deadly rip area. How I love the Australian attitude of *she'll be right, mate*: so different to the North American, *I can't help you just in case I screw it up and you sue me* attitude. Kev does his usual face-first semi-dive into the water and is immediately dragged along the beach by the longshore drift and, swimming desperately, his legs trailing like an anchor, gains some ground. Reassured by his progress, I put on my flippers to join him and we spend the afternoon chasing fish, swimming and laughing — fortunately without being sucked out through the reef into the never-never of the open ocean.

Up the steep embankment we labour, sweating, swearing and gasping, my feet struggling for purchase in the deep, unstable sand as I pull Kev's wheelchair, Tim pushes and Kev spins his wheels in futility. Several times he tips headfirst into the sand as Tim pushes with a rabid, desperate fervour. After what feels like riding a bicycle across the Sahara after a sandstorm, we make it to the top of the embankment.

'Thanks guys,' puffs Kev as Tim and I collapse onto the sand, gulping hot water greedily from plastic bottles. Slowly, my heart rate decreases and the rhythmic thumping in my ears fades away.

Late afternoon when we return to camp, Kev helps me tidy up the picnic table where our stuff sprawls. Washing the dishes in a small plastic tub, I momentarily leave the dishwater in the basin to run back to the tent. Within minutes, a kangaroo noses the basin, slurping up the dirty, soapy water. Soon, another, larger, kangaroo joins the first and they begin to fight over the water, spilling it in the process. I feel like King Solomon, and instead of punishing the kangaroos for fighting, and for their immorality, greed or whatever, I refill the basin and watch the male kangaroo chase off the female and drink all the water. After chasing the male away, I pour more water from our jugs so the female can tentatively return to slurp it up.

With all our water in the bellies of kangaroos, Kev and I drive through the twilight to Exmouth in search of a tap. I can tell he visibly restrains himself from saying, 'You fucking idiot, I can't believe you fed all our water to the kangaroos'. It is not easy to fill twenty-five-litre containers, and most places tell me to shove off because they don't want someone hogging their tap for ages. Eventually, a storekeeper directs me to a tap in the middle of a park where, through extensive tilting and manoeuvring of the container, I am able to fill them.

* * *

The condom catheters Kev bought in Melbourne deteriorate in the heat; the adhesive breaks down, causing them to fall off easily. Even when Kev manages to attach one, it comes off almost immediately during the first pee. Consequently, each time Kev pees he thrusts his hand down his pants to hold the condom on, regardless of circumstances or company. Nonetheless, accidents occur frequently and I wash the bedding daily.

'Thanks, Baby, I'm sorry,' he says sadly, his face burning in shame. Something inside me hardens as I hang the sheets in the trees behind our tent and the wind blows red dust across them; the once lush sheepskin I had viewed with envy droops, a bedraggled rag stained with pee and red dirt. I know I should tell him it's okay, that I don't mind and that I know a little piece of him dies every time he needs to ask me to wash sheets or clothing, scrub out the bathroom bucket or clean his leg bags. But sometimes I can't. It upsets me too, I guess. I never thought I'd be washing pee-stained clothing and linen every second day for my 25-year-old boyfriend. From never even seeing him sit on the toilet and not wanting to hold hands until he sanitised after peeing in the bush, to helping him onto the toilet and into the shower, of seeing his penis attached to a hose, has been a shock that is still raw. He promises it will get better. As he grows stronger and healthier, as time passes and he learns how to compensate for his injury and as his balance improves, he will become independent and won't need my help.

'You wouldn't have to do that if we stayed at Millennium Place,' he said one morning as I soaked up a pool of urine from the floor of the tent with my towel.

'I don't even know if we would still be together if we stayed in

Millennium Place,' I replied, 'don't you remember all the fighting?'
Kev was silent for a moment.

'It's not like we don't fight now, Em. Is this any better for our relationship?'

'I don't know; I don't know what's best for our relationship,' I said crossly, throwing the sodden towel into the blue bucket.

He was right though. If we lived in a fully accessible house equipped with grab-bars, higher toilets and wide, open bathrooms, Kev would be independent and there would be more separation between his bathroom routine and me. And with time he won't even need all of those accessibility features; he is adaptable and resourceful and growing stronger each day. Soon, he will not need to rely on me. It is only because we are travelling at a time when many spinal cord injury patients remain in rehabilitation hospital. If we were to do this trip in five years' time, it would be a very different story. The psychological lift travelling and camping gives us is measured against the toll it takes to maintain. So far, travelling is winning.

Having left rehab before he learnt how to get into his wheelchair from the floor, Kev needs help up into his chair each morning. After trying a number of times by himself, I inevitably grab the back of his pants and haul him into the seat. Being unable to get back into his wheelchair if he falls out terrifies him: he's stranded until help comes along. The ability to get up himself represents independence.

Attempting a floor-to-chair transfer for the five-millionth time, Kev sits in front of his chair, legs perpendicular to the footplate. Pulling his legs into his chest, he leans forward and rocks into a crouching position with his bottom a few inches from the ground. Again, he rocks forward and simultaneously pushes down with one arm, thrusting his bum into the air, and steadying himself with his other arm on the chair frame. Face scrunched in effort and cords of his neck visible, his bum nudges the front of the chair slightly below the seat cushion. Pushing down forcefully with his arms, his bum rises almost imperceptibly, nudging onto the cushion. I watch tensely; it's a slow, arduous process, painful to observe and to perform, but — for the first time — Kev gets up from the ground and into his chair independently. It's a huge milestone.

'Farrk,' says Kev, 'what a mission!' Dancing around him in triumph, I yell excitedly to Tim that Kev just got himself into his chair.

* * *

Travelling inland from Exmouth to Karijini National Park, the only sign of habitation we pass all day is Nanutarra Roadhouse and the heat is indescribable. Even the plastic chairs in the shade are too hot to touch. The air burns my lungs as though I'm breathing inches from a large, smoky bushfire, and my sweat is not so much excreted, as extracted forcefully from my body — akin to transpiration losses in a photosynthesising plant. Somehow I stand, despite lacking energy to support myself. My eyes flick to Kev who sits in the shade, breathing shallowly and dabbing sweat from his shiny face with his hat. The black push rims of his wheelchair burn his hands, much as the steering wheel scalds my hands as I drive.

'It's cooler today: only forty-seven degrees; it hit fifty yesterday,' the unfortunate shopkeeper inside the roadhouse tells us with relish. It's a miserable place in the middle of absolutely nowhere but it's in this desolate setting that Kev begins his miraculous recovery.

Priming the big toe of his left foot by pumping it back and forth, Kev looks up at me and says, 'Watch this, Em … watch,' pump, pump, pump. 'Look — it moved!' Pump, pump, pump. 'See — did you see it move?' Pump, pump, pump. I watch silently as the toe twitches ever so slightly — the only movement that can be mustered from his smashed spinal column. Something has changed and hope nudges me gently.

From Nanutarra we turn east, venturing further into the Pilbara towards the Hamersley Ranges, Karijini National Park and Tom Price, a staging town for Rio Tinto's Mount Tom Price Iron Ore Mine, located just outside the boundary of Karijini National Park.

I know Tom Price can't be far away when suddenly we are surrounded by lots of trucks — really busy little trucks, with many lights and radio transmitters, swarming like angry little wasps. It's scary having to drive with traffic again when I'm used to having the road to myself. Turning into the petrol station, the trucks part reluctantly to allow us to pull up beside one of the few bowsers and more trucks buzz impatiently behind. After filling up with diesel and grabbing some luxuriously cold water from the shop as I paid, I leap back into the truck and click on my seatbelt.

'Where are the keys?' I ask, receiving blank looks in reply. Shit. I check all my pockets repeatedly, then tear the store apart. 'Seriously guys, I can't find the keys.' Accustomed to my absentmindedness and frequent announcements that I have lost something, Tim and Kev do not jump to attention.

'Did you look in your pockets?'

'Yes Kev,' I reply sarcastically. 'I'm not a fucking moron.'

After blocking the bowser for about twenty minutes and holding up increasingly impatient truck drivers, one large, fierce-looking guy in a big white truck lays on his horn. Flustered, I start to panic because I don't have a spare set of car keys. 'Fuck fuckity-fuck fuck,' I fling maps and books and hats and glasses and rubbish through the car like a tornado and after another frantic ten minutes I find the keys under the front seat. The car roars to life to the sarcastic clapping of the truck drivers, and I gratefully pull out of the Tom Price petrol station.

Tom Price itself is an odd little town, bounded on all sides by harsh, inhospitable desert: an oasis where green lawns stretch forward invitingly at town boundaries with shorts-wearing men pushing lawnmowers across them. A lush, green suburbia with picket fences, garden gnomes, swimming pools, primary schools and gardens watered copiously with sprinklers blooming around carefully cared-for homes. It's quite a surreal feeling to suddenly come across an outpost of human existence so far from civilisation.

22

Although Karijini is so remote and difficult to get to, it is immensely popular due to the rugged beauty of the landscape and, of course, the ideal time to visit is pretty much any other time. During the blistering heat of high summer the park brochures recommend avoiding travel in the area because temperatures frequently soar to forty degrees. But happily, summer (the wet season) is also the best time to see plentiful waterfalls with water surging over glistening red rocks, and the site of sullen, dark, thunderous clouds storming over a parched red desert-scape is something worth seeing, indeed.

The park houses an abundance of birds, red kangaroos, euros, rock wallabies, echidnas and bats. Enchanting, but rare, pebble-mound mice collect small rocks into mounds which are seen occasionally in the spinifex country and geckos, goannas, legless lizards, pythons and other snakes are plentiful. Dotted across the landscape, termite mounds stand as sentinels. But the gorges which have eroded and cut through the ancient Banded Iron Formations (formations consisting of layers of iron oxides interbedded between iron-poor sedimentary rocks) make up the most spectacular part of the park, some plunging to depths greater than 100 metres with widths of less than an arm span at the base. The Hammersley Ranges are softly rounded and worn-down due to weathering over millennia; green bands of vegetation stand out on some of the softer, sloping, less resistant layers, while the more resistant layers form sharp cliffs.

The country is the colour of rust: the colour of Aboriginal paintings. The warm pigments of ochre tint the landscape yellow, various hues of red, cinnamon, brown and grey — deep and rich under the immense, impossibly blue, cloudless sky. The less spectacularly coloured iron oxides, black and white, are also common and segment the reds and browns into layers, resulting in vivid bands visible in the deep, heavily weathered, canyons. In the soft, wavering light of early morning, sunset or twilight, the country takes on a life of its own; colours flow and blend into one another like a watercolour painting and the smattering of green from the gum leaves, new grasses and the circular bunches of spinifex stand stark and bright against the backdrop of the termite mounds, canyons and deep, blood-red earth.

It is close to dark when we finally pull into the campground. Ants have established a large nest in the outhouse behind our campsite and Tim and I both avoid it, peeing in the bush instead; fortunately, we are the only campers. I unpack the car and set up the tent, neglecting the fly: rain seems about as likely as a violent snowstorm.

After dinner, Kev rolls a joint. Inhaling steadily, I relish the smoke deep in my lungs, the tightness in my lower back loosening slightly as my face turns up into the familiar night sky. The blanket of stars shines bright and intense. Suddenly, Tim says, 'Can you believe this! We are in the middle of nowhere, WA … absolute nowhere!' He is so excited, so animated. I smile and let the pot settle comfortably into my brain; middle of nowhere sounds pretty good to me. Taking a drink from one of the water bottles, I spill a mouthful and it instantly vaporises on the red, rocky ground.

'Hey guys check it out,' I pour more water onto the rock and watch as it vanishes almost instantly. Leaning down to feel the rocks, they are quite warm to the touch. 'That's what we're sleeping on tonight, like as if it isn't bloody hot enough already.' Sleeping on iron-rich deposits that retain heat as well as a barbeque is like reclining on a huge electric blanket, in one of the hottest places in the world.

Lying on my Therm-a-Rest in the tent, I watch as ants rush purposefully to and fro across the outside of the tent, too numerous to count. The endless procession swarming across the tent is somewhat hypnotic; it gives me the same feeling as being tucked up nice and warm and comfortable in bed during a violent storm. But, I am not comfortable. Not even close; I am hot, tired and pissed off because I have to pee and I know that eventually I will have to get up and brave the ants. Looking over at Kev sleeping contently I feel an insane, irrational stab of jealousy over his night-drainage bag and I wish that I could pee in a bag. Goddamn ants, when do they sleep?

Crouching, I unzip the door and squirm out of the tent, placing my bare feet on the warm red dirt and immediately, I feel the ants surge up my legs like a hot flush. I swat frantically but it is no use: when one is killed, four more appear to take its place. Squatting, I pee quickly, messily, not appreciating that any trace of my pee disappears from the dirt within fifteen seconds, and fling myself back into the tent with dozens of horrible little hitchhikers clinging to my legs. Kev wakes in alarm, mumbling sleepily as I land heavily beside him. Finally, I fall asleep and dream of water: cold, copious, clear water flows into my mouth and across my sunburnt body.

Waking with a mouth as parched as the Dead Sea scrolls, I feel as though I drank six beers, gobbled salted meat and nuts and then slept with my mouth open all night. Squinting myopically from one eye then the other, I blink exaggeratedly, and gulp the last mouthful from my water bottle, detaching my tongue from the roof of my mouth. The air inside the tent is fetid with bad breath and filthy bedding, already hot, even though the sun is yet to appear. Wriggling out of the tent, I'm surprised Kev did not wake with my clumsy, tent-shaking dressing and appreciate the solitude of the quiet morning.

A group of grey wallabies graze on a patch of grass behind our campsite and they hop away when they see me emerge and stretch. The sun has not yet peaked over the ranges, shadows are long and deep in the almost cool air and, surprisingly, a hint of moisture follows the wind. But the heat is near, radiating up from the warm earth. My palpable dread of the heat that I know will soon blast away the almost coolness, nearly spoils the perfect moment. I walk down into Dales Gorge, past Fortescue Falls (the only permanent waterfall in Karijini), and on to Fern Pool, a large deep pool at the bottom of the gorge, fed by a small waterfall and shaded by many large trees growing, somewhat tilted, out of the base of the red cliffs. A small wooden dock stretches out into the water and I walk to the end, kneeling at the water's edge.

There is something primal and primordial about the pool: the dark, still waters, the isolation, the arid, red escarpments and the many small, black fish that dart menacingly towards my fingertips as I brush them through the water. The rocks are Precambrian in age — older than all but the simplest forms of life — and imagining the changes that have occurred since their deposition is overwhelming. They witnessed the evolution of life from single-celled organisms, to crawling land animals, the glorious dinosaurs and their demise, through to the rise of the mammals, and eventually, as a mere blip in the vast cosmos of time, the appearance of hominids. I strip down to my bikini, determined to swim in this magical place, my toes ripple the surface and are mobbed by nibbling, mouthing fish. It puts me in mind of piranhas stripping a cow to the bone in two minutes. *I am not scared of you*, I think defiantly, kicking until they scatter. And in that instant, I plunge into the shockingly cool waters.

Having not felt cool in recent memory, the water invigorates me with a cold fire burning on my screaming skin as if I had leapt from a hot tub to roll in the snow. I start back up the steep track to our campsite where Tim and Kev are stirring. Kev wheels into the ant nest toilet and Tim and I share a glance.

The road stretches endlessly ahead and is lost in a sea of swirling red sand, marred only by scrubby trees and blue-green bushes. Occasionally cars appear in the distance as flashing sparks, elongated and distorted by the heat, gradually morphing into recognisable shapes only to vanish into the shimmering haze behind us. Four huge, deep gorges meet at Oxer's Lookout: the Hancock, Weano, Joffre and Red. Tim, Kev and I peer out from the lookout, each momentarily silenced by the splendour.

'How about we head down there,' proposes Tim, pointing to the bottom of the Gorge. We descend, leaving Kev to wait with his book, some lukewarm water, the heat, the dust and the flies.

It pains me to see him unable to do something he previously would have done enthusiastically and his receding figure, shaded by the day shelter, pulls upon my eye till lost over the mouth of the canyon. Tim is nonchalant about Kev's inability to go into the canyon, and says, 'Well that's just life,' as I try to disguise my tears from him. It's easy for Tim to be nonchalant because he doesn't love Kev; he doesn't feel the pain of Kev's exclusion almost as much as Kev himself, and does not find himself looking around for Kev, trying desperately to remember every detail, every interesting thing to tell him, and simply missing sharing the experience with him. Tim's concerns with Kev's disability are purely logistical: 'Am I physically capable of carrying him up ten steps or 150 metres down a dodgy path?' There is no, 'Is it going to upset me more to go and leave him, than to just not go at all?' conundrum for Tim. Tim is always going to go.

Before Tim and I sink into the gorge, I set up the hand controls on the car in case we don't return and Kev needs to go for help. We start down the steep trail, down into the deep, red canyon, crawling, wading and climbing our way along the base of the canyon. It is liberating for me. I can still live my life the way I want to: I am not limited by Kev's disability. I'm excited to tell Kev. Tim and I slip and slide down the steep, treacherous path, tramp through thigh-deep water and shuffle awkwardly forward, straddling the deep creek where the canyon narrows, and finally reach a section where the water funnels down the rock, not unlike a slippery-slide, and cascades into a large, round pool about six metres below. We need to clamber down and then leap out blindly into the pool, which I'm uncomfortable doing. Tim climbs like an agile little monkey and is able to continue past me. The gorge is narrow and the rock upon which I lie is as smooth as metal, water pressure builds behind my head, massaging my scalp then spilling over my face and shoulders. Within half an hour Tim returns, having reached his own impasse, and we climb back up the gorge to Kev.

23

The headlights cut the night as we approach Port Hedland. As Tim drives, I search for somewhere to sleep, ringing hostels about wheelchair accessible rooms.

'Love,' a man's voice says patiently, 'you are the first person in seven years to ask about wheelchair accessible backpacker accommodation. Last year new rules came in forcing us to put in alterations to accommodate wheelchairs and I just couldn't afford it, so I shut-up shop.' His voice is tinged with more than a tad of bitterness, as if I, and my wheelchair-using friends, were personally responsible for the closure of his business. Finally, another guy I call says slowly, 'Yeah, we are wheelchair accessible here,' in the same tone a little boy with a chocolate-smeared face uses to protest that he didn't eat any of the chocolate cake. But I am too tired to care because Kev is not doing well. The bladder infection he has been fighting has worsened and the nausea and vomiting have returned, which means it is fairly well advanced, and he churns through his antibiotics with new infections coming on the heels of the old. He was unable to do regular catheters in Karijini because of the dust on the wind, and the ants in the campground toilet biting and swarming across his immobile legs, chasing him out. So, to civilisation we go, with (relatively) clean and (relatively) ant-free toilets and wash basins.

As I step out of the air-conditioned car, the humidity hits me like a slap in the face with a heavy, wet towel. Ripe, oversaturated air hangs over Port Hedland, which boasts an immigration detention centre, a 'big' wheelbarrow and undeniably the worst nachos I, or anyone else for that matter, has ever eaten. Our hostel is a dingy little affair with all visible surfaces painted lurid primary colours in a vain attempt to fight off the shabbiness and the strange feeling of inherent loneliness. Caged parrots line the walls: blue, green, and white budgies, yellow and grey cockatiels, pink galahs, rosellas, corellas, sulphur-crested cockatoos, *pink cockatoos*, even black cockatoos and one sad, sickly looking bird of prey — possibly a type of hawk — sitting gloomily on his perch watching the parrots as they fluff around, safe in their wire prisons. The noise is tremendous. The entire hostel smells like wet bird and mildew. Insects and lizards scurry everywhere; I would have thought all the goddamn parrots would have taken care of them. Our room is a tiny, humid cell with twin beds pushed flush against walls the colour of boiled cod, studded with isolated colonies of evil-looking mould. A narrow shaft of moonlight stabs through a tiny window, illuminating a rectangle high on the opposite wall. Unsurprisingly, the door is narrow and Kev only just squeezes through without losing too much skin off his knuckles. I sigh in relief as I see the twin beds: finally I will sleep without Kev's legs constantly twitching and spasming all night.

* * *

We go out in search of the culture of Port Hedland and sadly we never find any. Instead, we find a pub with several lazily swirling fans and a large, open patio stocked with pool tables, a crappy local band and cold, cold beer.

'I'll have nachos,' orders Kev in a fit of homesickness, and the waitress returns far too quickly, plunking over-microwaved corn chips slathered in cheese and pasta sauce in front of him. He looks at me as if it's some type of sick, Australian joke that he doesn't get. Smirking, I eat my fish and chips — the one thing crappy pubs can't screw up too much. Tim and Kev order jug after jug of beer and I'm quite drunk by the time we stagger back to the hostel.

We are all looking forward to getting to Broome, in the fabled Kimberley region, and Yota churns up the miles, lulling us into a state that I imagine long-haul truckies know quite well, concerning me each time a road train hurtles towards us. Watery mirages dance across the road in the distance and, musing on the cause, Tim and Kev rush over themselves to enlighten me: 'Actually, it's an optical phenomenon that creates the illusion of water due to the distortion of light by alternating layers of hot and cool air.' Who would have thought that travelling with two physicists would have an upside? As we drive into Broome, it begins to rain. It has been some time since I've actually seen rain and the wipers groan in protest. Fat drops cut through the dust caking our windscreen and soon all we see is red mud smeared like blood across the glass.

The Last Resort is a sprawling backpacker establishment with a swimming pool surrounded by palm trees and a large, open bar with long, wooden tables, corrugated iron walls and requisite bar flies — which in this case happen to be the manager, Rhino, and his friends. A small, wiry man of indeterminate age, Rhino has straight blond hair almost to his waist and skin like well-cured leather. I never see him wear shoes and he rarely wears a shirt.

Kev and I book a private room to get some time away from Tim. Kev flops down on the bed underneath the coin-operated air conditioning unit, and I ferry stuff in from the car until our room brims with bags and smells damp, dirty and horrible, then slump, exhausted, beside him.

Rhino is drunk, very drunk, and the sun is barely overhead. He lounges on a stool, leaning back against the bar as he chats to his equally drunk mate, Glenn, and periodically scrambles over the bar like a ferret to make himself or Glenn a drink.

They watch impassively as I carry the bathroom bucket, toilet seat and shower chair up a small step and into the men's toilets and Kev nods as he passes them. His ability to pop-up curbs and steps has improved, but as yet he does not fly up the curbs the way the wheelchair basketball player from Melbourne does, and steps remain challenging. Charging the step, Kev fails to make it and rolls backwards, almost teetering over onto his back, as Glenn and Rhino watch like vultures.

'What are you up to for the day?' I ask Glenn, attempting to break his focused stare.

'Nuthin,' he replies without taking his eyes off Kev, attempting the step for the third time. 'I'm planning on sitting right here and laughing at Kev as he tries to get up that step,' he chuckles wickedly. Therein lies an integral difference between Australians and, well, pretty much everyone else: only an Australian will sit and laugh as a disabled guy tries to get up a step. Glenn is the kind of guy who will bet on a three-legged puppy race, who probably pulled wings off butterflies as a child and will happily buy Kev a beer if he eventually manages to make it up the step. But he will not help him unless he is asked explicitly. Attempting to justify himself, Glenn rants drunkenly, 'I don't care, chair or no chair, you are all fair game you fucker, fuck, fuck ...'

Finally, Kev makes it up the step, to the sarcastic, but good natured applause of Rhino and Glenn. He disappears into the bathroom for half an hour and when he emerges, Rhino calls, 'Let me buy you a drink,' and slaps a sizeable vodka down on the wooden bar above Kev's head. 'Look at your hair, you look like a fucking hippy,' charges Rhino. The humidity has sent Kev's hair crazy and it has become an almost spherical 'fro of blond curls: a halo billowing around his head, frizzy and fabulous.

'You're one to talk,' replies Kev.

'And that shirt, what the fuck man?' Kev looks down at his blue Nordica shirt which he has worn in many tropical places,

'What?'

'Wear this,' Rhino throws a red singlet with *feel the love* and *Broome's Last Resort* plastered across the front and back respectively and Kev obligingly pulls it over his head to hoots of approval.

'Stand up,' yells Rhino after several more shots.

'I can't stand up, I am a paraplegic,' explains Kev patiently, despite the copious amount of alcohol he has by now consumed.

'Fucking stand up,' Rhino repeats loudly.

'I can't,' Kev says again.

'Bullshit,' yells Rhino, 'you're going to stand. Glenn help me get him up!' Staggering from his stool, he speaks with the voice of a priest proclaiming 'the power of Christ compels you'. Rhino sidles up to me and says, 'Is this okay?' Realising through his drunken haze that perhaps he is going too far.

'It's okay,' I say, 'but if you hurt him, I'll kill you.' He peers rheumy-eyed at me, nods once and lurches back to Glenn and Kev. Then, with Rhino on one side and Glenn on the other, Kev stands for the first time since his injury. The three of them sway and stumble around the patio, all holding out their thumbs in a triage of thumbs up before Kev is deposited heavily back into the chair, almost flipping over backwards.

Seeing him standing moves me more than I thought it would: the three drunken faces, the three thumbs up, the long hair and board shorts. They look like three friends standing together for a photo — three ordinary guys, no pain, no spasms, no limitations, no incontinence and no disability.

'Why do you stay with him?' Rhino asks later.

'Because I love him,' I sigh. 'Sometimes I wish I didn't … and my life would probably be easier … but I do and I can't change that.' For once Rhino is at a loss as to what to say. He reels over to Kev, leans down till his forehead rests against Kev's, and then he slurs,

'Mate … I have only seen true love once or twice and that's it man! You should marry that girl.' Kev looks at me over the bar and our eyes meet for a moment. He smiles and I smile in return.

'I will, mate,' he says, 'one day.'

* * *

By the fourth round, I've discerned that the huge Maori guy with the green facial tattoos cheats at cards. I nudge Kev, indicating that he should probably mention it, when the Maori guy slams down his cards, looks at us with bulging eyes and says, 'People say I cheat and do you know what I do?'

'What?' I ask hesitantly.

'I smack 'em,' he yells, slamming his meaty fist into the table. My eyes slide to Kev and I shake my head.

'How did you get fucked up?' He asks suddenly.

'I'm not very good at riding motorbikes.'

'Are you going to get better? Like, will you ever walk again?'

'Unfortunately, that's unlikely,' says Kev.

The Maori guy nods his head, digesting. 'I have a friend like you … He's permanently fucked, too. I used to make sure he got into all the right clubs just by saying he is with me,' he declares proudly thumping his chest.

'Permanently fucked'! It conjures up images of cricket bats snapped in half, televisions with kicked-in screens leaking wires like intestines, or large appliances smashed forlornly, but spectacularly, at the base of a huge, rocky cliff. Things irreparably broken. Things like Kev.

'Permanently fucked?' Kev says, tasting the words with his tongue. 'I like that! Sounds way better than handicapped, disabled, mobility challenged or even paralysed.' For Kev, it seems strangely apt.

In a crazy coincidence, Fraser, one of Rhino's friends, is related to a guy Kev worked with at Mt Hotham Ski Resort in Victoria a few years ago.

'Matty is my cousin,' says Fraser delighted, 'if you're friends with Matty, then you're friends of mine and I'd love to take you camel riding where I work at Ships of the Desert tomorrow.' So the following day, Tim, Kev and I head down a narrow, sandy track, reaching a large paddock where several dozen one-humped camels mill around and a bunch of guys lounge, smoking in the shade of a dilapidated shack. Some of the camels are fitted with saddles made for two people to sit in tandem, separated by a sturdy handle. The camels have been trained to sit down so ungainly tourists can climb onto their still formidably high backs.

'This is Abdul,' says Fraser, introducing us to a tubby, Akubra-wearing man, 'my boss and the owner of Ships of the Desert.'

'Call me Cass,' says Abdul. 'You,' he says, pointing at me, 'will be on Belle,' indicating a smallish camel with long black eyelashes and muddy brown eyes. 'You,' pointing at Tim, 'will be on him,' gesturing to a somewhat larger camel, 'and you my friend, will ride Imran,' says Cass, pointing at the biggest camel of them all, which seems ludicrous to me; why give the guy *most* likely to fall off, the camel with the greatest distance to fall? Undaunted, Kev wheels up to Imran, who glares evilly, and a couple of the lounging, smoking guys throw him into the saddle.

Cass leaps onto the head camel with the finesse of Tom Burlinson in *The Man from Snowy River*, gives the 'stand' command and his camel lurches to its feet. He rides the turbulence like a surfer on a wave. As my camel, 'Belle', stands, I am pitched forward and back, coming dangerously close to tumbling off and immediately fret about Imran standing — Kev will be thrown around like a tin shack in an earthquake. But as Imran stands, Kev somehow manages to hang on. There are no helmets suggested or provided; liability is clearly not a huge concern of Cass's. Fraser runs barefoot next to the camels carrying a ridiculously tiny stick that would be about as helpful disciplining a camel as a rolled-up piece of newspaper.

Our camel train is seven long: at the front is Cass with his proud camel that knows it is first and prances arrogantly with its head held high, then me on Belle, Kev on Imran, Tim on his camel two spare camels and a baby camel brings up the rear. Rumours inform us that Cass sources his camels from Alice Springs and that he, his wife and family walk to Alice, catch wild camels, then the family and the browbeaten camels troop back to Broome and calmly convey the fat arses of tourists day after day along the same strip of beach. I don't know how much truth there is in this claim, because almost every story in the North is exaggerated by at least 300 percent. Cass looks like a hard-ass but I have seen wild camels and they look like hard-asses too. I certainly would not try to tackle one.

As we mill at the turning around point, Tim asks, 'So, do the wild camels ever buck people off and run for the bush or do they just become docile once captured?'

'There have been some incidents over the years,' mumbles Cass, launching into story after story of camel train carnage. Tim is enthralled.

'Really?' He asks. 'The boy was stomped by the camels — camels do that?' I keep glancing back at Kev who hangs on to Imran tooth-and-nail and grins widely under his 'fro.

'I'm fine, Baby!' He yells, yet visions of Imran rearing up at a dog, trying to hump another camel or viciously biting him spin through my mind.

After about a week in Broome, I'm sad to be leaving the Last Resort, having grown comfortable here. I will miss lounging in the hammock, watching the green tree frogs and geckos climb the walls, chatting and drinking too much in the bar and reading in air conditioned bliss while Kev and Tim play cards with other backpackers. I ring Mum and Dad.

'We are all betting on when you will turn around, give up and come back home,' Dad says. 'Gramps picked Broome.' My uncle Geoff who lived in Karratha for some time had scoffed, 'madness, pure madness: the heat will kill them,' upon hearing our plans and had said we wouldn't last past Karratha. Dad had said Perth; the bastards! I am stubborn by nature but this makes me positively recalcitrant. Now, about halfway around, we *will* make it, goddamn it.

24

Back on the Great Northern Highway, we drive across the Dampier Peninsula — an eerily beautiful landscape with swollen boab trees silhouetted against a darkening sky and huge, lumpy termite mounds abounding — eventually reaching Derby, the bright green grass standing stark against the rusted red rocks and soil. It may be unyieldingly hot during the wet season but it is also beautiful. The boab trees are flowering with green canopies blossoming above their round Buddha tummies like hair on a Troll doll, waterfalls cascade and swimming holes are brimming, while thunderous, grey clouds roll like avalanches across the parched land and great, fat drops of rain leave craters in the red sand as lizards, dragonflies and multicoloured birds scramble for cover. It is a stunning, timeless land.

Northern Australia essentially has two seasons: the *dry* and the *wet*. The dry season runs April to November and southerners swarm northward; campsites are cramped, tours are crowded and there is never a spare camel or an empty pond. During the wet season, from December to March, the monsoonal rains come battering down from Asia and drown the region with most of its annual rainfall. Dry, barren riverbeds become raging torrents and roads become impassable due to the swirling tide of muddy red water flooding down from the North. The build-up to the wet season from October to November is a tense time for locals, where the term 'gone troppo' originated, as people become slightly squirrely due to the oppressive heat and humidity. The wet season is the least preferred time to travel to Northern Australia: no one's mad enough to go north in the wet.

Reaching Derby, Tim and I walk into the only pub in town, the Spinifex Hotel, in search of a cheap bed. If we unscrew the inward-opening bathroom door from hinges seized in a prison of paint, then give Kev a titanic push up the step, it becomes an accessible room. Tim doesn't worry about how Kev will get in and out of places, he has a 'let's give it a bash' attitude and treats Kev no differently than he did before. He does not hover or pander, assuming if Kev needs help he'll ask. Perhaps it is the way Tim would like to have been treated had the accident happened to him.

Derby has Australia's highest tide — at about eleven metres — and a long, high pier snakes across water-covered mud flats visible at low tide. The sun sets over the muddy, turbulent waters and Tim fishes as if his dinner depends on it. Every log or piece of floating rubbish swirled and sucked this way and that by the vicious currents is a crocodile, and my fingers clench the rail as I peer downwards.

As Tim, Kev and I return to the Spini, Tim empty-handed, I feel good. It's such an unexpected feeling. Six months ago I thought I would never be happy again. Even though this is not a particularly joyous or auspicious place — a crummy, fleabag hotel room, where you want to lay a sheet down before you allow any of your belongings to touch the floor, bed or table — I am happy. It gives me hope that perhaps things will get better and maybe in a year I will be even happier, and be able to look back at the dark times without complete despair.

The brown carpet squishes as I step into the Spini's bar — a bar made for drinking and hosing out later. Several sad, spindly plants reach for the meagre artificial light, pots full of dead bugs and cigarette butts. After eating something deep fried, we have a few beers and start to get to know the ten or so other people lounging on the bar or rocking in plastic lawn chairs at the scuffed formica tables around us. A red faced, weather-beaten man introduces himself as 'Jacko from the Kimberley' and constantly harangues all the other patrons to do shots, including a handsome young Aboriginal tour guide from the Pilbara. A skinny, charismatic and flamboyantly gay barman from Adelaide, looking barely legal, pours drinks from behind the bar while snapping scathing comebacks to two grizzled men teasing him about hair gel consumption. A young married couple, both school teachers from Perth, occasionally help the bartender but mostly sit on their stools drinking solidly.

The owners of the Spini are in Perth for a few weeks and have entrusted the barman and the school teachers with looking after the bar, which they do with aplomb, and the free booze streams forth. As the night wears on, the bar becomes exponentially louder and more raucous than would be expected from eight or nine people, then suddenly, the entire bar is doing tequila shots — not only tequila shots, but tequila stuntman shots: lemon juice in the eye, salt snorted up the nose and shot gulped down the throat. Shots keep appearing in front of me like magic tricks and soon I am stupidly drunk. Both at least as drunk as me, Tim yells and challenges people to arm wrestles while Kev slops beer down the front of his blue shirt and asks for a prairie fire, made from Tabasco sauce and tequila. With the appearance of the Tabasco sauce, the crazy dares soon escalate. Jacko (from the Kimberley) dares the young tour guide (from the Pilbara) to snort Tabasco sauce then drink his shot. Being from the Pilbara is seen as a failing in the Kimberley, and it's a deadly insult to mistake someone from the Kimberley for someone from the Pilbara. Consequently, Jacko and the tour guide are mortal enemies and will duel to the death with warm tequila.

The tour guide, his friend and Jacko each line up their shots along the bar and squirt a generous amount of Tabaco into their hands, each man squirting a little more into the hollow between their thumb and pointer finger than the previous man, and then glancing around for approval. The stuntmen gulp down their shots then snort the tabasco like eighties' movie stars snorting coke. Predictably, it is incredibly uncomfortable; Jacko grabs desperately at a jug of beer in front of the male school teacher and splashes it onto his face. The tour guide and his friend swear profusely, dry retching, eyes and noses streaming, and splash volumes of water on their faces.

After several minutes, the burning appears to settle and Jacko's bravado returns. 'That wasn't too bad, huh fellas? Dare you to squirt Tabasco into your eye and then do the shot.' A hush falls over the bar as if a knight has just thrown down a gauntlet. The young tour guide raises his head, hair dripping, eyes reddened nose running and he says, 'You're on, mate.' The friend wisely decides to sit this one out. Tabasco is produced and shots are poured by a subdued bartender.

At this moment, the alcoholic fog clouding my better judgement momentarily parts and I leap up yelling, 'You can't be serious, Tabasco in the eye is seriously dangerous, you can go blind, this is insane, and it needs to stop.'

'Bullshit,' bellows Jacko. 'We will be fine — if he wants to pussy out that's fine but I am doing it.' The school teacher also rouses from his spell and echoes my point gently, prising the Tabasco from Jacko's hands. Jacko is crestfallen and there is lots of yelling 'harden up, harden up'. An orange, three-legged heeler limps through the bar and sits at Kev's feet. It's quite surreal.

I am up at about 8.30am banging on Tim's door yelling, 'Why aren't you ready?' He appears, bleary-eyed, and climbs carefully into the car, asking for the music to be played at low volume, thanks.

25

We had planned to take the scenic, remote Gibb River Road all the way through to Kununurra from Derby, but being the wet season it is completely impassable and we're forced to follow the Great Northern Highway through Fitzroy Crossing and Halls Creek instead. A sharp rock results in a flat tyre and Tim and I pull out our only spare. With no garages until Fitzroy Crossing, I drive carefully. It takes a while to find the tyre place because it looks more like a junkyard than a mechanic shop, but they certainly know how to charge $210 for a crappy tyre! A crowd of men comes over and, looking at the tyre, informs me, 'That's a good price for a tyre, won't find better around here.'

'I know that!' I want to yell. 'Where the hell else am I going to go?' With Yota's undercarriage heavier with a well-used tyre and my wallet considerably lighter, I pull into the parking lot of the Crossing

Inn, a wide veranda-encircled building adorned with Aboriginal art. After slowly and carefully explaining that I want wheelchair accessible accommodation, I'm given a room with seven large steep steps.

'I — need — a — room — without — stairs,' I say, carefully enunciating each word.

'There aren't many steps into your room,' says the receptionist.

'But, there's at least seven,' I splutter, 'why can't I have that room that has no steps?' I point at a ground level room.

'Oh no, that's our staff accommodation; it's not nearly nice enough for you to stay in.'

I eventually convince her that we are definitely scummy enough to stay in the staff accommodation, which doesn't have any steps but does have a resident frog inhabiting the neglected toilet where black specks of mould float ominously. Each time we flush, the frog is pushed down a little from underneath the rim and his leg and thigh briefly appear. Once the bathroom door is removed, Tim and Kev keep flushing until all the water pressure is gone and we are rewarded with a brief view of the frog before he scrambles up under the rim.

Walking up into the Crossing Inn bar, a huge Aboriginal man greets us; truly a mountain of a man, at least 150 kilograms with wild grey hair and an impressive beard. Seeing Kev wheeling up the gentle ramp through the gate, he makes a guttural noise, bellowing, pointing and gesturing wildly to Kev. He rushes towards Kev and I involuntarily take a step backwards as the man reaches Kev and grabs him in a huge bear hug, temporally lifting him and his chair off the ground.

Kev looks hesitant as the man continues to yell incomprehensibly, grabbing every part of his body and feeling and shaking it, then lumbers behind him, pushing him into the bar. A tall, thin Aboriginal man with an Akubra perched forward on his head appears at my side. 'That's Mikey,' he says, nodding towards the huge man. 'He's deaf and dumb. He wants to buy your friend a drink.' Kev and Mikey are by this stage at the bar and in the process of buying two Emu lagers. Being the wet season, there are not as many tourists around Fitzroy Crossing, due to the very real potential of getting trapped there for several weeks if the rains come. Consequently, the locals are starved of outside company so we are a curious novelty and everyone in the crowded bar introduces themselves and their families to us.

Sparse in furniture that is not tied or bolted to the ground, the bar is made of brick and solid enough to sustain emersion in rushing floodwaters. A couple of fat Aboriginal women squat, laughing and chatting, on one of the eight wooden picnic tables. A cage of wire with a locked gate surrounds the bar, through which an old Aboriginal man fights loudly with his equally old wife until she starts to jab him with a stick through the wire. On seeing this, the small Asian bar girl yells 'Yes!' triumphantly.

An almighty racket can be heard from the indoor area of the bar and occasionally people stumble out looking as though they have been propelled by something from within.

'You don't want to go in there; in there is not nice, stay out here,' advises Phil, who I had met when unpacking the car. Phil, a kind, quiet Aboriginal man who grew up in the region, is drinking with his wife Joyce, an attractive woman in her late forties who has spent her life working on cattle stations.

Phil tells us about the region, about poisonous creatures and the Aboriginal names for everything. Naturally, Tim asks about snakes — Tim loves hearing about snakes and how deadly, aggressive or plentiful they are. Once, Phil said, he was bitten by a King Brown snake and he sports a nasty scar on his leg from the bite. Apparently, he chuckles, he had been so drunk at the time that he didn't even realise he had been bitten and only survived because Joyce had seen the snake bite him and got him to a doctor. Phil asks Kev if he can do some magic on him and uses the pressure points on Kev's head while clicking with his tongue, making strange clucking noises in the back of his throat, and blowing on Kev's head. Then me, for luck — it feels good, like a head massage.

Talking to the locals I discover that this year is an unusually dry year. Often at this time of year, Fitzroy Crossing can be cut off and the bar can only be visited in a boat due to the flooding of the Fitzroy River. The small barmaid leans across the bar, which reaches up to her chest, and adds, straight-faced, that during the floods she has to catch crocodiles in the bar and throw them out. The damn toilet frog that I thought was quaint croaks all night and I lie awake waiting for the next loud, happy croak.

* * *

My back hurts all the time — even when I sleep, a dull pain thuds in my lower back and turns into white-hot agony with the slightest uncalculated movement. It's hard for me not to resent all the lifting, all the packing, all the work I have to do when my back hurts, even though I know Kev would gladly give his right arm to be doing those tasks for me. Although it's a struggle having to unpack, set up and repack Kev's chair every time we stop, I want him to get out and experience everything.

Bending to remove the wheels from Kev's chair, pain in my back flares like fire and I am stuck — bent like a fishhook. I can't move up, can't move down, and I grasp the wheelchair as though it is a lifebuoy. It is some time before I'm able to climb gingerly into the back seat, stuffing pillows behind my back while Tim speeds us to Kununurra. That night, I cry to myself, wishing for a strong, healthy boyfriend who can do all the lifting for me.

We rise early for a scenic flight over Purnululu National Park (formerly known as the Bungle Bungles) from the Kununurra airstrip. Apparently, there is less turbulence in the morning, which I'm all for because I have a history of getting airsick in little planes, and strenuous vomiting might aggravate my back further. We all scramble into the small plane, with Tim sitting shotgun next to the pilot and Kev and I jammed together in the back. The little plane hangs over Lake Argyle and the Argyle Diamond mine, a huge strip mine burrowing into a Kimberlite pipe, and then swoops down to give us a close-up view of the spectacular rock formations and deep canyons of Purnululu. My stomach rolls and reels with the plane, then thankfully I fall asleep, hearing Kev mumbling, 'I am glad we paid for you to be on the plane.'

Near Kununurra, there is a local swimming hole called Black Rocks, to which Tim piggybacks Kev. For his slender frame, Tim is ridiculously strong, like a climber, and jumps nimbly from rock to rock with the not inconsiderable weight of Kev on his back. Huge, black, jagged basalt boulders, tall shady trees and lush greenery surround the pool into which a large waterfall cascades. The water ripples dark and cool and spray hangs in the air like fog: a perfect little oasis. Tim and I swim as Kev sits on the rocks, watching; unaware his right leg is leaning against the burning hot black rocks that give the pool its name.

According to the locals, only 'friendly crocs' live in the water: freshwater crocodiles. Freshies, as they are colloquially known, are smaller and less aggressive than their salt water counterparts, but are still able to liberate you of your limbs and consequently, your life. On the cartoon warning signs posted around most swimming holes in the north, freshies are depicted with small teeth and their mouths politely closed, whereas salties are shown with large sharp teeth and big, wide, threatening mouths. Just in case you were tempted to try and pat them, the sign advises against it noting 'do not approach these animals'. Fortunately, we don't see any and after a lazy afternoon we head back towards Kununurra and our hostel.

The road abruptly disappears into a wide, fast flowing river and I slowly bring Yota to a halt. Beside me, Kev shrugs his shoulders and winds down his window, letting the heat rush in, then settles down to wait as Tim and I climb out to explore. The river is the mighty

Ord and levels are high, with water thundering over a ford and down into a turbulent, rocky pool below. Throwing sticks into the water and trying to spot crocodiles with Tim, I'm startled to see a snorkel-equipped Landcruiser troopy moving slowly and purposefully through the rushing river from the far side, a bow wave fanning out from the bonnet and drawing a wide wake behind, and I scramble to move Yota out of the way. As the troopy emerges dripping from the river, the driver, a hard-looking man wearing a stained and dusty Akubra, raises his hand in greeting.

'Did you see that?' Yells Tim, his plummy British accent strong in his excitement. 'That was so cool! We should do that!'

'Yeah, right,' I reply, 'there is no way I am driving across there without a snorkel. It's way too deep, we will conk out for sure. And what about you, Kev? How are you going to get out if we are swept over the ford?'

'We won't get swept over, anyway I could probably get out in time,' he says dismissively. *He has got to be kidding me*, I think as we watch another troopy breeze past and plunge into the river. 'Probably get out in time'? It wouldn't even be close. If Yota goes down, then Kev is going down too. Barely three months have passed since he was released from G.F., sitting in a shiny, new wheelchair he didn't know how to use, and barely six since the accident that left him a paraplegic. Tim and Kev watch a blue Pajero drive steadily across the ford and it's obvious they both desperately want to drive across, but the hand controls are suspect at best and Tim, having almost flipped the car off-roading north of Perth, has even less chance. If anyone drives across, it will be me.

Anyway, just how deep is too deep? Having not driven through much more than a generous puddle in the past — just enough to get water spraying impressively from the wheel wells so that self-congratulatory photos could be taken — it's pretty clear that I'm not only in a different league to these hard-looking, troopy-driving men, but playing a completely different game. As the Pajero ploughs its way through the last few metres, Tim and Kev begin their campaign.

'A Pajero! Come on Em, if a Pajero can do it, we can totally make it. A Hilux is more hardcore than a Pajero.'

'No,' I say emphatically with my *and that is the end of it* voice, yet they persevere, pleading and cajoling like a couple of whiny school kids on a sugar high.

'Go on, you can make it, come on: Em! Em! Em! Em! It will be fine. Don't be a chicken.' And finally I am worn down. I don't so much believe 'that everything will be fine,' or 'for sure we will totally make it,' I just want them to stop. I want to feel as though the decision is out of my hands. My foot nudges the accelerator with a feeling of disconnection — the same feeling you have when flirting with the impulse to jam on the accelerator at inappropriate times (such as at red traffic lights), while listening to that naughty little voice that whispers in your ear, 'I wonder what would happen if … '.

Each of our windows wound part-way down; up is good because it keeps the water out but bad because it keeps us in if water floods the engine and cuts out the electric windows. I drive slowly into the swollen Ord, trembling and terrified. Tim, seatbelt unclipped, leans far forward between the two front seats, his long, skinny neck craned like a tortoise and his eyes shining brighter than a kid's on Christmas morning. My foot presses harder as the water surrounds Yota, terrifyingly high, and peering out the window I feel as though I am in a boat.

The water pressure is immense and Yota struggles for purchase. The generated bow wave threatens to spill over the bonnet and, frightened, I push the accelerator down. Driving through flooded rivers requires a calm, confident driver, capable and composed. I am none of those things. I have changed my mind; I don't want to do it, I want to go back — maybe I can stop and reverse: shit, shit, shit. I want it to be over. Even though I can see the other side of the river, it might as well be New Zealand it seems so far away. I can hear Kev's voice, dim and distant, saying, 'Good job, Baby, keep going, you're doing great.' It is getting deeper, oh my God, oh my fucking God. How much deeper can it get? Maybe if I go faster it will be over sooner. The bow wave on our bonnet is almost at break point. Where the hell is the air intake? Water will flow into the engine, it'll conk out and we'll be swept off the ford into the pool below. Fuck, Kev is going to drown, or worse, get eaten by a crocodile. And it is all my fault.

Eventually, after what feels like an eternity experiencing 'you are going to die and kill your friends' guilt and remorse, the tyre traction increases and the water pressure lessens. Hallelujah, it's getting shallower; we are actually going to make it. A group of men stand waist deep in the river throwing out fishing nets directly underneath a 'danger: saltwater crocodiles' sign and they wave as I drive from the river. One guy yells, 'You were going too fast and had a really big bow wave, we thought you were going to conk out: that would have been funny.' My heart stops. I am completely insane.

Back at the hostel, Kev notices a really nasty burn, blistered and bleeding, over an area about the size of my palm on his calf where it had been leaning against the black rocks. I grab a couple of burn pads from the first-aid kit and dab the wound with Savlon as his spasms go crazy.

'Does that hurt, Kev?'

'No, it's okay. I can't really feel it.'

His leg had fried to the point of large, yellow blisters and sloughing skin, yet he didn't even notice. My hands shake as I squeeze out the Savlon.

26

Between Katherine and Darwin lies Litchfield National Park, covering an area of about 1500 square kilometres of eucalypts, banksia and grevillea woodland, stunning gorges brimming with rainforest, gushing waterfalls, termite mounds aligned with the earth's magnetic field, rare horseshoe bats, dingoes, wallabies and a multitude of other wildlife.

We eat lunch at Buley Rockhole — Kev fighting to keep his sandwich from lizards and kookaburras, while Tim and I leap into the interconnected circular pools of dark water and stroll along quiet, walking paths serenaded by hundreds of birds and devoured by billions of mosquitoes. The view of Florence Falls, where dual waterfalls spill into a wide, deep pool of emerald green, carved into orange rock fringed by rainforest is hard not to admire. As Tim and I pass the base of Wangi Falls following a trail looping around the top, five or six Aboriginal guys bathe in the shallows sharing a slab of beer and, surprised, I wave. 'Are you sure you guys should be swimming in there? I thought there were crocodiles.'

'Nah it's all good,' they reply in unison.

'Okay, see you later.' Although every refreshing pool in the top end should be assumed to shelter a voracious crocodile, certain swimming holes are considered safe if regulated by the wildlife service or if it's the dry season, when crocodiles are unable to access them. During the wet season, many pools considered safe in the dry teem with crocodiles.

The guys are gone when Tim and I return, hot and sweaty, to the base to meet up with Kev.

'Surely a little dip wouldn't hurt,' suggests Tim and I nod enthusiastically. 'You keep watch while I jump in.'

My eyes earnestly scan the still water for the tell-tale protruding eyes of lurking crocodiles. My keeping watch is supposed to allow me enough time to yell 'Tim, lookout: crocodile,' before he is seized and dragged to his watery doom, totally redundant. Tim is in and out in seconds. I'm climbing, dripping, from the pool when a stern-faced ranger appears and, frowning, delivers a scalding reprimand.

'What the hell are you doing? Can't you read?' He says, pointing to the 'danger: saltwater crocodile' sign right in front of me.

'I … Ah … Oh …' I want to say, 'Where the hell were you a couple of hours ago? You didn't yell at the guys who were having a party in the pool,' but restrain myself.

'Do you have any idea how dangerous saltwater crocodiles are? How fast? How easily they could rip you limb from limb and hoard you underwater till you're nice and soft and tender?'

'No … I'm sorry.'

Tim and I look down, almost expecting a smart smack on the bottom for our stupidity.

* * *

Darwin is the capital of the Northern Territory and has a population of about 142,300 people, yet it feels like a large country town. Architecturally, Darwin is fairly modern, due to being flattened twice — once by Japanese bombs in World War II and again by Tropical Cyclone Tracy roaring in on Christmas Eve 1974, killing over sixty people and damaging almost everything. Monsoonal Darwin has intense, shockingly sudden, downpours causing people to scatter like rolling marbles and blasting birds from the sky.

It's so hot, I feel poached. All my energy is sucked away, oozing from my body like sweat; walking through the dense, viscous air feels more like swimming. The heat is getting to me, making me stupid, drugged, narcotic. I have lost my appetite. Kev and Tim feel the same. 'People seem to get over it though,' notices Tim, as a particularly rotund pair of women wander slowly past us.

Fortunately, our tiny, messy room is air-conditioned and Kev and I return, to my intense relief. We should be out sightseeing but all we want to do is lie in air conditioning or sit inside in yet another air-conditioned pub. It is rumoured that the Territorians are, per capita, the biggest drinkers in Australia and I can see why. If I could choose between doing something, anything, or sitting in an air-conditioned pub, I would hands down choose the latter.

Kev and I walk to downtown Darwin, all two blocks of it, on a mission to find sushi — not something I can just whip up on our camp stove. It is as though we have employed the wasters at the hostel who are drinking with Tim as babysitters and Kev and I are having a night alone together.

'That one's mine!' I say, as Kev and I clash chopsticks, fighting over the sushi passing by on the train. It's nice to share delectable treats and forget how sad we are for a while.

Walking back into the hostel we pass the swimming pool, dark and still in the moonlight. 'Do you want to go for a swim?' I'm expecting he'll say no, that he is in too much pain or that it will be a mission to get in and then take off the leg bag so it is best not to bother, but surprisingly he says yes. I peel down to my bikini and Kev takes off his t-shirt and delicately lowers himself to the ground and into the pool. We swim around in the silent darkness, dunking each other and coming up together at the edge of the pool. The air is warm and still and we are somewhat tipsy from dinner. Making out on the side of the pool, we feel like carefree teenagers.

Later, we have sex. It has been a while — we are both scared it will be too weird because we have had failures before, but it is great. A sudden tropical storm rages outside, torrential rain and lightning adding to the atmosphere.

Kev claims he really enjoys having sex but I still wonder whether he is doing it just for me and how much he actually feels. Thinking of it like this upsets me and it often ends after awkward fumbling and an emotionally agonising crying fit. He is convinced I don't want him, and I am convinced he doesn't want me — that he is enduring intolerable amounts of pain for negligible enjoyment. It is frustrating for him that I do not seem to understand how much he wants and enjoys sex. There is so much build-up and pressure when we actually do have sex because he thinks that if he screws it up I am going to sleep with someone else. The pressure for it to succeed completely overwhelms the act itself. We have had so many fights and circular discussions about sex, with Kev saying how he is emotionally screwed-up by his disability and the changes it has caused in our sex life.

In the past couple of months, Kev has started to get used to his new body, and his strength and mobility have increased, boosting his confidence. I, too, have grown accustomed to the changes in his body and we are rediscovering our intimacy as the weirdness fades. Kev is almost, but not quite, to the point of laughing about our first disastrous attempts. Somehow, I think he will never laugh about that. Each time sex is great for us, we heal a little as a couple.

27

'Hey … It's been ages. Kev, mate … I was sorry to hear about your accident.' Says James, a friend of Kev's from Darwin as he grips Kev's hand between his. Seeing his familiar face is a reminder of happier times.

We first met James when living in a trailer park in Queenstown, New Zealand a couple of years ago; Kev and James were both ski instructors at Coronet Peak. Accommodation was expensive in Queenstown and even the trailer park was well out of our price range but was our only option.

Our trailer park house was a two room, fibro cement shack with an outside loo and a water heater the size of a large bucket. I had merely thought the open fire quaint and cute when first inspecting the house, but it was the only thing that kept us alive as we slept huddled together and fully dressed on our mattress. The first night we discovered that the heater was full of asbestos and took about twenty-four hours to get hot (after we flicked the power switch on and off, not understanding why the goddamn heater wasn't getting warm). The walls were a lurid purple and plastered with photos and pictures, the oven was older than time with temperature settings of 'hot', 'warm' and 'cold', and several possums lived in the roof, to Kev's delight. It was cold, crappy and absolute extortion, but it was our first house together and I loved every inch of it for the winter we lived there. The view was magnificent: over Lake Wakatipu with the jagged peaks of the Remarkables forming a backdrop.

James lived down the path from us in another crappy little shack but it was clear from the outset that he came from money, serious money, and the shack was just casual slumming. He was arrogant, abrasive, and brash but also a really nice guy and heaps of fun. Tall, with a sharp face and nose like the beak of an eagle, he styled his hair regally and was well practiced in the art of looking down one's nose.

When James appeared to meet us in the crowded bar, he couldn't look less like the dirtbag ski instructor we knew back then. All the barmen know him. Every well-dressed businessman nods to him and his mobile phone screeches all night from the pocket of his grey dress pants. I think about the last few days in Darwin and remember seeing his surname on quite a few nice boats and buildings so I ask, 'What exactly is it that you do?'

'My family own the largest pearling company in the South Pacific,' he replies.

'You're kidding,' I say, and he just looks at me long and hard as his perfectly cut hair tickles the neck of an immaculately tailored shirt designed to look both casual and extremely expensive. James, Kev and I reminisce about our season in New Zealand and Tim asks loads of questions about boats, snorkelling and pearls, listening enthralled to James' endless stories. We feel like the ski bums that we had been when we first met — when we'd lived for booze, sex, travel and skiing. Tim, Kev and James pile drunkenly into a taxi as I walk back to the hostel. They are bound for James' house to raid his wine cellar, smoke fancy Cuban cigars and live for a minute like millionaires instead of penniless backpackers. I grab Tim's arm as he climbs into the back of the taxi, 'Look after him,' I nod at Kev.

'I will,' he says equally seriously and then they are gone.

James' fancy, modern, multi-levelled waterfront house is huge, with a three-car garage full of fast, expensive cars and one friendly Rottweiler puppy. Kev and I have our own suite that we corrupt with all of our dirty, mildew-stinking belongings. I could get used to the lifestyle of the mega rich: lounging on the deck, paddling in the kayak or watching TV on the home theatre. Time passes quickly and for our final night in Darwin we have beer and pizza on James' waterfront patio. He leaves tomorrow on another business trip and so it is time for us to move on.

We head east from Darwin on the Arnhem highway towards the beautiful World Heritage listed Kakadu National Park, bursting with wildlife, wetlands, birds and a huge collection of Aboriginal rock art. Large yellow billboards advertising 'jumping crocodile cruises' appear at regular intervals, sparking excited discussions between Tim and Kev, and about an hour out of Darwin we reach the Adelaide River where the jumping croc billboards urge me to turn.

The entire premise of a jumping croc tour is to attract crocodiles to a dangerously over-crowded boat on the crocodile-infested Adelaide River, and teach them to jump out of the water at chunks of meat hanging from the boat; not unlike the way the guy next to me hangs over the edge with his camera. The crocodiles burst from the muddy water, thrusting their muscular bodies upwards so that most of their body is visible, before falling back into the water with the meat clasped in their jaws. The tourists (us included) charge like an attacking army from side to side when a croc appears, causing the boat to lurch alarmingly and my heart to flutter, but fortunately it remains resolutely upright.

James had suggested we go out in his 'tinnie' to see the crocs on the Adelaide River and I'm grateful we hadn't done that. I refused after a visit to the Darwin museum where I met 'Sweetheart', a five-

and-a-half metre saltwater crocodile that became famous in the late seventies because he couldn't tolerate the sound of outboard motors and attacked more than fifteen aluminium tinnies on the Finnis River south of Darwin. No one was killed but many people were terribly frightened during Sweetheart's five-year rampage. Eventually rangers captured him, intending to take him to a local croc farm but accidentally drowned him when a rope holding his mouth closed snagged underwater. Sweetheart was estimated to be about sixty years old when he died — an impressive feat for an aggressively territorial crocodile with no apparent fear of humans during a time crocodiles were hunted almost to extinction. Since 1971, crocodiles in Australia's Northern Territory have been protected, which has allowed a new generation of crocs to grow to significant sizes and even learn to jump for their meat!

Passing through Jabiru, the only Australian town established in a national park, we continue to Nourlangie Rock. While the ochre rock art at Anbangbang Gallery of Nourlangie Rock was painted in the sixties by an Aboriginal artist named Barramundi Charley, rock shelters at Nourlangie Rock date back 20,000 years. Kev wheels a 1.5 kilometre trail as Tim and I scramble over the rocks on adjoining trails.

'Closed' signs hang on all the campgrounds; with boat access to Jim Jim Falls and Twin Falls unavailable, the entire park seems to have wound down for the wet season. As such, we are forced to stay in a huge resort-type-place at Cooinda, with solid, clay-coloured cabins enveloped by greenery and undergoing renovations. Dinner is served in a portable room (with three steps up to it) full of workmen tucking into a large, but bland, buffet and we join the line-up, somewhat resentful of our less than five-star treatment.

Nothing much is open in Kakadu during the wet season. Everywhere we go we see signs for amazing and interesting places and things that are all closed. Clearly it is not the best time to see Kakadu in all her glory, although it is nice not to have hordes of tourists everywhere. Minutes from the resort is the Yellow Waters

Billabong, a wetland area where melaleuca trees droop into swamps and crocodiles lie on the muddy shore, or peer like submarines from carpets of white and purple water flowers. From the bow of a tour boat, we watch long-legged egrets spread their snowy wings and eagles soaring thermals above. Kev smiles wanly, he wants to enjoy the wetland cruise, but struggling with a bladder infection, even the simplest actions exhaust him.

* * *

Huge bats inundate the trees surrounding the hostel in Katherine and the guy next door shoots off a gun periodically to scare them. They all take flight into the twilight sky, fluttering around for a few minutes, then resettling in the exact same tree they recently vacated. He fights a losing battle.

Unpacking our stuff from the car, something stinks more than the usual background smell of horridness. 'What stinks?' I ask, passing Tim and Kev laden with bedding and backpacks.

'I don't smell anything,' says Tim.

'Me neither,' adds Kev.

'Well I do,' I empty the contents of the car onto the ground, inspecting and tentatively sniffing, each item individually, and, upon opening the food box, the putrid stench makes me recoil in disgust: it smells so bad I can taste it. 'Arrriggghhh,' I spring backwards and indiscriminately fling blemished and unblemished items into the rubbish bin, realising it has been a while since we have camped so the food box has been sealed for some time. Cans have exploded due to the heat and oozed out in vile slurry. I'd just had a go at Tim, accusing him of causing the smell, and my face burns thinking of how I yelled that 'I was going to throw his fucking foul bucket in the rubbish'. Simply pouring the brown, lumpy liquid onto the grass makes me dry retch. Kev offers to hose it out while I wipe down the few salvageable items. Tim comes over once the box is clean and put away.

'Do you think my bucket could be saved then?' He asks mildly.

We are heading to Alice where Tim will leave and Kev and I will carry on alone. I crave time alone with Kev. I need to talk about my dreams, fears and how we both feel life will be for us in the future. And even if there is an 'us' anymore. I am looking forward to Tim leaving, and count the days to Alice: Tennant Creek, one day down; Wauchope, another day.

Almost there, almost there, almost there becomes my mantra as we get closer and closer to Alice Springs, the biggest town since Darwin. Surely once we talk about stuff we can be happy, right?

The road is hypnotic: nothing changes. I feel like I am driving around in circles. Have I seen that rock before? I am pretty sure I have seen that rock before. Occasionally the radio crackles into life, entering a discussion about drenching sheep or religious people ranting about the end of the world, but mostly we drive in silence, sick of the sound of each other's voices. We stop for petrol in Wycliffe Wells, a blip on the Stuart Highway and, apparently, the UFO capital of Australia, with a weird alien museum, murals and lurid green figurines lurking around the petrol bowsers — then onwards we go.

Incredibly, farms exist out here stocked with scrawny, starving sheep capable of drinking saline bore water and gaunt, pointy cows, all angularity and skin, no muscle. But it is the feral animals that thrive; tough, hardy goats high in trees nibbling leaves and plentiful rabbits darting across the road. The only break in the monotony of the red, parched landscape comes with the appearance of several large, bloated bovine corpses — at least ten red, white and black bodies littered by the side of road — and we speculate by what means these poor creatures met their ends.

'It was totally the aliens from Wycliffe Wells doing fucked up experiments,' surmises Tim, and we all muse broodingly as we speed by with only the stench of death to remind us of their presence.

28

Alice Springs, the second biggest town in the Northern Territory, originated as a telegraph station on the Darwin–Adelaide telegraph line and is rich in history, museums and cultural centres. It is also unconscionably hot and dusty, so everyone lurks in the shade.

Robyn, a friend of Monica's, lives in Alice. Tall and slim with light brown hair in a pixie haircut framing a face blessed with the bone structure of a Norse goddess, Robyn was led to the red centre of Australia by a bad breakup. It seems like almost everyone in Alice Springs is running away from something or someone; places as isolated as Central Australia or Northern Canada are full of people running away.

'I'm sorry my house is not very comfortable at the moment,' says Robyn, gesturing to empty rooms. On the verge of moving, her house is sparse and everything is packed neatly in piles of meticulously labelled boxes. Open and clean with knotted hardwood floors and shuttered windows, Robyn's house resounds with the melody of the Waifs, an Australian folk band. It is surprisingly cool inside, like a spa. Robyn keeps eighty-five percent cocoa chocolate in her fridge and all her spices in multi-shaped jars labelled in her elegant cursive, and has nine different types of tea crowding her shelves; I want to stay forever.

Kev and I sleep on our Therm-a-Rests in a spare bedroom. His spasms kept him awake most of the night. It is so hot, but he finally nods off, only to have me wake him with my fretting over his spasticity. His spasms scare me; they are uncontrollable and are getting worse. While Kev was in hospital I'd heard about a guy with spasms so severe he was forced to surgically severe his spinal cord. And that is what I fear. I like Kev being able to feel my touch — I don't want to lose that and neither does he.

Waving goodbye to Robyn in the morning, Tim, Kev and I drive further into the red centre towards Uluru, the largest monolith in the world, which at 348 metres, is taller than the Eiffel Tower. Uluru is composed of almost vertically inclined sedimentary rocks deposited in a river environment during the time Australia was part of the supercontinent Gondwana. The sediment was crumpled and folded like a carpet during a period of mountain building, then eroded over millions of years, leaving Uluru as part of one limb of a large U-shaped chunk of rock called a syncline, most of which is hidden underground. Uluru is simply, so to speak, the tip of the iceberg. But it looks like it was simply plonked in the middle of the desert like an enormous paperweight because there is nothing quite like it (with the exception of Kata Tjuta) for miles and miles.

At first sight, Uluru is a breathtaking, magical, exquisite place full of way too many tourists. Rigorously structured, there's a place for sunrise viewings, for sunset viewings and for midday viewings. Apparently, this is the quiet season; I can't imagine the crowds at peak season. Kev wheels beside me around the base of Uluru as Tim runs ahead and we pause to gaze at several large indentations eroded into the surface of the rock. The flies are merciless, as relentless as the furies, and the sun drills a hole into the back of my skull.

'Wouldn't it be amazing to ski those rollers?' I look at Kev who stares with something akin to love at the iron-oxide blighted, red valleys. Is he high? If any place is unlikely to see snow, surely it's the red centre of Australia. And yet, in the centre of one of the hottest and driest countries in the world — a country ridiculed for its snow — he still dreams of skiing.

The Anangu people, the Aboriginal traditional owners, request that people do not climb the rock as it is an intensely spiritual place, but it seems to be another of the check-mark boxes of life accomplishments for some people, and incredibly, a line of people crawl up the rock. Tim, Kev and I instead take a beautiful walk around the base. Watching the rock lit by the setting sun in the allotted place, I can't help thinking it would be even prettier one hundred metres down the road, without a crowd of people breathing down my neck.

Two days later, we set up camp just north of Uluru at a Kings Canyon campground and lying in the tent, I can hear bats — large bats, scary bats with warm bodies and sticky wings. Unlike Uluru, Kings Canyon does not have a designated sunset viewing platform, but people congregate nonetheless. It seems that people are gravitationally attracted to each other nearing the hour of sunset — like watching a sunset alone is somehow prohibited. Tim, Kev and I smoke a joint as the sunset approaches and head toward the crowd gathered at the 'sunset spot.' Kev lags behind, ploughing through the sand. A middle-aged man runs to him and starts pushing the chair through the deep sand despite Kev's assurance that he's fine. 'Let go,' Kev finally snaps when the man refuses to relinquish control of the chair.

Some people seem to think that anyone in a wheelchair always needs help, no matter what they are doing — that they would prefer to be pushed up hills and along paths instead of wheeling themselves. Imagine your reaction, as an able-bodied person, if a stranger approached you and, without a word, picked you up and carried you up a hill because you were walking a bit too slow for their liking. It is insulting and presumptuous — but it is part of life in a wheelchair that many people think you are incapable of simple tasks.

I set the alarm for 5.30am so we can pack up and be on the road before the oppressive heat has time to crush our spirit, enthusiasm and resolve. I pack loudly, slamming car doors and yelling to Kev, deliberately making enough noise to wake Tim — who emerges from his tent red-eyed, just in time to quickly pack his tent and get in the car. The rocks glow red in the morning sun, displaying amazing samples of ripple marks, cross bedding and beautiful stratified layers. There are few trees, all gnarled from lack of water, and the only other greenery comes from prickly spinifex bushes, which sprout from the rocks in clumps. The rocks themselves form large, bulbous shapes, giving the landscape an eerie moonscape appearance.

Fortunately, we are on the Canyon Rim trail slightly before most of the tourist buses disgorge their rowdy camera-wielding cargo, but nonetheless there are piles and piles of people everywhere, crawling on the rocks, yelling to each other, dropping and throwing stuff and generally being a nuisance: busload after busload of people, all wearing fly-nets just like Tim's. With every step, more flies rise to greet me, hovering around my face in great irritating clouds and coating my back, turning my white t-shirt a writhing black. Tim walks fast, he is competitive — he even ran the Inca Trail just to try and hike it faster than his friend. I'm also competitive and I'd rather risk a heart attack than ask him to slow down. We complete the six kilometre Kings Canyon hike in just over an hour.

As Tim and I march, Kev wheels along the bottom of the canyon, finishing his own hike in the recommended time of one hour. I still tend to hover over him and worry about him constantly because his injury is so new, but with time my excessive fussing is fading. At the start of our trip I would never have left him to go hiking while he went down a gravel path.

We drive back to Alice, a long and rambling route that takes us past the Henbury meteor impact crater near the McDonald Ranges and Tim heroically piggybacks Kev down to a dirty, brown swimming hole at Glen Helen Gorge that smells strongly of cow shit. Dodging carefully through the cowpat piles littering the shoreline into the dark reedy waters, I swim out rapidly, beyond the reeds, and float contentedly on my back. Kev ploughs through the cowpats on his bottom, leaving a wide, erratic trail. Once we are away from the shoreline, the water is clear and cool and we wash away the sweat of the morning's exertions, all becoming sunburnt.

Kev climbs onto Tim's back in the pond and, emerging from the water, the flies fall upon our wet bodies with delirious joy. Tim plonks Kev down on a rock while he wipes his face and I offer to piggyback Kev the rest of the way. As soon as Kev climbs on, I feel something crack and shift deep within my lower back, accompanied by a searing surge of pure agony. Staggering forward, I collapse to the ground, Kev falling unceremoniously on top of me, crushing my face into the warm sand and narrowly missing a large cow shit. Breathing shallowly, I kneel for a moment to assess the damage. When I can stand without too much pain, we slowly walk back to the car, Tim carrying Kev. I'm able to walk without the lightning bolt of pain; it has faded to a dull, niggling ache that threatens *I will be back, be careful what you do, because I will be back.*

Robyn has moved out of her house and it sits sad, empty and alone, a shell of its former self. We knew that she was moving and staying with friends but none of us organised alternative accommodation, assuming everything would be good and something would turn up. With all the hostels booked, we finally find a room in a motel. As I unlock the door, I notice it has been forced on more than one occasion and I'm immediately assailed by a nasty, fart smell unmistakably recognisable as something recently dead. Walking into the room, I see a large, bloated mouse lying on the filthy carpet, clearly at least partly the source of the smell.

'Phoowar,' says Tim, disposing of the mouse and I think with a pang of the serene abode of Robyn, which now exists only in my mind.

I'm a little scared to go into the bathroom and Kev beats me to it, emerging: 'I knocked the towel rack off the wall and the sink doesn't drain, it must be clogged with something.' Peering into the bathroom, I imagine all the horrible things that could be lurking just around the U-bend, noting with disgust that the sink is rimmed with grunge and something black grows in the toilet, flecks floating ominously upward.

Braving the shower and washing my hair for the first time in weeks, I feel great. As I am drying my hair with the greyish threadbare towel, my fingers run seamlessly — my ring, does not grab tendrils of hair: it's missing. Dropping to the floor of the shower and pawing the horribly clogged and rusted drain yields nothing; no pile of matted hair just below the plug has caught my ring. I'm inconsolable. The rings represent our strength, our connection, our resilience and now that has gone, lost down the murky drain of a fleabag hotel in central Australia.

'I've lost my ring!' I cry to Kev.

'It doesn't matter,' he says. 'It doesn't mean we're doomed as a couple, it was simply a symbol and the root feeling is still there.'

'Can you try and get it back for me?' I ask plaintively and he pulls out the toolbox and starts to take the drain apart, a nasty, dirty job, without complaint. After removing the filter, he jams his thick fingers down the slimy, gross drain and feels around for a little silver ring.

'I'm sorry Em, but it's gone.' I start to cry again.

* * *

It's so malevolently hot. I want to surrender, lie down and die, then be baked into the earth, preserved through desiccation — become a desert mummy for future generations to laugh at my weird clothes and dyed hair, and wonder if it was a status thing instead of a prematurely greying thing. Tim, Kev and I had ambitious plans to go to the Alice Springs Desert Park, the Alice Springs Reptile Centre and the Royal Flying Doctor Service Museum, but weary from heat we nip into a cheesy pub for lunch and there we stay. Tim befriends an elderly couple from the UK on holiday and starts to teach them origami with the napkins, making an elegant swan, a boat and an aeroplane — although the aeroplane is not strictly origami. We laugh and talk over many beers and someone brings out a baby joey, which we all nurse.

Later, I climb into the nasty, sagging bed and Kev throws my ring at me, landing with a little thump on my stomach. 'Where did you find it?'

'It was lying on the lower bunk, so I'm sure glad that I put my fingers down that nasty drain last night,' he replies. Leaping up, I sit on his lap and kiss him.

'Thank you, thank you, thank you.' He laughs as I slide the ring back onto my finger.

Tim talks of the WOMAD Festival in Adelaide he plans to catch while we head north to Tennant Creek and across to Townsville on the east coast. Now Tim is actually going, I'm afraid. I'm anxious about being alone with Kev — anxious it will be just the two of us, with no Tim to help lift Kev upstairs or piggyback him across rocks. Kev and I will be the Two Musketeers: sad, broken and incomplete. I don't want people feeling sorry for us.

As Tim hoists his pack out of the back of the car I hug him goodbye, sad to see him go. He says, 'Look after yourself, too.' Kev and I wave as Tim disappears into the bus station and we head north as he heads south.

PART V

ALONE

29

Being alone is intimidating and frightening. We feel vulnerable. Everything is just a little more daunting without the buffer of Mum or Tim who had given us a safety net that won't always be there. They were diversions, a distraction from issues we don't want to — and are not yet ready — to face. But this is how life is going to be for us from now on. Can Kev and I manage, just the two of us?

The spasms are becoming unbearable. Kev's legs continually shake, violently kicking themselves off his footplate as he wheels, forcing him to increase the amount of neuro-suppessors he takes to try and keep them under control. With the increase in neuro-suppressors, all movement becomes somewhat muted, including the subtle movement of his big toe and hence, any recovery he might be experiencing. He feels an absurd amount of pride in being able to move his toe, the movement showing a tangible connection between his mind and his feet. It's so much more than just a brief flicker of movement in his toe or a cheap party trick; to Kev it represents hope. Hope that perhaps one day, maybe a year from now or maybe twenty years, he may walk again. The toe is the beginning, a nucleus around which other muscular recovery could propagate. Even though nothing has changed since he first discovered the movement, it's nonetheless encouraging. And suddenly he is forced to give up that movement, to give up that hope. How can he tell if he is getting better if he is so drugged that he can't feel it? Increasing the medication upsets him more than he will say. He is becoming obsessed with moving his toe; often I catch him priming it, back and forth and then desperately trying to move it, concentrating intensely like Uma Thurman in *Kill Bill*, as if it could be that easy. He feels as if he is going backwards in his recovery, that things are getting worse when they should be getting better.

The drugs not only affect his body but also his mind. As much as they calm and numb his legs, they also numb his mind, wrapping his brain in a foggy net of cottonwool. It has always been difficult for Kev to get up in the morning but with the increased neuro-suppressors coursing through his veins, it is becoming arduous. He's reluctant to move out of bed because he knows as soon as he moves the spasms will kick-in and fight him, throwing his body this way and that. He requires copious quantities of strong, sweet coffee before he is able to tackle the morning routine of getting dressed, trying to get into his chair, going to the bathroom and finally getting in the car. Coffee activates him, stirring him briefly out of his drug-induced stupor, like a tired old turtle sticking his head out for a tasty morsel and then retreating back into the comfort and familiarity of his shell. So does Kev's mind retreat back into a comfortable numbness as the drugs and the caffeine struggle and wrestle for cognitive control. I know the drugs affect him and make it difficult for him to get anything done, but it's still frustrating. I want him to get up and try and help me, instead of having me literally drag him from his bed

I drive north up Stuart Highway to Tennant Creek, where Kev and I will turn east to Mount Isa and across to the coast to Townsville. At Tennant Creek, we book into a warm, homey hostel with a communal kitchen, circa 1960, and I almost expect to see Carol Brady in there cooking up a tasty stew. There is a small TV room crammed with noisy British teenagers and a rough, bearded Irishman.

Our room contains a double bed, with a bright doona straight from the eighties, pushed snugly up against the single window, a stand-alone fan and a hard, uncomfortable, straight-backed chair. I climb heavily onto the bed and put the Tempur on the side nearest the window, lying down on the side furthest away from the window.

'Can I lie down too?' Kev asks, wheeling over. There is not enough room between the end of the bed and the wall for Kev to wheel in and climb on so I reluctantly move, my lower back twinging as I shift onto the Tempur. Kev climbs in on 'my' side, away from the window, and effectively blocks my access to the rest of the room. I can't walk along the base of the bed because the bed and the room are almost the exact same width. I am trapped. I hate sleeping on the far side of the bed because I inevitably have to get up to go to the toilet several times during the night and climbing over Kev is awkward, forcing him to move, wince, groan or inhale sharply in pain.

'It's not fair, you always get the good side of the bed and I get the crap side. You are the 'special' one now,' I snap, leaping from the bed. In my mind, I see that if I move the bed into the middle of the room then we would both have access to a walkway beside our bed, and hence both be happy.

But the room is small and tight and the bed is reluctant to move. It scrapes along the far wall as I yank angrily and finally, it ceases to move all together. Jammed across the room, the bed now impedes access to the bathroom, and then Kev cracks. He pushes his mattress over to the crap side and shifts across, cramming the Foley night drainage bag down the crack formed between the window and the bed, then snatches a pillow. We lie down, both feeling we have surrendered. And between us the Tempur looms like the Great Wall of China.

I stare at the smooth, white ceiling, trying to regulate my breathing, trying to meditate, trying to be goddamn fucking calm and Kev's legs immediately begin kicking. I lie fuming, anticipating every new kick and twitch, and finally jack-knife up, grab both pillows and throw them onto the ground. I re-orientate the standing fan so that it points directly at the space on the floor between the bed and the bathroom door, and lie down with my feet stretching out underneath the bed.

Kev sits up in bed and looks at me lying uncomfortably on the hard, dirty carpet. Upset, he says, 'Em, let me sleep on the floor.'

'You will get a pressure sore,' I snort dismissively.

'Let me be a man,' he yells furiously, in anger, guilt and pure frustration, red spots appearing under his eyes and across his cheeks. I climb back into bed beside him. I didn't realise how much it would hurt him to see me lying on the ground and be unable to do anything about it. To know that I was lying there because his spasms were uncontrollable and that his body was betraying him, yet again.

Kev smiles a sad little smile and gently rubs his rough palm along my bare legs, 'Em, you have always been the special one; no matter what happens to me, you will always be the special one, and as much as I can, I will make sure you get the best of everything. Remember south-east Asia when you had the fan under your mosquito net and I was just hot; or how I had the lumpy bed in New Zealand so your back didn't hurt as much; and whenever any food fell on the floor that was immediately my food? I am glad this happened to me and not to you.'

I look up at him with his curly hair and sad eyes and my heart softens, my frustration fades, and I remember that I love him. I snuggle up underneath his arm and put my head on his broad, hairy chest, and he wraps both arms around me and eventually, we sleep.

30

MARCH 2005

I drive till my eyes hurt from staring at the vanishing point of the road and then Kev takes the wheel. We seem to be driving forever, not seeing anything or anyone. The landscape is so flat I almost see the arc of the Earth, and mirages dance in every direction. A huge sky stretches forever and ever — the particular hue of deep blue only seen above red sand dunes or sparkling carpets of flawless snow. Although Montana has a claim on the term 'Big Sky Country', Montana has nothing on outback Queensland; truly nowhere else has skies like these. The road degrades as soon as we cross the NT–QLD border, changing from a nicely paved, wide, open road to a rough potholed strip of bitumen, with a narrow, dodgy shoulder. Clearly Queenslanders have better things to spend their money on than road maintenance. On the upside, petrol becomes significantly cheaper due to extensive subsidies demanded by the population of the sunshine state. Road trains pound the road: three or four trailers, sometimes more, roar towards us, forcing us to skid from the bitumen onto the gravel shoulder.

Almost 700 kilometres later, Mount Isa comes into view and, opening the guidebook, I direct Kev to a hostel. Several steps lead up to the door and my back, worsened by the drive, thuds rhythmically when I see them. Kev's in too much pain to crawl up the stairs himself, so we return to the car to find somewhere else to stay. Both hot, stiff and exhausted, we start fighting — all pleasantries degraded by fatigue. All I want is a bed: nothing fancy, just a bed … and maybe a kettle and a bathroom. We blame each other: 'You should have booked.'

'Well you should have organised something, too,' and finally, in desperation, we go back to the first hostel with the five steps up into reception. The bearded Irish guy from Tennant Creek checks his email on the computer when I walk in and we nod in recognition. I explain to the receptionist that I want a double room on the first floor, and then ask Beardo if he can give me a hand. He says, 'Yeah, yeah give us about fifteen minutes,' and I stand behind him, shocked and upset. He clearly thinks I want help unloading the car, not help carrying my boyfriend up the stairs as Kev waits forlornly at the bottom. As I stand waiting, Beardo gets the message and leaps up, apologising, and together we lift Kev. At this point, Kev and I both realise how vulnerable we are without Tim or Mum and how much we need to rely on other people as he recovers. The tactless receptionist launches into a story about the last disabled person who stayed at the hostel: an American geologist.

'She was amazing,' the receptionist continues blindly. 'She could be left by herself looking at rocks out in the bush. How incredible is that?' She looks at me as if the woman was a dementia patient who had no business being alone in the outback looking at rocks, not a highly-trained professional. Clearly, in her view, the woman should have been parked securely up against a large picture window in the care home she so sorely needed to be living in. 'She dragged the wheelchair up behind her as she crawled up the stairs: amazing, just amazing,' she says, shaking her head as if still in wonder. Kev and I look down. We both feel weak and hopeless and want her to shut the hell up. I want to say to the receptionist, 'He was only just injured. He is still healing, still learning. We both are.' We feel like failures because Kev is not yet as independent as he would like to be and he needs me — a lot. Neither of us wants to admit that. We are scared it will last forever and he'll come to depend upon me.

I grab the key from the infernal woman, choking off the next instalment of the amazing crippled Yankee geologist with a terse, 'Yeah that's really interesting.' I walk down to our room, unlock the door and flop gratefully down on the bed, exhausted. Kev wheels over to bathroom, returning quickly.

'You are going to hate me.'

'Why?' I sigh, and he explains he can't fit through the door into the bathroom. For one second I think desperately *what can I do with him? Where can I leave him? I need someone to come and take him away from me* and in that instant, I almost hate him. Slowly, I get up, check out and Kev and I are back sitting stonily in Yota. My back is a molten pool of agony and every movement enlivens the pain. Kev is starting to get sick again, sweating and panting with a bladder infection. It is all too much. My entire body aches with weariness felt only after a long day of hard physical work and I just want to sleep in a real bed with a real mattress and a real pillow. But finally, we decide we will have to camp.

Kev and I start to set up the tent at a crowded caravan park with a couple of vacant tent lots. He knows I'm upset and feels guilty. 'I'm so sorry Em … I'm so sorry,' he says as he watches me struggle with the tent and the unpacking.

'It's not your fault Isa sucks.' Desperate to help, he starts wheeling around the sandy soil to put in tent pegs, and in his haste, tips over backwards. Frustrated and angry, he lies there, like a tortoise stuck on its back. I pass him the last cold beer from the fridge which cheers him, and he drags himself into a sitting position on the sand, and watches me pile the last of our stuff into the tent.

I'm awake, hot and stiff, at 5am after a night of constant dog barking. Even Kev wakes up early. We are trying to make it to Townsville as fast as possible because he's running out of condom catheters and other medical supplies. We leave Mount Isa without a backwards glance and start towards Townsville. It is our longest day yet: 912 kilometres. Kev does most of the driving — he can drive for hours and hours and it doesn't seem to be an onerous chore for him. He sits in the driver's seat for so long I worry about pressure sores. I try to sleep while he is driving because the hand controls are adequate at best; I don't really trust them not to fall off (they can be removed with the loosening of a single clamp). It is always in my mind that if that clamp fails and we are going at 110 …

To make matters worse, Kev experiences spasms in his abdominal muscles, which throw him backwards, forwards or from side to side depending on the muscle group activated and, as such, we can be driving along, chatting pleasantly, and suddenly he will be gripped by a full-body spasm, his body pitched backwards into the seat. He doesn't say anything but simply grimaces and groans as he's flung around like a chew toy by muscles that have become strong due to the constant spasms. Worry gnaws at me like a rat; my fingernails torn and bitten savagely to the point of sensitivity to touch. The spasms do not respect the fact we are passing a speeding road train, a time when Kev needs to be in control of the car. When he actively tries to suppress the spasms, they manifest themselves in a particularly violent way, kicking and flexing like a raging child. It reminds me of a person with Tourette syndrome trying to suppress their tics while sitting in church and causing a resounding outburst of 'fuck, cocksucker, whore'.

On the straight stretches, he tries to relieve pressure on his tailbone through weight shifts; balancing one arm on the door and the other on the steering wheel, he sort of topples forward sometimes so that his head touches the wheel. Then he flops back and wrenches the car back onto the road. I have visions of him flopping forward and losing control during a weight shift, or a particularly violent spasm resulting in little Yota slamming headlong into a tree or an oncoming vehicle, but I am so tired that I am just as likely to crash, too. So we draw our cards and take our chances. Eventually, after thinking we surely must have driven across the entire centre of Australia, we reach the twinkling lights of Townsville and turn into the hostel: hot, hungry, exhausted and covered in a thick layer of red dirt. I feel dirty, dishevelled and stiff, and, stepping out of the car, I walk unsteadily. Unpacking the car, I can smell the ocean, and feel a slight breeze. I have made it to the east coast and it feels like coming home.

31

With everything located on the ground floor, the open-plan Townsville hostel works well for Kev and he cooks spaghetti bolognaise while I unpack. I'm pleased to see the room has twin beds so I won't be disturbed by Kev's spasms. I fall asleep almost immediately and sleep till late the next morning when the sun is high and fierce. Hauling water jugs out of the truck to clean the damp carpet underneath, I catch a glimpse of a couple of Scandinavian girls staring in awe at our extensive water supply and our red desert dust-coated truck, strange and incongruous on the lush, green east coast. Pouring the water onto the grass, it glugs and burps out horrible algae-tainted fluid and I'm pleased I hadn't needed to drink it.

We are passing through Townsville on our way to Cairns, using it as a pit stop — somewhere to clean ourselves and the car and pick up more medical supplies at the GPO. It's fortunate they have arrived because Kev is using the last of the deteriorated ones, which were ruined way back in Broome, and have spent the last few weeks stewing in the humid medical box, the last remnants of their adhesive dissolved. By the time I've packed the new medical supplies securely in the medical box, it's early afternoon and any motivation to play tourist has melted away with the rivulet of sweat trickling down my back.

As a result, the only sites of Townsville Kev and I experience are the insides of air-conditioned pubs. I am concerned about our drinking, though. We use our problems as an excuse and drinking as a distraction; I drink so I can forget what's going on in my life. I want to feel numb because feeling numb is preferable to feeling sad, anxious and out of control. When I drink, I feel happy. I feel free. I feel like I did before; as if I can do anything. The disability doesn't matter, all that matters is that Kev has beautiful blue eyes, and looking into them makes me happy. When I'm drunk, I can't see people looking or staring at us; all I can see is Kev, the man I love. I don't see Kev, disabled, sick, and fucked-up. I see with a clarity that is denied to me when I am sober. I see only what I need to see, what I want to see; the doubts, the anxiety, the fears, the anger, fall away like water. That's why we need to rein in our drinking. Rationally, I know that it is an empty, temporary solution, which makes me feel worse — but I am not a rational person, I'm emotional. I drink to escape.

* * *

The drive from Townsville to Cairns is a stunning kaleidoscope of colour, texture and people: so green and lush. The abundance of colour overstimulates my senses — I am so used to the red, desolate landscape of the desert, it's difficult to focus on all the sites, smells and sounds bombarding me. All I've seen for weeks and weeks are different shades of brown and red with smatterings of green grass and leaves but here, on the verdant east coast, there are flowers, trees, vines and people — Hawaiian-shirt-wearing people. Kev and I pass through mile after mile of tall, neat-as-pins cane fields and banana plantations with black bags wrapped around the bananas to protect them from pests.

Gecko's Backpackers in Cairns has a disabled toilet at the end of the hall and double rooms with twin beds. I don't even need to carry the toilet bucket to the bathroom because Kev can balance it on his lap — a little glimpse of normal life. He rises before me this morning, amazing considering the number of neuro-suppressors he's taking, and tickles my feet with breakfast in hand.

'Morning,' he says, handing me porridge in bed. I can't believe it. He is never up first and in that moment, I feel pampered. And I like it.

The fabled Great Barrier Reef lies just off Cairns and Kev and I are keen to experience it through scuba diving.

'We'd like to enrol in the three day, live-aboard, PADI (Professional Association of Diving Instructors) certification course,' I tell the young guy at a dive shop.

'Is it going to be a problem that I'm in a wheelchair?' Asks Kev.

'Nah, shouldn't be a problem,' says the guy. 'Ring this number to book your spots,' he says, handing me a pamphlet with the number of their head office.

'Aah,' says the guy at head office upon hearing Kev's a paraplegic 'our boat isn't wheelchair accessible you know.'

'Yeah, I know, but he is pretty strong and he's used to wheelchair unfriendly places.'

'Yes, but there are stairs.'

'So, he'll crawl.'

'It's very wheelchair unfriendly. His carer will have to do a lot to make it work for him.'

Carer? This guy is trying to talk me out of it — douche bag! On the west coast everyone was more than happy to help out and keen Kev was interested in going on their tour.

'It'll be fine,' I say 'I will ring you back when we have our medical checks done.'

Somewhat miffed, Kev and I arrive at a walk-in clinic to get a medical check up for our PADI certification. Apparently, I am medically fine but sadly, Kev's not fit to dive.

'I'm not comfortable with you scuba diving as long as you are taking baclofen,' the doctor says, referring to Kev's anti-spasticity neuro-suppressor. 'You also have diminished lung capacity due to your injury, which also concerns me.'

'Fine,' he says, 'I will find someone else.'

'No doctor will pass you while you are taking baclofen,' she says.

Historically, baclofen was developed as a drug to treat epileptics, which is why it is on the scuba diving 'banned' list of drugs. A seizure at sixty feet underwater is a scary thought and consequently, diving is not a good idea for epileptics. It isn't as if it's an option for Kev to stop taking baclofen either; the spasms are worsening even as he increases his dosage to compensate. There is no way he can stop taking it, no matter how much he wants to go scuba diving.

The sheet listing the side effects of baclofen says that high doses of the drug are known to cause drowsiness, which can interfere with daily function. I watch Kev as he listens to the doctor. His head slowly, almost imperceptibly droops lower and lower, whereby the strain on his neck kicks in, alerting him that his head is almost on his knees, and he jerks it up again, eyes wide and shocked. Once the shock passes, his blinking becomes slow and measured, and he's clearly struggling to stay awake let alone focus. He looks positively narcoleptic, which isn't on the bloody side effect list.

But Kev and I don't care about explanations or justifications, however reasonable and logical. We care about proving to ourselves that we can do anything and everything. Undaunted, Kev makes an appointment to see another doctor, an elderly old-school guy, who claims it is a requirement that Kev stand up before he will pass him: something even less likely to happen than Kev suddenly stopping popping baclofen like candy. So we drop out of the three day, live-aboard PADI course to the delight of the instructor. It just isn't going to happen; Kev can't get a clean bill of health and I shouldn't have because my back is a train wreck. I worry that dropping out of the dive course is a bit of a cop-out, and scared of getting into the mindset of, 'Oh we can't do that because it will be hard'.

Later, I make a curry and we eat mangoes in the spacious communal kitchen. Kev is really helpful here, making me a cup of tea, getting me snacks and cooking sausages — I love it. It's a surprise how normal life feels when Kev and I are in a situation where things are easy to him and the disability seems less of a big deal.

The evening comes warm and clear and Kev and I reach the Green Ant Cantina, a cute little pub just down the road. As the night wears on, we squeeze through the crowd to the pool table and watch as a long-haired hippy wearing blue stripy pants and a Ben Harper t-shirt is soundly beaten by his friend. We challenge them to the next game. Even though Kev has to balance without any core muscles while holding a pool cue to take a shot, and I'm generally just crap at pool, incredibly we win. It is the first time we have won at pool playing together post-injury and are ridiculously pleased. Although, to be fair, our opponents are pretty baked and I think even the stationary balls were moving to them. Kev asks Stripy Pants for pot and he yells, jumping around and pointing at Kev, 'I knew it man, the second I saw you, I knew you would ask me for pot!'

Kev empties his leg bag into a flowerpot until he realises he can get into the bar's toilet. Being able to get into the toilets is an unexpected pleasure, as generally they are up or down stairs or through narrow corridors. Tropical plants are brushed aside to enter the beer garden and my fingers stroke the grout between tiles on the stunning sunflower-mosaic table at which Kev and I sit.

Now that it's just the two of us, Kev speaks about when he was hurt, for the first time in ages. 'When I first came to after I fell, I knew immediately I had a spinal injury: my belly felt strange and tingly and I couldn't move my legs. My high school biology teacher had said you could make a spinal injury so much worse if you moved. So I was trying to be really, really still.' His eyes drop to the table where his beer has left a ring of condensation across one yellow-tiled petal, and he smudges at it with his pointer finger. 'But then I was lying there for longer and longer, listening for animals crashing through the brush and I had a lot of time to think. I knew I was badly injured and that my life might end there, at twenty-four. I realised I didn't have control over much, which made me feel calm, and I made a conscious decision not to panic.'

'I was glad I'd spent so much time skiing and travelling, enjoying my life, and I didn't have any regrets. Knowing that something like this can happen anytime, I want to live the rest of my life in such a way that I don't have any regrets.'

Nodding, I take a sip of my beer.

'Yeah, there is a lot of stuff I can't do now — and of course I wish this had never happened — but there is a hell of a lot that I can do. I'm going to do my best to not get upset about stuff I can't do until I have run through all the things that I can.'

He shrugs, 'I dunno, I'll just try and shift my focus away from limitations and onto possibilities.' His sanguinity is as integral to him as his personality, yet something has recently shifted and he seems more at peace than I have seen him since the accident. Joy blossoms in my stomach and I barely recognise it.

The stereo switches to the Beatles' 'Free as a bird' and someone inside turns up the volume. Most of the other people in the beer garden also know the lyrics and everyone sings along in friendly camaraderie. It's reminiscent of the end of season bash at Big White Ski Resort the year Kev and I met; 'Hey Jude' by the Beatles was the final song played at Snowshoe Sam's bar and Kev, the rest of my friends and I linked shoulders and rocked drunkenly, roaring the words at the top of our lungs.

I often think about how bad it was when Kev was first hospitalised and the only place I had to cry was in the shower. I remember the feelings of helplessness and total despair; the problems with Kev's lungs requiring him to use the sucky-hose and how it would get clogged, and he would wake up and call my name frantically when he was unable to find his 'pain button'; how sleeping next to him was so hard because he was afraid and didn't want to be alone. I have to keep reminding myself that it has only been seven and a half months since those nights, that it is a pretty drastic change and things will continue to improve. It was the worst time of my life and we speak of what we have come through together, still a couple, still limping along. It is so nice without Tim; Kev and I are able to talk. Had Tim been here I have no doubt we would have been playing some crazy game with a bunch of people, chatting, laughing and having fun but we would not be accepting, healing and moving on.

We stagger back to the hostel, completely wasted, and fall into bed, snoring the emphatic snores of the very drunk.

32

On our way to the Atherton Tablelands, we stop for lunch in a cool little restaurant in a quaint little town inland of Cairns. The proprietor is an old hippy woman — the type who almost sits down with you to chat when she brings your food — and we order the last two servings of veggie lasagne but one is mangled in the delivery, which she pointedly gives to Kev. I am absurdly pleased she gives him the crap lasagne, treating him like a man, not a disabled man.

Countless walking trails snake through the rainforest and we turn back when we inevitably encounter a barrier. One path through the trees overlooks a series of exquisite rock pools where a blond couple swim — they are beautiful: she is tall, slim and tanned, wearing a turquoise bikini, and he is young, athletic and handsome, wearing a pair of red board shorts. Laughing and smiling, they climb out of the water and sit on the rocks as she squeezes water from her long, straight hair, occasionally flashing him a luminous smile and, like me, he can't take his eyes from her. He rubs her neck and shoulders as she leans back into his strong, muscular body down which water rolls like oil. I watch them both longingly, stabbed by an overwhelming feeling of pure, unadulterated envy. They are so healthy — they have everything in the world. I'm so jealous I can hardly breathe.

Kev yells from behind me, 'Hey Baby, do you think I would get down there?' He hasn't seen the couple and wonders what's taking me so long as I lurk like a voyeur in the trees above the pool. They turn at the sound of his voice and, seeing me, smile. A wave of sadness and loss crushes me. I want to go down to them, swim with them — hell, I want to *be* them. Instead, I turn and walk back up the path to Kev, and he slowly struggles along the rough, bumpy trail back down to the car.

Both deflated and defeated, we focus on the fact that we can't get down to the pools instead of savouring the sights and smells of the lush green rainforest we're immersed in. Instead of hearing the bird calls as a magnificent soundtrack, we hear them as mocking, 'You can't get over here either, or here, or here'. I resent we can't go down to the pool together, that I can't swim with my boyfriend — that he can't massage my shoulders as I sit wearing a turquoise bikini on the rocks. But I'm not yet ready to leave him alone and do things by myself because it feels like a desertion. So I stay with him, even when I don't want to. Over time I know that will change, but just not yet.

Kev and I travel in heavy silence, both hoping the other will speak first. Kev says abruptly, 'Sometimes I think I am happy and sometimes I think it is all a fucking joke and I would not blame you if you left me … this is my journey Em, not yours. Why don't you leave me? I want you to: you can still have a good life, you deserve better than this.'

'I deserve to be with a man who loves me.'

'It's because I love you that I want you to leave me. I want you to be happy and I don't think you can be happy with me.'

'Like I am suddenly going to be happy with someone else, and just completely forget about you! That is not going to happen.'

Sometimes I wish I could leave him and forget him forever, erase my memories like Clementine in *Eternal Sunshine of the Spotless Mind*. Is the absence of pain worth the absence of love, of having been loved? Sometimes it is. Sometimes I wish I had never met Kev. In those dark times, I see myself with someone else, the idyllic imaginary partner. If I could forget, I could just get on with my life: live a normal life. However, I cannot do it without some amnesia-inducing drug to erase him completely, otherwise he will always be there and I'll always wonder what my life would have been like had the accident never happened and we'd stayed together. He is wrong when he says it is his journey, not mine. It is my journey too.

'I am so fucking sick of looking on the bright side. This is not good, nothing about this is good, it's fucked — our lives are fucked!'

'I know,' Kev says quietly, 'but I have to look on the bright side and appreciate all the good things that I can do because if I don't, and I give into the dark thoughts, I'll wheel myself off a fucking bridge.'

Not only does he have his disability to adjust to but also a multitude of associated woes: the constant neuropathic pain, the debilitating spasms and the never-ending bladder infections. He walks a tightrope and if he stumbles, he will be lost forever.

I fall to pieces. My heart breaks when I thought it could break no more. 'Please don't,' I blurt out, sobbing. 'I love you.'

'I am not going to off myself just yet,' he says, 'I was just trying to explain why I can't let myself fall into a well of self-pity. I have lost so much, more than most people realise, but Em, if I lose the ability to make you smile, then I will have lost everything.'

Somehow, we come to an understanding that we cannot expect to be happy right now because something awful has happened to us. If we ever want to be happy we need to appreciate each other here and now, instead of hoping, dreaming and remembering what we used to do. It doesn't matter what Kev could do before, what matters is what he can do now.

It would actually be easier if I met him as a paraplegic man instead of knowing him before his accident: I hold the memory of Kev walking locked away like a captive in a secret place, now reduced to snatches and flashes — Kev running down the stairs of our house in Edmonton, silhouetted on a ridge in New Zealand, and walking beside me hand-in-hand along the footpath in Breckenridge. Bit by bit, slowly but inevitably, I am losing those memories as they fade and are warped by time. It's becoming hard to bring to mind Kev running, almost as if it had never happened. It is a loss that makes me feel the greater loss of his ability more keenly, as my previous life becomes intangible, floating away as a wisp of smoke.

I guess I think if only I had ten tall, blond, shirtless men following me around attending to my every whim, that I would be happy. But instead of worrying about the fragility of my boyfriend, I would fret over my weight or the appearance of an errant black hair on my bikini line. I adjust to my circumstances: if I don't have any real reasons to worry, then I'll invent some, because that's what I do. I have no doubt that there are many people in the world who would consider my own problems trivial, after all I have a man who adores me, and family who love and support me. In my happier moments, I can see that I am doing okay. It is just that my happier moments are few and far between.

I hate that I am jealous of other couples and that if I went down to the pool it would be alone. I don't want Kev to be left out. I struggle to accept there are things I can do that he no longer can, but that doesn't mean I shouldn't do them. Kev encourages me to go and do the things we used to do together, to walk the path less trodden, or un-wheelable. He never says, 'it's not fair, I can't do that'. He's not bitter or jealous of my ability, which would make me feel guilty and resentful and would ultimately break us up. He feels no anger over his injury and copes with admirable resilience, which makes it easy to love him.

33

Daintree is a quaint little town on the forbidding edge of the mighty Daintree Wilderness area: the sort of town you find yourself saying, 'this is nice, I could live here.' The ecologically diverse Daintree Rainforest is Australia's largest area of unbroken rainforest spanning about point-one percent of Australia, but containing about thirty percent of our frog, marsupial and reptile species, sixty-five percent of butterfly and bat species and twenty percent of Australian bird species.

We walk through the rainforest, stopping when we reach stairs. My face darkens and Kev takes my hand, 'Let's just appreciate that we're in a beautiful rainforest together listening to echoing birdcalls.' Under the shade of the rainforest canopy far above, I lean on Kev's wheelchair, rest my chin on the top of his head, as he wraps his arms around my waist, and we are quiet.

Driving over a small ford, as we delve deeper into the Daintree, I'm thrilled as a crocodile skids into the water by the side of the road and Kev plasters himself to the window after we pass a 'slow down: cassowaries' sign. Pulling into a campground at Cape Tribulation, I wander into the reception, looking for a campsite.

'Are you kidding?' The girl behind the desk asks.

'No … why?' I reply suspiciously.

'Haven't you heard about the cyclone? It's coinciding with a king tide; all the campsites are closed due to flooding.' Grudgingly, I book a double room and we check out the deserted beach, wild in the early throes of a category five cyclone. Coconut trees crowd the sand and the mangrove flats, with their twisted pneumatic roots, are alive with crabs and insects. The ancient forest positively thrums with bugs, spiders and other creepy-crawlies and, sitting by its edge, I feel it reaching out to me, trying to envelop me in its green, leafy arms. Everywhere I look or sit something is going about its daily business, usually a grotesquely huge version of the Victorian bugs, such as a giant cockroach or a monstrous huntsman. It is the type of place where you need to keep your tent zipped up tightly or, better still, spray insect repellent around the legs of your bed if you are lucky enough to be sleeping inside. Kev and I sit on the beach for a while and feel at peace: nothing needs to be said. It is rejuvenating looking at the grey, foamy waters churning and surging furiously and the pewter sky, angry and threatening overhead. The violence of nature soothes me, making me feel better about my own anger.

Back at the hostel, everyone is freaking out, rushing about in a seemingly disorganised and haphazard manner. A small, dark-haired Israeli girl runs up to me as I unlock our room and asks accusingly, 'So when are you leaving?'

'What do you mean? I only just got here.'

'Haven't you heard about the cyclone?' She says as if explaining to a toddler and launches into how dangerous it is, how much flooding there will be, and how her tremendously unreasonable tour company has refused to come and pick her up until tomorrow. By then, she continues, the Cape could potentially be cut off because the storm is predicted to hit during the early hours of the morning.

'Okay,' I say. 'This changes things somewhat. I need to consider this.'

'Do you have any room in your car?' She asks.

'Yep, we have room for one more.' She frowns. Entering the adjacent shop, I pick up *The Cairns Post* and the headline screams: 'The big blow: Cape braces for Cyclone Ingrid's onslaught' in huge capital letters beside a grainy satellite image showing a cyclone heading directly for Cape Flattery (slightly north of where I am standing with paper in hand), and I sigh. How did Kev and I not hear about this before now? Do we have our heads so far in the sand that we don't even know about a category five cyclone heading for our very destination? It would have been nice if someone in Cairns had mentioned this before we left. We don't read the newspapers, we don't watch TV, and so we are essentially isolated from the outside world, lost in our own problems. We don't have time to consider such trivialities as cyclones. The grizzled old Queenslander who owns the shop is scared, worried about his shop flooding, and this in turn makes me scared.

'I think we should leave,' Kev and I both blurt out as we step outside and, with substantial relief, check out of the hostel. Six people gather in the communal area and watch me load the car. I hadn't noticed how eerily deserted the place was and I make a mental note to start paying more attention. The six appear divided into three groups of two: the Israeli girl and her British friend, two young men from Sydney and a Swedish couple, all on a booked tour of Australia. The bus was supposed to return for them in a few days after they had explored Cape Tribulation but they have been desperately ringing their guide to come and evacuate them before the cyclone hits. Everyone who could leave has already left.

I nod as the male half of the Swedish couple asks whether we're leaving and he follows with, 'Do you have any room in your car?' The Israeli woman shoots him a sharp, angry look.

'We have room for one.' Actually, with all of the medical equipment, wheelchair and wheelchair accessories, we barely have room for one. The room falls quiet, the atmosphere tense, as the six stranded backpackers slowly look at each other. It reminds me of the final graveyard scene in *The Good, the Bad and the Ugly* where the camera flicks rapidly between the three cowboys.

'I'm sorry, I wish we had more room …' The Israeli girl glares at me. I try to rearrange everything in the car but it's no use, there's just not enough room. I see their sad, scared faces watching me as I slowly pack Kev's chair into the back seat and start Yota. I know the Israeli girl is thinking, *there would be room for two if you left the goddamn wheelchair behind.* Driving away, I feel like a traitor.

We drive sombrely back to Cairns, mostly in silence, both thinking about the stranded backpackers.

'Would you leave me?' I ask finally.

'Are you kidding? I would never leave you, Baby. I would endure 10,000 cyclones for you.' I am pleased because I saw in the eyes of the Israeli girl's friend that he wanted to leave her but his well-bred manners prevented him.

In the pouring pre-cyclone rain, I stop at a roadhouse and call Geckos to ask for our room back, then drive through the night as the downpour turns into a gentle shower. I am so tired; no one has ever been more tired than me — I am more tired and frustrated than Sisyphus with his infernal boulder. I unpack everything I painstakingly packed this morning and ferry it back into the nicely cleaned room. Falling into bed, I jam my hand underneath my hips in a vain attempt to alleviate the pain in my back, where my anxieties about Kev are stored.

Over breakfast this morning I hear the water has risen above the road in sections of the Cape; had we not left, we would have been stuck like the other backpackers, car or no car. Cyclone Ingrid seems to be heading further north and is turning into a bit of an anticlimax.

My back is stuffed; the final straw lain. After doing the preliminary groundwork involved in screwing up my back, all it takes is bending down to pick up my wallet. It's the longest bend in history as white fire jets up my nerve endings and I stop. I can go neither up nor down, and I hang in horrible limbo, trying not to breathe. The only thing that makes me feel somewhat better is that at least I was not getting up off the toilet, as happened to my cousin: the last thing I need is ridicule.

I'm still awake and crying at 3am. No matter how I lie, I can't get comfortable. Only people who have experienced back pain truly understand how tremendously painful it is; my back is involved in every movement I make, even breathing and actions I thought were completely unrelated, send spasms of pain through my body. Staggering over to Kev's bed, he rubs it for a while. At 5.30am I get up and stand, like a heavily pregnant woman, slowly dress, with Kev putting on my socks and tying my shoelaces and go in search of drugs. Shuffling the deserted streets, I feel sad. Every step brings more pain and I know that before the accident it would've been him walking through the darkness in search of pain-killing drugs; I feel a pang for the pre-injury relationship. Wrenching open the bottle of Panadol while still at the counter of a 7-Eleven, I swallow four tablets.

'Are you okay?' Asks the kid behind the counter.

'Nope, but I will be once these kick in.'

I take tonnes of Panadol — way more than the packet recommends — and I can hear Dad's voice echoing in my head, 'Drugs are bad. You are going to get liver cancer.'

I spend the next day lying in bed — all day in bed, in a tiny, windowless, hostel room. And I feel worse: my back seizes and stiffens. So I move. I move like an arthritic old woman. First just to and fro from the bathroom or kitchen, then tentatively venture outside into the sunshine and slowly I regain my confidence. After three days, we are ready to go on.

It rains the entire 350 kilometres to Townsville, making the drive slippery and treacherous. Yota creeps along the freeway tailgated by a conga line of infuriated Queenslanders. In some places I slow to sixty kilometres per hour because I literally cannot see out of my windshield. The procession of cars following me must have better wipers because at every opportunity they roar past, glaring and occasionally giving me the finger, as we drive through endless fields of sugar cane fronting misty mountains buried under lush green forests.

About sixty kilometres south of Cairns, Kev and I stop at Babinda Boulders, a swimming hole formed when a series of large granite boulders impeded the fast-flowing current, causing the river to widen into a big, deep pool. Under the shadow of Queensland's highest peak, Mount Bartle Frere, the pool is crowded on all sides by dense rainforest.

Kev plunges into the water and fights his way upstream, to where long vines trail prettily in the current and trees grow thickly over the water. The pool is empty; the last couple are climbing back up the stairs with their belongings bunched in their arms. We are completely alone as the rain patters silently on the water, muffling all sounds. Grabbing hold of a vine, intending to trail in the water like a fishing lure, I receive a handful of sharp little barbs and instantly release it. Kev grabs another vine with his rough leathery hands, invulnerable to little splinters, and we float in the current, Kev holding the vine with one hand and my waist with the other, and I wrap my arms around his shoulders. The rain continues softly patting my upturned face as the current spills over my hair and water swirls around my ears. The damp smell of the algae-coated rocks, the wet undergrowth of the rainforest, and the saltiness of Kev's skin as he nuzzles my cheek with his lips, relaxes me. And I breathe slowly, losing myself in this perfect moment.

The rain intensifies and by the time we swim back to the bottom of the stairs, it buckets down. With our towels as heavy, sodden masses flung over our shoulders and Kev's terry towelling hat drooping limp and wet like a rag on his head, I walk beside him through the rain while water carves rivers through the gravel track and droplets shine as glass on the verdant greenery.

Racing the storm, we make it back to Townsville. We need more happy memories like being at the Boulders today. I am so sick of crying and being unhappy. I just want to go an entire day without crying.

* * *

I've found myself thinking about other men for the first time in ages, like Constance Chatterley dreaming of her gamekeeper, hungrily accepting the smallest attentions of other men. I want to be hugged, kissed and touched; to feel loved. I don't want our relationship to become platonic — staying with him out of guilt, regret or pity — and sex reinforces that we love each other. Occasionally I do pity him, hating myself for it. Sometimes I even think he looks hopeless when he struggles with something difficult but at the same time I am so immensely proud of him, his dignity and positivity, and how well he copes. My conflicting feelings of pride, pity, love and resentment are hard to define. I wish I were more emotionally stable and less emotionally schizophrenic: imagining a white picket fence and a lifetime together one minute and then leaving him the next. It's a manic-depressive relationship; both of us still shell-shocked and screwed up.

Kev says he can cope with the staring, and the pity and people not meeting his eyes, but sex is one of the hardest things for him to deal with. He wants it back to *normal* so badly and he thinks that it is crap for me because it is not the same as before his injury, but that simply isn't true. I love having sex with him. I just want him to enjoy it too — to stop worrying about me worrying about him. When everything goes well, as occurred tonight, Kev and I laugh and smile and exchange small kisses as we admonish each other for not doing it more often.

* * *

Monica leaves a garbled message on my phone. Instead of dancing under Moreton Bay figs and Wollemi pine to the sounds of drums and pipes, Tim is back in Melbourne fighting for his wife and relationship. From the message, I gather Mon has met someone else: her name is Donna, and she moved into the share house while Tim was travelling with us. When I speak with Mon she is with Tim, trying to talk things out. Tim takes the phone with sad finality in his voice, 'All hell has broken loose here; nothing's left for me here and I'm flying home in three days. Thanks for the fun times and maybe see you guys again sometime.' In the background I hear Mon sobbing.

It is a horrible, protracted dissolution of a six-year relationship. I feel as though my parents are breaking up. Mon and Tim have always been a constant — a couple I modelled my own relationship upon, reasoning that they have their issues, like every couple, but they are still together, so maybe Kev and I will last too.

Whenever a couple who have been together for a long time break up, it makes me examine my own relationship and wonder if it will be able to weather the storms of time. Kev and I discuss Tim and Mon's break up and I jokingly say, 'Well, we're together until someone better comes along.' Kev becomes really paranoid that I am going to leave him for the first man who *walks* by. He doesn't seem to realise that I love him and I am not going to leave him. If I was going to leave him, I would have done it months ago and spared myself all this shit. Not to mention, you never know what is going to happen in the future, as we have been so brutally shown.

In the words of Janis Joplin, 'If you've got a cat for one day, that one day better be your life, because you can cry about the other 364, but you're gonna lose that one day, and that's all you've got — you've gotta call that love.' Yes, Janis was a hopelessly drug-addled hippy, but in that sentiment there is a piercing clarity: we have love. And according to John Lennon, that is all you need. Kev and I need to appreciate our one day together and stop crying about the other 364. Can I see myself with Kev for the rest of my life? For the rest of his life? Can I picture myself raising children with him, growing old with him? Sometimes I can, but the picture of old-man Kev in a wheelchair is hazy and indistinct, as if it doesn't, and never will, exist. I fear that he will die of an infection long before that.

Being with Kev has given me my happiest and my saddest moments in life. He once said to me under very different circumstances, 'The downside of loving you Em, is that you can break my heart with a look.' Now he is doing the same to me.

34

Morale is low. I can't sit unless perfectly straight, hands bunched into fists in the arch of my back, and any movement aggravates the pain. Kev constantly has tasks for me and the requests seem to be worsening as he becomes more and more wasted on baclofen. Pain has degraded the barriers of civility and makes me snappy, Kev tentatively gauges my mood before asking, 'Em, I left my night bag in the car, do you think you could go and grab it for me?'

Searching through the car for his night drainage bag, I shove the medical box aside, spilling tubes of lubricating goo, white powder and packets of bandaids. *If only he was a bit more goddamn considerate*, I fume, slamming the lid on the food box and rummaging through the pile of loose junk in the boot. All I want is for him to ensure he has everything he needs so I don't have to go searching for stuff a million times every night. Kneeling on the downturned tailgate, I fling things out of the car as viciously as my back allows, and with every item, I grow angrier and more resentful, thinking of Kev stretched out and reading on the queen bed, sandals off, enjoying the air conditioning. Finally, I find the drainage bag, wrapped in plastic, and tucked under the back seat. Repacking, I wish for someone to look after me.

An old English woman in Broome solemnly said to me in one of the hostel kitchens, 'Carers always get angry.' I don't want staying with Kev to turn me into a twisted, bitter person and sometimes, I feel it is. Kev hates the fact that his injury is responsible for me changing, becoming angrier, less fun and more of a bitch. I hate it too because I don't want to spend my life being angry, jealous and resentful, but this journey is changing us both. And I can't talk to him about it: how do you start a conversation like that? *I am angry at you because my life did not work out the way I had planned, because I am jealous of other women and I resent the workload placed on me. I am angry because you are disabled.* It's not exactly the type of conversation I really want to get into — not just for the simple fact that it's not as though he deliberately broke his back and maliciously put himself through months and months of pain and emotional agony just to piss me off, but also because of how the thought makes me feel. It paints a disturbing picture.

* * *

Night falls slowly and it's by soft starlight that Kev and I arrive in the backpacker's Mecca of Airlie Beach. A few kilometres from Airlie itself, Bush Village Backpackers' Resort is quiet, green and leafy, set back from the road among palm trees and jungle, just out of Cannonvale. Kev and I share a two-bedroom cabin with two American girls from Kentucky and Florida respectively and a Canadian girl from Winnipeg. Chatting to the girls, somehow Kev's leg bag begins to leak and, unbeknownst to him, a large puddle of urine forms on the kitchen floor under his chair, inching slowly towards the pink, exquisitely manicured, toes of the girl from Kentucky as she flexes up and down like a dancer. Realising, Kev looks at me in dismay. He'd been mildly flirting with the girls, enjoying their interest in our trip, and his eyes implore me to do something, to please fix it. Stricken, I want to hug him and say it'll be okay. Instead, I deliberately drop my water bottle, spilling a litre of water across the floor, which flows like a tide into the puddle.

'Shit, sorry,' I say, grabbing a mop to clean it up as the girls move aside, unaware of Kev's accident. He smiles sadly and mouths, 'thanks' and I squeeze his shoulder as I wring the mop into the toilet.

Tonight, I have three pillows: one for my head, one to wrap my arms around, and one for between my knees to help my back, leaving just the lumpy one for Kev. In my dream, he says, 'Em, I'm getting better,' and it is so vivid, and feels so real, that I wake believing it. Pure disappointment crashes upon me when I realise it was only a dream — I want it so badly. His spasms are so painful and people stare without even trying to disguise it anymore. He worries that I'm embarrassed to be seen with him and, sometimes, I am. Sometimes I want to walk away and pretend I'm not with him, but instead, I stand behind him, glaring at the starers, who quickly avert their gaze when their eyes meet mine, burning in defensive anger.

I roll onto my side and hug my knees to my chest, muffling my cries with a pillow so as not to wake Kev, who snores softly in the darkness beside me. I cry until all I can do is hiccup softly and my eyes are red and swollen. Someone once said that crying helps make you feel better. But I do not feel better: I feel alone. And finally, I sleep and dream of nothing.

* * *

Gateway to the beautiful Whitsunday Islands and the Great Barrier Reef, Airlie Beach is undeniably abundant in natural beauty, despite the crowds, noise and tacky souvenir shops lining the main avenue.

Kev and I are keen to get out onto the reef for some snorkelling and from the billions of boats clamouring for our business, we select a company called Manta Ray. Rick, the dive instructor, takes Kev and me out in the tinny spotting sea turtles, while everyone else is wandering around in the scrum down on Whitehaven Beach. It's glorious — way more fun than the conga line hike to the lookout or the beach — and for once we are doing something better than everyone else because of Kev's disability. The rest of the tourists arrive back a couple of hours later and after we have had a bit of a swim, a fabulous lunch is served while the boat cruises over to Mantaray Bay for some post-lunch snorkelling. As all the old people faff around looking for nose clamps and earplugs and size XXL stinger suits, the captain says patronisingly to Kev, 'Now will you be able to go in the water?'

'I think I should be able to manage,' Kev replies, struggling with his awkwardly small, worn and decidedly unattractive stinger suit. 'What about my face and head?' Kev says, pulling on the suit. Good point.

'What happens if we get stung on our head or face?' I ask Rick.

'Oh, that is pretty unlikely,' he says dismissively, 'although we had one guy once who was stung on the lips and that was pretty nasty.'

Oh awesome, it will be just my luck to get stung on the head by a bloody great box jellyfish and be medevaced to who knows where. Kev lunges past all the old people sorting out their masks and snorkels, and tumbles into the water. The captain says anxiously, 'Does he need a noodle? Will he be okay? Can he swim?'

I reply laconically, 'I dunno, I guess we'll find out,' earning myself a sharp glance.

The coral is spectacular and otherworldly and comes in every shape imaginable; more than 350 different types of coral grow on the Great Barrier Reef. There are large staghorn corals, like deer's antlers; soft, wavy types that sway with the current, similar to leaves on a tree; bright, complicated, brain-shaped corals; and large, precarious, slab corals teetering on pedestals. Animal life is plentiful: colourful, fleshy, giant clams that snap shut when touched; schools of fish moving instinctively as one; bright eels peeking from crevices in underwater ravines; large, majestic turtles; reef sharks; and colourful little clown fish darting to and from the safety of their anemone home. It is a magical world and, together, we float over the coral wonderland, watching our shadows darken the water beneath us as the fish dart tolerantly around us. The remaining people in the boat throw handfuls of food to the fish, and I swim lazily, drifting through the frenzy of fins as they bash into my face and mask in their desperation. It is a great day and as night falls, we crash into bed sunburnt and exhausted.

Packed and on the road early, onwards we go, down the coast past Rockhampton to Seventeen Seventy, a small coastal town near Agnes Waters. A long day of driving, Kev holds the wheel until his spasms become so violent, he kicks at the brake, despite the yoga strap binding his legs to the underside of the seat.

'My hip is hurting,' he says conversationally, 'so the spasms are bad. I first noticed a weird feeling there a while back, and I am pretty sure it's pain.'

Worrying, I am silent. For him to feel pain with his dulled sensation it must be quite substantial. Has he fractured it somehow in one of his many falls? Dislocated it? What the hell is wrong with it?

'I've started to take more gabapentin for the pain as well as baclofen. It helps, but it makes me so wasted.'

I mumble a reply, restraining myself from saying he should immediately see a doctor, and stress about his worsening pain all the way to Seventeen Seventy.

After paying for a little patch of grass under towering gums and palm trees a few meters off the beach, I set up our tent and unpack.

Later, we sit on the beach and smoke a joint together in the darkness while the occasional breaths of a soft, cool breeze caress our sunburnt cheeks. The bay is perfectly still, a wide pathway across the water is reflected by the moonlight, through which a single pelican floats gracefully. The only sounds are the distant clanging of masts as the anchored boats in the small mariner sway gently with the waves, and the infrequent, indignant squawks of squabbling seagulls. I dig a little hollow in the sand with the back of my head: soft and warm against my neck, sand mats into my hair, and looking up at the wide expanse of stars above me, a shooting star blazes across the sky. Kev meets my gaze and his teeth flash into a simple, happy smile.

Kev befriends an old guy at the campsite called Len, who had both his legs blown off above the knee during the Malayan War and also uses a wheelchair to get around. Kev and Len share the key to the wheelchair bathroom, neither of them are thrilled about sharing 'their' private bathroom. Len and his wife Jen camp in a different realm than Kev and I; more living outside than camping, their caravan has several rooms and a sturdy carpeted veranda sheltering a barbecue, dinner table and all sorts of other fancy stuff. There is no sand, no dirt, and no filthy bush turkeys scratching around their campsite. They even have a vacuum cleaner, which evidently, they use pretty often.

As Kev and I sit around the outside dinner table sipping beers, waving away mosquitoes and coveting their camping set up. Len appears with a pile of beers on his lap and Jen carries a plateful of barbecued prawns and crab cakes. Jen caught the crabs and prawns earlier that day, seasoned and barbecued them, and I restrain myself from licking my fingers. We sit around chatting and drinking beer until the early hours of the morning, discussing geology and travelling, disabilities and war, among other things. I feel as though I've known them forever. Their life gives me a glimpse of a possible future for Kev and me. When Jen goes off to do something that Len can't, such as swim in the Atherton Tablelands pools, she says, 'Len will mind the car park.' I like that. So much time has passed since Len's injury it has simply become part of life.

Having been injured during military service, Len used to be required to front-up each year to the military office in order to receive his disability pension and explain that his legs are still blown off. Constructed prior to legislation requiring disabled access to buildings, the office had a tonne of steps, requiring Len to leave his wheelchair at the base of the steps, crawl up into the office and say, 'I still have no legs, give me my money.'

'I was lucky because my legs were blown off.'

Not something I would consider particularly lucky, myself. Len turns to Kev, 'You have to lug those useless chunks of meat around with you everywhere: you'd be better off without them.'

I, for one, am quite fond of Kev's legs; useless chunks of meat they may be, but they give him symmetry. Of course, Len is right: dragging a paralysed lower body around everywhere is about as convenient as a conjoined twin. Piggybacks, transfers and swimming would all be made infinitely easier without the added weight of Kev's immobile legs.

'I need them as a counterweight for my beer belly, and my feet are so hot I just couldn't bear to part with them.'

Somewhat improved since leaving Melbourne, Kev's feet remain grotesque due to changes in his circulation, intertwining with his sandals like a tree and a strangler fig. Great puffy mounds of flesh protrude from the sandals, and at least one sort of fungus has colonised his toes. Kev may joke about cutting off his legs occasionally, much as the way he jokes about severing his spinal cord to stop the spasms, but he isn't really serious and the whole idea of losing his legs or remaining feeling is abhorrent to him. When we finally get back to our tent, we startle a large goanna in the process of nosing its way in and as it scurries away, I wonder what else has slithered in.

Len comes around early to say goodbye to Kev and me, then I

drive through Bundaberg to Hervey Bay, and finally, onto the ferry to Fraser Island.

A World Heritage listed island just off the coast of Hervey Bay, Fraser Island is the largest sand island in the world. As the ramp slowly rises for departure, our car is alone on the ferry to the island. That Kev feels pain in his hip yet didn't feel any pain when burned in Darwin, makes me think it must be really, really bad and that he is pushing his body too far. He in turn worries about me because I am worrying about everything. We almost didn't come out on the ferry and argued in the car park for some time about whether it was a good idea or not — something we have been doing a lot lately. We're always asking each other whether or not we need to cut the trip short, and I guess on some level, we both would like to just drive straight back to Melbourne, because it would be easier. I carefully drive off the deserted ferry, lower the tyre pressure, and follow the narrow sandy path into the dark forest.

35

Cicadas trill in the tall eucalypts surrounding Central Station campsite as Kev cooks spaghetti, and lying on my yoga mat, stretched out across the sand, branches obscure the stars, yet my heart is light. It doesn't even annoy me as much as it usually would that the campsite down the road is jammed with two Landcruiser troopy loads of English backpackers, in the process of getting well and truly shitfaced. Their loud, happily drunken accents echo through the once-silent forest. Having just finished off the last of our pot from Cairns, I'm mellow and stoned.

The most beautiful bird calls, clear and crisp as a bell, but melodic like a music box, chime through the early-morning forest as I lie beside a sleeping Kev. The backpackers got pretty noisy last night and my yoga-Zen glow didn't last. Kev had to talk me out of storming over to their campsite and demanding they shut the hell up. The morning spoils us with clear blue skies and after breakfast, packing up and the long process of Kev getting ready, I enthusiastically leap into Yota and roar out of Central Station, taking a perverse satisfaction at gunning the throaty diesel as I pass the beer-can-littered campsite of the backpackers. Through thick forest, keeping within the narrow, but established wheel tracks, and brushing Yota's undercarriage on the tall pile of sand in between, the driving is challenging. On meeting other four-wheel drives, mostly Landcruisers crammed with ten or twelve people, I carefully reverse along the track until I can pull off for them to pass.

There are no speed limits, road signs, or cops that I notice, to enforce anything, so it is no surprise that people have been killed in car accidents on the island. Over 120 serious accidents have occurred since 2003, mostly involving backpackers unfamiliar with four-wheel drives or driving on sand. As I steer along Seventy-Five Mile Beach, I keep on the hard sand and away from the waves that sweep rapidly onto shore causing several other cars to swerve violently. Everyone travels fast and troopies race along the beach as arms, hands and sometimes bare bums, are thrust out windows.

Lake McKenzie, one of Fraser Island's many clear and exceptionally pure freshwater lakes, is stunningly blue against the dazzlingly white sand dune it perches on. The white sand itself is almost entirely composed of quartz. An oasis in the forest, the area teems with animal life including wallabies and dingoes, for which the island is renowned. Arriving reasonably early, Kev and I have time to appreciate the beauty of the lake before the tourist onslaught. Within a quarter of an hour or so, the troopies begin to arrive, one after another — an almost never-ending line — and the clean, white beach becomes crowded with people jostling for space to lay a towel. A path of deep, loose sand interspaced with several wide steps leads down to the lake and presents a bit of a mission for Kev.

'I can give you a hand; it'd be a bit faster.'

'I will do a couple then get your help so that we get there before it's too crowded.'

He drops a few stairs, and I sort of crash him down a few more, and he wheels a long, sandy stretch down to the water, one excruciating push after another. When he finally reaches the water's edge he plunges in, despite his spasms doing their best to drown him. We swim over to the other side of the lake away from the crowds wallowing in the shallows, watching bodies swarm across the far beach. I can hear them, muffled somewhat by the distance, and see Kev's chair empty on the shore.

As Kev struggles back up the path, a French woman passes and says, 'Respect, respect,' without stopping. It touches Kev, she acknowledges his struggle but doesn't try to push him, carry him or patronize him, intuitively knowing that things are difficult for him, but if he wants help, he will ask. It is a good attitude.

We are the only campers at Lake Allom, a small, quiet camping area with three sites, and renowned for short-necked turtles, which are, apparently, plentiful in the still waters of the lake, stained dark with melaleuca tannin. Yet, I manage not to spot a single one.

No fence prevents wild dingoes from rummaging through our stuff and eating scraps at Allom Lake the way it did at Central Station, and it crosses my mind that Kev may be attacked and mauled by a particularly large and aggressive dingo. 'You know, I'm a bit worried about you and the dingoes: a kid was killed by dingoes here not that long ago.'

'Are you kidding me? I'm a bit insulted by that, I can fight off a dingo easy,' Kev replies indignantly.

The pamphlets handed out by the National Park's service may have made me a bit paranoid, and while caution is prudent and essential, it is easy to forget that a dingo is just a small dog. The Fraser Island dingoes, though, are the most purebred dingoes in Australia because being isolated on an island, they have never interbred with domestic dogs.

A cute little yellow bird flits and fluffs around while I set up the tent and hang the stinking tarp between a couple of trees to shelter the picnic table from the dripping trees and ominous, bruise-coloured sky. In no time, a curry bubbles away happily and I leave Kev in charge of stirring as I throw all our sleeping gear into the tent.

'Fuck!' Kev curses loudly behind me and I turn as the curry topples over and crashes messily onto the muddy ground. There is to be no salvage and, irritated, I throw together another can of chickpeas, tomatoes and tin of curry sauce in the empty saucepan, worrying about whether dingoes are attracted to chickpea curries. I say patronisingly, 'Make sure you watch it properly this time.'

'I know, I know: I won't spill this one or I will have to have porridge for dinner, and I hate porridge.' As I busy myself with unpacking and re-tying ropes here and there, Kev watches the bubbling curry like a cat watches a canary.

I was expecting rain, but when it comes, it is with a terrifying vengeance. Never have I seen such rain, so heavy and sudden, and soon rivers flow along the ground and water pools on the tarp, causing it to bow alarmingly. As the water quickly accumulates, the weight becomes too much for the ropes to bear and the tarp collapses, sending water cascading onto our heads and flowing as if from a bucket onto the cooking equipment on the table.

'ARRHH! I need to get the tarp back up!' Shedding clothes, I run into the downpour to replace the pegs, hoping to create some form of shelter. Instantly drenched, my hair is plastered to my face and the pounding of the rain on my head makes it difficult to see and hear, as though I'm in a wind tunnel. The roar of the rain is everywhere. Water runs into my eyes, ears, and nose and it's hard to breathe. The almighty racket this rain would make on a corrugated tin roof is unimaginable. The air is warm but the rain is cold, and purple blotches and goose pimples erupt on my skin when I dive under the re-strung tarp, and jam my muddy feet into Kev's lap to be warmed up.

During the melee, somehow the curry plummets to the ground and is lost. Kev looks at me in despair, 'Shit, will we have to eat porridge now?' I nod, feeling somewhat pleased that at least *I* like porridge. After porridge, we huddle in the tent as the crazy storm rages outside and the tent shakes with the force of the rain. 'Well the tarp seems to be holding up okay,' says Kev hopefully as we peer gloomily from our canvas prison into the dark and angry sky, periodically illuminated with bright gashes of jagged lightening. Incredibly, there is no water in the tent: I'd set it up facing downhill, so we watch the water flow past like a flood.

The rainstorm of the night turns into a thick, blanketing mist by morning that I feel I can almost brush aside with my fingers like parting a curtain. The dense, low mist shrouds the forest and everything is still. Wandering down the muddy rivulet-cut path towards the lake that gives the campsite its name, the air smells of eucalyptus and fresh, damp dirt. A lone duck carves arrows through the perfectly still surface of Allom Lake, sending ripples cascading to the shore as it dives purposefully for food. Calmed by the vista, I climb over roots and squeeze by trees on the narrow path, still hoping to spy one of the goddamn turtles. Bird calls toll, sounding then echoing forever.

When I return to the tent, Kev has cleaned up most of the mess from the previous night and is almost ready for me to help him into his chair. Everything is wet and stinks: the sheets, the sleeping bags, all our clothes and we really, really stink. I just throw everything in the back of the car without even bothering to pack, wind down the window and try to ignore it. I hate the smell of wet clothing; it is almost as bad as wet dog.

We head back across the ferry to Hervey Bay and on to Brisbane where we will be able to chill-out for a while and clean ourselves up. My Aunty Marie and Uncle Manfred live in Brisbane with the youngest of their three daughters, Simone. Marie, my mother's sister, is a fragile little woman, almost bird-like with tiny wrists, and belts with enormous buckles to keep her trousers from pooling around her delicate ankles.

'It's good to see you Em,' she says, kissing my cheek. In contrast, Manfred is a huge, moustachioed Swiss man, who has a propensity to lecture on subjects as diverse as the best type of cheese to have on a sandwich, and whether a retirement saving plan is a better investment than the housing market.

Marie and Manfred's house is an old Queenslander: up on stilts and, because it is constructed on a slope, only has a few steps up to the front. It is fabulous sleeping in a bed and just slobbing around the house, doing nothing all day except watching inane, stupid TV. We appreciate all the modern conveniences, like fridges, in which delicious perishable items such as ice-cream, soft cheeses and, especially, butter are kept. I didn't realise how much I missed having butter and milk and I can't stop drinking the cold, fresh milk. It is amazing how mundane items become so delicious when you're deprived of them for a while, during rationing, I would've been one of the hoarders, the cheaters, and the black market dairy customers. I love butter like Midas loved gold.

The rest from constant lifting, packing and unpacking helps my back and happily, Kev's hip doesn't seem to be getting any worse. He has a nasty bite on his leg that looks sore and infected and we're both hoping it's not some type of weird tropical parasite. Marie's washing machine churns endlessly through our wet, stinking camping gear and once vacuumed then Windex-ed, Yota gleams, and smells like a pine forest.

Before they moved to Queensland, Marie and Manfred lived across the creek from my house in the country and I grew up with their eldest daughter, Shannon, essentially my sister. On our second night, Shan and her girlfriend Holly come over and we all walk to the pub together.

Much about Shan is big: big boobs, big opinions, big voice and big heart— she cultivates an intimidating exterior to mask her soft, sensitive interior. Her hair shifts from black to blue as she moves underneath the streetlamps, and her right shoulder, strong from rowing, sports an intricate tribal tattoo.

Holly's hair is dyed a vibrant red, shaved at the back and falling forward in a floppy fringe. She has multiple piercings, crooked teeth endearingly smeared with scarlet lipstick, a frequent, happy smile and carries her own personal soapbox with her. She does not so much attract your attention as grabs it with both hands and stuffs it into her oversized purple handbag.

Shan has not seen me since Kev's accident and, at first, we mostly talk of our time in Vancouver, of the recovery, our trip and Kev's health. Holly turns to me and says, 'This must be so hard on you Emma,' and something inside of me wakens and begins to sing — a tiny bird that has been caged so deep for so long is finally released and I choke slightly on my beer. Her brown eyes are soft and kind as she stares levelly at me. It is the first time that someone has put my feelings above Kev's and thought of me first, and of the pressure and responsibility I carry. It *is* hard for me, and Holly sees that. She validates my feelings of anger, resentment and frustration without judgement, regarding me calmly with her soulful brown eyes that say, 'I understand, I know what you are feeling.' I want to put my head on her large, soft breasts so she can stroke my hair gently, while softly crooning 'it's going to be alright' in my ear.

36

Kev and I are so focused on reaching Taree, south of Port Macquarie, to meet Gramps who is on vacation there with his cousin Elaine, that somehow we drive straight past the Big Oyster without seeing it. We are both exhausted by the time we reach Old Bar, about twenty kilometres from Taree, where Gramps is staying in a caravan park, impressively secured by a boom gate at the entrance. I park and wander through the darkness looking for Gramps' car, ringing him several times without answer.

Damn Gramps, I think, *this is so typical*. After searching in the darkness for what feels like hours, I give up; I can't find his car and I have a complete breakdown.

'I don't want to search everywhere for a room at 10.30 at night when everything in this little town is closed down; I'm tired, I want to go to bed.'

'I'll drive to Newcastle and we can sleep there,' Kev says.

Drained, we fight and snap at each other. I climb heavily back into Yota, rubbing my back, and am driving back into Taree when a set of headlights flashes past and, I catch a glimpse of the number plate: 'Gramps!' Chucking a U-turn, I chase the taillights back into Old Bar and to the gates of the caravan park.

Gramps is fiddling with the swipe card at the boom gate as I leap out of Yota and run to the passenger window, startling Elaine, who has had a few too many wines with dinner and thinks I am someone looking for spare change. 'Kath!' Yells Gramps, 'You made it!'

The unit is much the same as most portable holiday units, with cheap faux wood covering most surfaces except the floor. Elaine inhabits the main bedroom and the rest of us sleep on bunk beds, which are three high, with Kev on the lower bunk, Gramps on the middle bunk and me on the highest.

After breakfast and a shower, Kev and I explore Old Bar, which doesn't take long: out of the caravan park, past the airstrip, past the chip shop and down to the beach. Grey, foamy waves crash to the rocky shoreline with a vehemence I'd not seen up north; a few people stroll along the rocky beach and several paddle between the lifesaving flags, visible in the distance. A high-energy current hurls the rocks about.

'So do you still want to go for a swim?' I ask Kev doubtfully.

'Sure,' he replies, and we descend to the beach. The waves are strong and the rip even stronger and we are caught between them: pulled out to sea and smashed onto the beach. I feel as though I'm in a giant washing machine. The bottom drops away not far from the shore, suddenly becoming quite deep, and Kev quickly finds himself out of his depth as he struggles with the blue boogie board intended to keep him afloat. The waves try to wrest the board away and Kev clings to it as the ocean churns around him and the cord entangles his hands, effectively hobbling him. Then he begins to sink. Buffeted by the waves, I force my way towards him, lunging for his arm as he flounders. Kev has the grip of a drowning man and I dive below the water, forcing him to let go of me. His hands tangled in the cord from the boogie board, I grab his pony tail, and drag him into the shallows. Angry waves are unrelenting — kneading and pummelling him, trying to rip us apart.

A crowd has gathered on the viewing platform above us and curious faces peer down as finally, we crawl onto the rocky beach and lay panting for a while, cheeks pressed against the wet rocks. The sand catcher in my bathers is full of small rocks and it feels like I have a little turd in the bottom of my pants. Adrenaline throbs through my body and my heart bangs against my ribs.

'Kev … are you okay?' He nods weakly in reply. We didn't swim between the flags. We had discussed it, and assumed, like assholes, that the lifeguards would save us when in fact the lifeguards have more than their hands full watching the swimmers between the flags. The only reason they knew we were there was because of the crowd jostling for space to watch the two stupid morons lying half drowned, on the beach.

'This is too much. This is beyond us both … it would have been beyond us before you were disabled and it's definitely beyond us now,' I pant.

Kev's hip and spasms worsen, maybe he shook something loose in the surf. The aggravating hip pain is the coup de grâce of the trip, and we decide to drive straight back to Melbourne.

Once past Sydney, Kev takes over driving and I collapse, sleeping, neck kinked against the window. We eat car food from petrol stations: heat-lamped, soggy potato cakes, hard, crispy spring rolls and dry, crunchy dim sims. We have tunnel vision and count the kilometres to Melbourne. Exhausted, we reach Albury after midnight and crash into bed, sleeping in our clothes, and rise early to cover the final stretch.

Driving the familiar Melbourne roads leading to my parents' house I feel like Odysseus after his return from the Trojan War. I have only been gone for three-and-a-half months, yet I am changed. Kev and I have been through so much together and the trip bought out both our best and worst qualities. If he is able to cope with life in a wheelchair in the middle of the Australian desert, then surely city-living will be a breeze.

'We made it Baby,' Kev says, taking my hand as I pull into the garage and laughing, we hug in disbelief. We actually made it, despite everything, and I am as light as air. While much has been lost, so much remains possible for us.

Mum and Dad are delighted to see us and fuss excessively. Mum puts the kettle on, 'Ahhhhh, yummy-cuppa-tea,' she says, taking a sip and the familiar irritation flares again: I am home.

EPILOGUE

After a few weeks in Melbourne, we flew back to Vancouver. Kev returned to G.F. as an outpatient, quickly built up his strength and learnt to get into his chair from the ground on his own. In an urban environment the disability was less of an issue and he became completely independent. With the help of G.F. physios, he learnt to brace walk, with his lower body strapped into a framework of metal braces that bend and lock, allowing him to walk slowly with crutches. Adjusting to reality was a challenge. After travelling, we assumed that life would be easy but that was not the case. For the first time, we were forced to deal with Kev's injury without the distraction of travel.

We spent a few months in Vancouver for Kev to complete rehab and then moved to Calgary where we were both enrolled at university. Using the scholarship he'd won prior to his accident, Kev shifted his focus from avalanche prediction to hydrogeophysics and investigated how geophysics could be used to remediate hydrocarbon-contaminated sites. I studied environmental geology. Life became ordinary.

After a while, *when Kev recovers* became *if he recovers*, and then was lost entirely. We went from thinking of the injury every moment of every day to barely thinking of it at all, and most of the time it was forgotten in the daily rush of life. Kev learnt how to sit-ski with the help of volunteers from the CADS program (Canadian Association for Disabled Skiing) and within months was better than me, racing on the provincial disabled team. He began to accumulate wheelchairs, including an off-road wheelchair and a hand-crank Varna handcycle to maintain his aerobic fitness. Over time, brace walking began to hurt Kev's hip, and he continued to struggle with severe spasms and bladder infections that frequently left him hospitalised.

An x-ray showed hip subluxation was the cause of the persistent hip pain: the joint had been worn smooth by constant partial dislocations as the spasms pulled and pushed at his leg. Brace walking ceased completely and Kev's name was added to a surgical waiting list to insert a baclofen pump into his abdomen that delivered baclofen directly into the intrathecal space. Because the medication was delivered directly into the spinal fluid, much less was required to have the same effect as oral medication, usually resulting in a decrease in the mind-numbing side effects.

Upon our return from a trip to Europe for my brother's wedding, Kev's spasms were so severe he could barely wheel twenty metres without his feet kicking off the footplate and, his legs thrummed against tables and hurled themselves about as he transferred, often cutting and injuring themselves in the process. Desperate for help, he spoke to an orthopaedic surgeon about a girdlestone resection that involved sawing off the head of the femur to prevent recurrent dislocations. The description was graphic, terrifying and seemed somewhat drastic. Kev decided to wait a while.

We had been in Calgary for about a year when, during one of our frequent trips to the foothills of the Rocky Mountains, Kev picked up a limestone pebble from the ground and took the battered wave-patterned ring from his finger.

'Em, I'm not perfect, you're not perfect and our life together probably won't be perfect, but I love you. You are the light in my universe, the wonderment in my life, and the inspiration for me to push as hard as I do. Will you marry me?'

He slipped the ring on my finger. 'Here's your engagement rock,' he said, passing me the pebble. With his arms around me, I sat on his lap, watching the last few yellow leaves fall from the larches beneath the huge, grey mountains.

After eighteen months on the waiting list, a baclofen pump was installed in Kev's stomach. The surgeons commented that even unconscious, under anaesthesia, his legs kicked and flexed, almost terminating the surgery. When he woke, the spasms had finally calmed. Along with the spasms went the severe bladder infections, changing from something consistently resulting in a hospital stay to something that could be dealt with just by drinking lots of fluids.

A few days before our wedding, Kev gave me a pendant he'd had a jeweller make from the limestone pebble that he'd snuck out of my box of special things. I wore it on a silver chain when we were married by a magician in the Fitzroy Gardens Conservatory in Melbourne. Our honeymoon was spent in a one-room driftwood shack in the Cook Islands, owned by an eccentric German guy who, with Kev's help, made a sketchy ramp from more driftwood. Within two days of arriving back in Calgary, we brought home an eight-week-old Bernese-mountain-dog puppy and named him Manny. With Manny on his lap, Kev met every woman within a two-mile radius.

We knew we both wanted kids in the future but it was the year I turned thirty that we made an appointment to see an IVF doctor to find out if it was possible. A testicular biopsy was necessary to extract Kev's sperm and the quality analysis took several anxious weeks. *Adequate* was the term the doctor used to describe Kev's sperm in his droll, humourless voice and, laughing, we replayed the message he left several times. We decided to freeze the sperm because, both being students, we were not ready to have a baby yet.

As Kev adjusted to his injury, our relationship drifted closer to how it was before. When camping — which we did often in the mountains — Kev helped set up the tent, made the fire, chopped the wood and carried the heavy stuff balanced on his lap. At home, he was always messing about in the garage, building something, tinkering with his chairs or bike and making practical solutions for challenges, such as sawing up a kid's snowboard to strap onto the front casters of his chair so he could glide across the snow. Many days were spent skiing together; being faster and better than most people, it was only on snow that Kev no longer felt disabled.

Despite the pump, the pain in Kev's hip remained significant and his medication volume was increased periodically until it reached 1200 micrograms per day — four times the amount anyone else in the region was taking. The pain made the girdlestone resection appear more reasonable and Kev underwent surgery once more. The surgery failed. Kev was left in considerable pain with the jagged end of a floating femur ramming into his sciatic nerve. The sole remaining option was a total hip replacement, which his surgeon was reluctant to perform on a paraplegic because hips are prone to dislocation even with muscle mass to hold them in. Consequently, conducting a hip replacement on a paraplegic with no muscle mass was uncertain; no one knew whether it would make him better or much worse. In constant agony, gulping back synthetic marijuana and oxycodone tablets, Kev was bound to the couch and spent countless hours researching hip replacements, finally speaking to a surgeon in the US who'd conducted several hip replacements on paraplegics. After looking at Kev's file, he recommended the surgery and advised Kev to seek out a surgeon willing to undertake it.

Kev continued to work on his PhD thesis from the couch with his computer balanced on his stomach as he waited for orthopaedic appointments. I graduated from university and started working as a hydrogeologist for an environmental engineering company. I worked for a while, writing reports, monitoring and drilling wells, driving ice-roads and conducting pump tests at minus forty degrees.

After a visit to a particularly contaminated gas plant, I decided I wanted children before being rendered permanently infertile and Kev and I returned to the IVF clinic.

Just as I filled my first prescription of IVF drugs, a surgeon in Calgary agreed to conduct the hip replacement and my girlfriend Joanie replaced Kev as my partner at all IVF appointments and procedures. Two eggs were fertilised with Kev's sperm and implanted into my uterus. A couple of weeks later I peed on a stick and discovered I was pregnant. Later that morning, the doctor smiled as he scanned my stomach and turned the monitor, showing a grainy image of two small, grey, fluttering balls.

'Heartbeats,' he said. 'Congratulations: you're having twins.'

Kev spent the first trimester of my pregnancy on the couch recovering from the hip replacement, unable to bend past ninety degrees and terrified of dislocating it. Fortunately, the surgery made a dramatic improvement in pain, spasticity and mobility and over time, all became manageable. He acquired a standing frame and an electro-stimulation cycle that pulses electricity into Kev's legs and enabled him to pedal a bike. The standing frame stretched his hips, weight bearing increased bone density and cycling built muscle mass, improved circulation and kept the hip joint secure.

When I was eight months pregnant, Kev submitted his final PhD thesis and successfully defended it, earning a Doctorate of Geophysics.

It snowed on the May day our fraternal twins, Kai and Naomi, were born.

Mum came over from Australia for two months to help with the babies, and when they were four months old Kev and I took them to Australia for the first time. Kev returned alone after six weeks to start a new job at an engineering company and I stayed with Mum and Dad for two months.

When Kai and Naomi were three, we moved to Melbourne (Manny too) to be closer to my family. Kev taught the kids to ride bikes, spending hours hanging out at the BMX track with them in his off-road chair, and riding for miles along the Maribyrnong River on his hand cycle. Ever since Kai and Naomi were born, Kev has rarely been without a child in his lap. They fight over who gets to sit there, especially when he flies down a hill or they're tired. During ski trips in both Australia and Canada, we taught Kai and Naomi how to ski from a snowboard and to sit-ski, and they are faster than I would like. We still frequently swim together and Kev has taken to ocean swimming, competing in the Lorne Pier to Pub in 2015, causing a commotion as he slowly wheeled himself through the sand and across the finish line.

Kev has his own business as a groundwater modeller and I am currently working on an engineering PhD at The University of Melbourne.

With the exception of a few hiccups — such as a broken baclofen pump and surgery for carpal tunnel in his hands — Kev has been strong, fit and healthy since the total hip replacement.

Tim never returned to Australia and now lives in London with his partner May and his two sons. He works as a physics teacher and still travels every chance he gets.

Monica and Donna were together for seven years before splitting and remain friends. Monica still lives in Melbourne and is working on her PhD.

Mum has not camped since.

Kev still moves his big toe.

ACKNOWLEDGMENTS

This book is based on my diary and the recollections of others. I am very grateful for the friends and family who not only helped and supported me during Kev's injury and our trip, but also helped me recall it later.

I want to extend my sincere thanks to everyone who encouraged me along the way. Specifically, I want to thank Monica O'Dwyer, Joanne Watson and Moira White for reading woeful early drafts and giving helpful comments.

Thank you to my editor, Pia Gaardboe, who made suggestions that greatly improved this book and to David Tenenbaum, my publisher, and everyone at Melbourne Books for believing in it.

Thanks to Tim Prior for travelling with us and being exactly what we needed. And, of course, Mum, who not only travelled stoically with us but also provided me with a huge amount of encouragement and her exceptional editing services — thanks Mum, you're the best.

Lastly, I want to thank Kevin Hayley for his strength and support; I love you more than everything.

THE AUTHOR

Emma White grew up in country Victoria and after completing a BA in Classics at The University of Melbourne travelled to Canada where she spent several years teaching snowboarding and working in ski fields in North America and New Zealand. After Kev's accident and their trip to Australia, she returned to university in Calgary and completed a BSc in Environmental Geology. She worked as a hydrogeologist for a few years at an engineering consulting company where she got to drive ice roads and drill wells in between writing hydraulic assessments. She is currently completing a PhD in Infrastructure Engineering at The University of Melbourne which she commenced after moving back to Australia with Kev. They now live in Melbourne with twins.

www.ingramcontent.com/pod-product-compliance
Lightning Source LLC
Chambersburg PA
CBHW021221090426
42740CB00006B/319